The Art of the One-Act

New Issues Poetry & Prose
The College of Arts and Sciences
Western Michigan University
Kalamazoo, Michigan 49008

An Inland Seas Book

 Inland Seas books are supported by a grant from
The Michigan Council for Arts and Cultural Affairs.

First Edition, 2007.

ISBN-10: 1-930974-60-4 (paperback)
ISBN-13: 978-1-930974-60-9 (paperback)

Library of Congress Cataloging-in-Publication Data:
Johnston, Arnold and Deborah Ann Percy
The Art of the One-Act/Arnold Johnston and Deborah Ann Percy
Library of Congress Control Number: 2006935272

Managing Editor: Marianne Swierenga
Copy Editor: Curtis VanDonkelaar
Art Director: Tricia Hennessy
Designers: Jason Punches, Rachel Farabaugh
Production Manager: Paul Sizer
                      The Design Center
                      School of Art
                      College of Fine Arts
                      Western Michigan University

THE ART OF THE ONE-ACT

Edited and with an introduction and commentary by

Arnold Johnston and Deborah Ann Percy

For Herb Scott

CONTENTS

SECTION TWO: LONGER ONE-ACT PLAYS

APPENDICES

POINTS TO CONSIDER IN ANALYZING A PLAY

PLOT STRUCTURE

SOME NOTES ON COMEDY

PLAYWRITING—SOME RECOMMENDATIONS

SCRIPT FORMAT AND RELATED MATTERS

HANDS FOR TOAST: AN EXCERPT IN THEATRICAL FORMAT

INTRODUCTION

Drama traces its beginnings to ritual: joyous celebrations of life, plenty, disorder, and chance; quiet or noisy rites to proclaim our need for order and to get us through the inevitable: death, loss, fear of the unknown. All or most of these rituals involved recitation, movement, costume, and interaction between congregation and priest-performers.

Theatre has retained these elements, but has added an essential dynamic: interruption of the ritual, whether that ritual be cultural, institutional, familial, or personal. Playwrights must supply an answer to their own variation on the Passover question ("Why is this night different from all other nights?"), and that question is, "Why today?" The answer virtually always identifies an interruption or disturbance of the status quo, something that changes the life of at least one character, sometimes irrevocably. And almost always the disturbance begins a struggle that ends in the reestablishment of the old order or a change to something new.

Hard times for Thebes and the Chorus's cries for succor disturb the reign of Oedipus and set into motion a tragic fate he not only cannot avoid, but to which he rushes headlong. Hamlet's gloomy mourning of his father's untimely death is galvanized by the Ghost into a halting but inexorable quest for vengeance that brings about his own ruin and the fall of the kingdom he might have inherited. And as the lights rise on Simon Gray's *Otherwise Engaged,* the main character Simon Hench has cleared the decks of all social obligations so he can enjoy, undisturbed, his newly-acquired recording of Wagner's *Parsifal.* His attempts to start the first disk are thwarted by a succession of characters, all bent on altering what they see as the selfish status quo of Simon's life.

These full-length plays feature conspicuous interruptions or disturbances leading to consequences we cannot fail to note. One-act plays—either very brief ones like the ten-minute plays in Section One of this anthology, or longer ones like the ten-to-thirty-minute plays in Section Two—may incorporate similarly plain dynamics, or may opt for a subtlety appropriate to their relatively slighter structure. Nonetheless, you will see in the pages that follow, in the most dissimilar of plays, the invariable but almost always surprising process of disturbance leading to change.

As the collection unfolds, we will also draw your attention to other elements of the playwright's craft through introductory comments on each play and in further observations on craft, technique, and format in the several appendices. Our aim is that this book will be useful and pleasurable to general readers, to teachers of literature, theatre, and playwriting, and to playwrights and other practitioners of the craft. We hope you'll agree with us that the twenty-six plays in this anthology, chosen from over five hundred submissions by playwrights from some forty states and several countries beyond the United States, stand as excellent examples of what we've called *The Art of the One-Act*.

—Arnold Johnston & Deborah Ann Percy

SECTION ONE: TEN-MINUTE ONE-ACT PLAYS

TEN-MINUTE PLAYS

The ten-minute one-act is a form related to the "curtain raisers" or "afterpieces" that in the nineteenth and twentieth centuries sometimes preceded or followed full-length plays, either to warm up an audience or to dispel the sobering effects of a serious or tragic piece.

At this point in theatrical history, the ten-minute play often serves as a "calling card" for playwrights, providing a quick way of showing off a writer's talents to agents or theatre companies. The form also offers a budget-friendly way for theatres to introduce new playwrights to the public through festivals or evenings of such one-acts. The plays are frequently selected from entries in a contest, the best-known of which is probably the Actors Theatre of Lousiville's National Ten-Minute Play Competition.

Some theatre people seem to feel that one can't write a "real" play in the space of ten minutes, that the best one can hope to create in such limited time is some sort of blackout sketch. The ten-minute plays in this collection demonstrate the fallacy of that proposition. Not only can a ten-minute play recapitulate, admittedly in miniature, the structure and effect of a full-length play, but writing one can also serve as excellent practice in constructing effective scenes. If more writers recognized that strong scenes—the building blocks of a full-length play—invariably share the dynamic of the larger structure, we'd see better full-length plays on the world's stages. And this holds true both for conventional scenes that begin or end with a lighting or set change to signal a shift of time or place or for French scenes that begin or end with a significant entrance or exit by a character.

As you'll discover, the contents of the following section, though varied in style and idiom, are not merely theatre pieces: they are complex, subtle, and satisfying plays.

Hands for Toast

This funny, disturbing play by Carey Daniels exemplifies a dynamic frequently observed in comic or tragicomic plays: that of the stranger in a strange land, an innocent or "normal" character who must cope with characters and customs that confound and/or threaten his welfare. The other side of this coin is the play that dramatizes the effects on a "normal" world of an unreasonable or "abnormal" character, the sort of character Henri Bergson called "the comic monster." In fact, Bergson, in *Laughter* (1890), found such rigidity and unsociability to be at the heart of the comic character.

In *Hands for Toast,* Baby Baby must deal with the grotesque world presided over by her father, Chester, and only partially mitigated by her stepmother, Darlene; and in the play's short span the only hope we can see for comically happy resolution stems from Baby Baby's defiant nature and the knowledge that her elder sister has escaped to lead a presumably "normal" life. In this respect, too, *Hands for Toast* demonstrates a notably subtle form of the several kinds of change vital to drama. From least subtle to most subtle, a character may experience change of situation (as from rags to riches), change of nature (as from coward to hero), or change of awareness (as from ignorance to knowledge). In those plays where nothing seems to change for any character, the writer works for a change of awareness in the audience, which—as in *Hands for Toast*—may recognize the possibility of future change or—as in *Waiting for Godot*—that true change may be illusory or simply unattainable.

Carey Daniels

Hands for Toast

CHARACTERS   CHESTER: a man in his mid-fifties, a corrections officer, built and fit like a man twenty years younger, wears glasses and a moustache, perpetually angry and dissatisfied but able to maintain a sense of civility on occasion.

DARLENE: Chester's wife, 40, with the demeanor and maturity of a seventeen-year-old, alternating between self-righteousness and petulance.

BABY BABY: Chester and Darlene's nine-year-old daughter, as yet unnamed.

SETTING   Chester and Darlene's modest two-bedroom, one-story house. It looks like something out of Levittown, slightly homey and with the exception of an expensive entertainment center, it hasn't quite moved out of the 1960s in terms of décor. A beige afghan rests on the back of a beat-up, old armchair that obviously belongs to Chester. A decorative table sits next to the armchair, adorned with a white doily and overgrown spider plant. Antique lamps with dusty lampshades rest on both end tables flanking a brown plaid upholstered sofa. Mainly we see the living room. Passageways in the back on either side of the stage lead to the kitchen (R) and bedroom/bathroom area (L). Alongside the house (L) a dark blue '88 Cadillac rusts away through the seasons, sadly missing one of its back tires. An eight-foot-tall fence, fashioned from old lumber and obviously constructed by hand by Chester separates the Caddy and rest of the house from whatever lies on the other side. Chester and Darlene would be able to look out the window facing the car and fence if the blinds were not always drawn.

TIME   A fine spring day. The present.

(*The bang of a screen door slamming shut is heard. CHESTER enters from the kitchen, in uniform, his jacket slung over one arm, sorting through a small stack of mail. He stops in the center of the living room, sorting the envelopes and frowning. He pauses to loosen his tie and toss his jacket onto his armchair.*)

CHESTER: It's hot in here. (*Pauses, looking around.*) Darlene! It's hot in here!

DARLENE: (*OS.*) What?

CHESTER: It's hot in here! Are you deaf?

(*DARLENE enters. She's wearing a pair of cutoff shorts and a tube top. Her skin is overly tan almost to the point of crispiness and her hair, naturally a medium brown, has been streaked blonde. She is barefoot, but gaudy gold chains adorn her neck and wrists, her long nailed fingers glittering with gold and jewels.*)

CHESTER: Damn woman, how hard is it to open a few windows in here? This place is like an oven.

DARLENE: (*DARLENE reaches under the blinds to open the window and then leaves through the kitchen to open more in there. She is still very audible offstage.*)

Don't start with me first thing, Chester! You just got home from work and haven't even been fuckin' drinkin' yet! I swear to Christ if you drink tonight I'm leaving you!

(*CHESTER ignores this and looking through his mail, he pulls out an envelope and tears it open, thoughtlessly handing the envelope to DARLENE as she re-enters.*)

And your mother called today.

(*DARLENE takes a cigarette out of the pack she got from the kitchen and lights up. She inhales as CHESTER reads his letter, blowing smoke out of the side of her mouth and picking up where she left off.*)

Your mother is a real piece of work, Chester. She was on about the kids again, bitching that you forgot Jason's birthday and didn't even call him—

CHESTER: (*Reading his letter, mumbling.*)

If he wanted me to talk to him on his birthday he would've called me. Him and his sister know how to pick up the damn phone and use it. If they want me to talk to them, they'll call.

DARLENE: (*Taking another drag off her cigarette.*)

Ungrateful brats. After all you did for them. Heather's been getting a lot of use outta that lawn chair you bought her for Christmas three years ago and not a word of thanks since. What kind of father buys something as useful as a lawn chair for his kids? One with a cupholder even? A damn thoughtful one, I tell you. No fucking respect.

(*Pausing to smoke as CHESTER ignores her, reading his letter.*)

What's in the mail?

CHESTER: (*Throws the letter to the floor in a rage.*)

Fucking bitch!

(DARLENE *moves to pick up the letter as CHESTER stomps into the kitchen with the rest of the mail. He returns quickly, opening a can of beer and taking a long drink.*)

That bitch wants me to help pay for Jason's college tuition.

(CHESTER *drinks his beer, fuming, as DARLENE reads the letter.*)

DARLENE: She says she'll take you to court to fight for it. Fucking bitch.

(*Beat. Then, confused.*)

Which wife is this?

CHESTER:	(*Drinks his beer.*)

First. The other two never had any kids—must've been something wrong with them. And then there was Gao Yung over in 'Nam . . . but that was never official. I wonder how little Choo or whatever her name is is doing these days. She's gotta be about nine or ten by now, but there's no proof she's mine anyway . . . Fucking bitches.

DARLENE: What more do they want from you? This is ridiculous, Chester. They're bleeding us dry and what right do they have? First Jason needed braces and Heather had to have that, that tumor removed or something. That cost a fucking arm and a leg. Then she wanted to go to college. Thank God we didn't have to pay for that—

CHESTER: That girl will never make anything of herself. After all I did for her too.

DARLENE: Damn right, honey. She might have a few degrees by now, but what good is that gonna do her? She might have an okay job at that university or whatever, but writing books for a living ain't gonna put food in her mouth for long. Ungrateful brat don't know the meaning of hard work.

CHESTER: After all I did for her.

DARLENE: She's gonna end up poor and miserable, mark my words. And then who's she gonna come crying to when she needs money?

CHESTER: It sure as hell better not be me. And Jason, what he needs is to join the Army. I was in the Army and I built character. He doesn't need a college education now—what kid needs to go to college at eighteen? What he needs is to be drafted. I went to the Army out of high school, fought in 'Nam and then went to college later.

(*With pride.*)

Went to college nights and worked full-time and look at me now. That's what that boy needs. What's he going to do in college at eighteen? He's going to be a lazy bum is what. Just like his sister. Neither one of them know the meaning of hard work. No respect.

(He eases himself into his armchair, resting his beer on the table.)

DARLENE: Chester, how many fucking times do I have to tell you to use a coaster? That table used to belong to Great-Grandma Sullivan and I swear to God if you put a mark in it—

CHESTER: Don't you have anything better to do than yell at me all day from the second I get home—

(They overlap, screaming at each other, DARLENE standing, practically shouting, in CHESTER's face, CHESTER yelling back but at the same time ignoring her proximity and not looking her in the eye.)

CHESTER: You're nothin' but a nag and I don't even know why I married you in the first place you don't do nothin' around here except take up space and complain that I don't buy you enough shit to keep you happy and yell at me about my drinkin' and complain about my mother like it's your business anyway—

DARLENE: I swear to God Chester I will leave you and divorce you so fast you won't even know what hit you you'll be sorry mister let me tell you 'cause I'll leave you and take Baby Baby with me just like all your other wives left you alone with no one to do your God damn cooking and cleaning—

BABY BABY: *(OS.)* Mom!!!!

(CHESTER and DARLENE stop fighting and DARLENE runs off R. to BABY BABY in the bathroom, yelling something incoherent yet obviously annoyed.)

CHESTER: *(Mumbling to himself, taking off his glasses and pinching the bridge of his nose as BABY BABY and DARLENE argue unintelligibly offstage.)*

Damn kids. I got too many of them if that ain't the truth. And I do everything for those kids. They're spoiled is what they are.

(Pauses, reading the letter.)

Emergency room bill! I swear these kids go to the doctor more than any damn kid I ever met in my life. Their mothers are fucking hypochondriacs. Appendicitis my ass. What that kid needs is aspirin and some cheese to go with his whine.

(DARLENE *re-enters.* CHESTER *gestures towards the bathroom.*)

What's her problem?

(CHESTER *tosses the letter to the floor and* DARLENE *picks it up, taking it into the kitchen.* CHESTER *takes another drink from his beer can.*)

DARLENE: (*Off.*) I'm trying to teach that girl to dye her hair properly.

(CHESTER *opens another letter, reads briefly as* DARLENE *re-enters.*)

She's in the bathroom with her head in the sink.

CHESTER: (*Annoyed.*) What's she dyeing her hair for? She's only five.

DARLENE: She's nine Chester, and she's gotta learn some time. And I tell you, going to the salon is a rip off. I mean, look at my hair—I've been doing it myself for years and you can't tell the difference. Same with the tanning. No daughter of mine is gonna waste her money at the tanning salon. Home Bake makes perfectly good tanning lotion and as soon as summer comes that girl is gonna work on her color.

CHESTER: She's only five.

DARLENE: She's nine. If she doesn't learn now, when will she ever? Chester, you're the one who made Jason go to Attica with you when he was four. And then he got in trouble for telling his kindergarten teacher about the convict who cut off his wife's hands and put them in the toaster—

CHESTER: The boy had to have an education, Darlene! That's the way the world works. The boy had to learn. There are people in the world who do things like that—use hands for toast, or cut off their spouse's and dog's heads and sew them to the other's body. Darlene, that's a lesson every kid needs to know, and four is hardly too young to learn it. On the other hand, Baby don't need to be dyeing her hair.

Next thing I know, you'll be putting her in a halter top and teaching her how to shop on the QVC.

> (CHESTER *pauses, looking at* DARLENE's *excessive jewelry collection, of which she seems to be wearing every piece.*)

As you seem to have done. With my credit card.

DARLENE: (*Fuming, as* CHESTER *goes back to reading his mail.*)

And all those collector's edition state quarters in their own special map with a numbered certificate of authenticity haven't been running up the bill any.

CHESTER: Those'll be worth something someday Darlene. It says so on the certificate.

DARLENE: (*Walking off L.*) Yeah, twenty-five cents.

CHESTER: (*Ripping open another envelope, smiling as he looks at the letter.*)

Two more payments and the Caddy will be all mine. That was one faithful car. I dunno what Heather needs with that new Volkswagen. Spoiled brat. I would have helped her pick out a nice used car. Nothing wrong with a used car. I been driving used cars all my life and look at me—I get around just fine. That girl don't know the value of a dollar wasting her money on some Japanese piece of shit that's gonna fall apart tomorrow. Now that Caddy was a good car. 278,000 miles before I put her out to pasture and I bought her at 110,000 for $800.

> (*Talking to himself now, lost in thought.*)

She probably woulda been begging me for money if her faggy lawyer husband hadn'ta bought it for her. Restraining order, my ass.

> (*Picks a postcard out of the pile and looks at it, frowning.*)

Darlene!

> (*There is a slight commotion off L. and the sound of* BABY BABY *protesting.*)

DARLENE: (*Off.*) Chester I'm busy helping Baby with her hair! What the fuck do you want?

CHESTER: Max is overdue for his vet's appointment!

(*Pause, and eventually DARLENE comes out of the bathroom.*)

DARLENE: (*Frowning at CHESTER, disturbed.*) That dog died two months ago, Chester.

CHESTER: (*Laughing at himself.*) Well, I guess he don't need to go to the vet's then.

DARLENE: (*Walking off L.*) You're sick, Chester.

CHESTER: That was a good dog, Darlene. He knew how to obey and never had to go to some stupid dog school. A nice swift kick was good enough for that dog. And he knew who his master was.

(*Instantly irritated, CHESTER jumps up from his chair and goes to the window, violently opening the blinds. He shouts through the screen.*)

And I know you fuckers killed him! I know all about you! There's a reason I built that fence and you know damn well what it is, killing my dog!

(*A very faint "Fuck you!" is heard from off R., beyond the Caddy and the fence. CHESTER moves back towards his chair, throwing himself into it and drinking the rest of his beer.*)

White trash sitting around in their house doing nothing but drinking beer and smoking cigarettes. And killing my dog.

(*CHESTER takes out a pack of cigarettes and smokes as he goes back to looking through his mail. A second, louder commotion is heard from off L. and BABY BABY stomps into the living room, carrying a book under her arm as DARLENE yells at her to get back in the bathroom. Her hair is in a wet, tangled, mess. She's wearing a haltertop and cut off shorts, much like her mother but unlike DARLENE, doesn't wear them naturally. BABY BABY fidgets and pulls at her shorts, trying to pull them farther down her legs, even walking a little bowlegged and uncomfortably. She sits on the couch and opens her book, reading, ignoring* CHESTER. *Initially,* CHESTER *ignores her as well.*)

CHESTER: (*Finally looking up from his mail.*) What do you think you're doing?

BABY BABY: (*Not looking at* CHESTER.) I'm reading a book. I don't like sitting in the bathroom with my head in the sink.

(CHESTER *gets up from his chair and snatches the book away from* BABY BABY.)

CHESTER: You don't need to be reading no book. You're only five—you don't know how to read.

BABY BABY: I'm nine! And I most certainly do know how to read.

(BABY BABY *gets up and takes the book back from her father.*)

CHESTER: Don't you lie to me! You're only five and you have no idea how to read!

(CHESTER *gets up and grabs the book back.*)

BABY BABY: I'm nine!

(BABY BABY *tries to take the book back from* CHESTER, *but he puts it up out of her reach and looks at it.*)

CHESTER: What is this junk anyway? The Moral Ass . . . Ass . . .

BABY BABY: *The Moral Aesthetics of Victorian England.* Heather wrote it and she gave it to me!

(*She jumps for the book and finally gets it out of* CHESTER's *hands, running off R.*)

CHESTER: (*Calling after* BABY BABY) Your sister's a deadbeat.

(*Pause.*)

And you're only five!

> (*We hear the slamming of a bedroom door as* CHESTER *sits back down in his chair and goes back to the mail.*)

I'm her father, I should know these things.

> (DARLENE *enters from L., wet down her front and splattered with dark stains from hair dye.*)

DARLENE: (*In one long streaming high pitched complaint.*)

Your daughter! Chester, you need to teach that girl some discipline! I'm not her slave she expects me to teach her how to dress like a lady and dye her hair and then has the nerve to complain about it and leave me in the bathroom to clean up her mess she complains about her shorts being too short and her top being too small and she don't wanna color her hair but if I don't teach her to look like a lady no one will God knows you won't! After all I do for that brat this is how she treats me!

> (CHESTER *looks up from his mail.*)

CHESTER: (*Shouting in* BABY BABY'*s general direction*) Baby Baby, respect your mother!

> (CHESTER *opens another envelope as* DARLENE *goes out to the kitchen to return with her cigarettes. She lights up as* CHESTER *lets out a grunt of surprise.*)

Well, speak of the devil. It's a notice from the federal government. Seems as though we haven't actually given Baby a proper name on her birth certificate. It looks like a problem for Social Security or somethin'.

DARLENE: Chester I've been bugging you for years now over what to name that girl. She's nine years old, she needs a name. We can't keep calling her Baby Baby forever.

CHESTER: She's five. I don't know what a five-year-old needs with a name anyway. No one calls five-year-olds on the phone. No one writes letters to five-year-olds. I don't see as how she needs something like a name right now. She'll get one in good time.

(BABY BABY *comes out of her bedroom and stands in the doorway, neither parent noticing her.*)

DARLENE: She's nine, Chester! And she needs a name!

BABY BABY: (*Whispering to herself, neither parent hearing her.*) I have a name. I call myself Cleopatra, the strongest woman in the world.

CHESTER: She isn't nine. I think I'd know it if she were.

DARLENE: Whether she's five or nine, she needs a name! And she needs to start going to school! You keep her cooped up in here like she's some sort of pet!

CHESTER: (*Agitated.*) Get me another beer, woman.

(DARLENE *angrily moves off R., towards the kitchen.*)

When I was five I worked as a mechanic in my father's shop. And I helped on the farm too. And I walked to work uphill both ways in the freezing snow in July with no shoes. Five-year-olds don't need to go to school—they need to know the meaning of hard work.

(DARLENE *re-enters with a beer and a coaster, smashing both down on the table by* CHESTER. *He opens the beer can, takes a long drink and sets it back on the table, ignoring the coaster.*)

And five-year-old girls certainly don't need to go to school. What she needs is a husband and a few kids to keep her busy.

DARLENE: She's nine!

CHESTER: Don't matter, Darlene. There are only three things a five-year-old girl or any girl needs to know. To cook, to clean, and to remember that there are people out there who will use hands for toast. And no amount of schooling is going to teach her that.

(BABY BABY *starts to cry and silently runs off L. and into her room.*)

It's a cold, hard world out there, Darlene. The sooner she learns these things the better. And she ain't gonna learn them at school

(DARLENE *walks off R., shaking her head and muttering to herself about* CHESTER *and the "drink."*)

Hands for toast, Darlene. That's all she needs to know.

(CHESTER *eases back into his chair and finishes his beer. The lights fade to black.*)

END

Carey Daniels has an MFA in playwriting from
Western Michigan University. *Hands for Toast*
is part of a series of plays about the different
people associated with the main character,
Chester. She dedicates this play to her mother
and brother.

Offering

In this brief encounter between a teacher and a student, Richard Keller shows how much may be accomplished by creating tension between the character as type and the character as individual. Mr. Wycoff, the Social Studies teacher, and Francis, the student being kept after class, begin immediately to say and do things that establish their uniqueness and lead to revelations and discoveries that are both credible and surprising. In fact, the play's action depends precisely on the characters' moving beyond their social roles and exposing to each other unexpected measures of vulnerability.

What begins as a familiar exercise of authority by a teacher becomes a complex and humorous negotiation in which the teacher risks that very authority and acknowledges his humanity. Mr. Wycoff's tentative foray into matchmaking between Francis and his younger daughter ends on a hopeful note, suggesting not merely that boy will meet girl, but also that establishing meaningful human relationships involves, in Ferlinghetti's phrase, "constantly risking absurdity."

Richard Keller

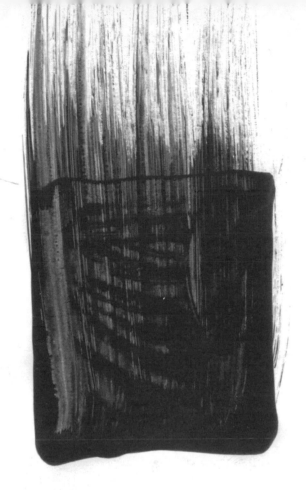

Offering

CHARACTERS   MR. WYCOFF.

FRANCIS.

SETTING   A high school classroom.

(Lights up on a tired-looking high school classroom. FRANCIS, an adolescent boy dressed in Goth style, including a cape, eye makeup, and dyed black hair, stands with his palms outstretched and his head tilted to the side. MR. WYCOFF, a balding, middle-aged teacher, enters.)

MR. WYCOFF: What's with the pose, Eddie?

FRANCIS: I'm exposing my wounds.

MR. WYCOFF: You know, I used to dye my hair. Yeah, when I had more to dye. Now I'm dying to have more. *(No response.)* Cool cape. You look like the Antichrist.

FRANCIS: I'm not working the Satan angle. I'm a Christian Goth. It's mostly about clothes and self-absorption.

MR. WYCOFF: What about the wounds?

FRANCIS: Stigmata tattoos. They wash off with alcohol. My name is Francis.

MR. WYCOFF: I know. I was ribbing you. Such a serious kid.

FRANCIS: Adolescent. Why do you always call me Eddie?

MR. WYCOFF: Eddie Munster. The ghoul. Hid under the kitchen sink. Eddie Munster? From *The Munsters?*

FRANCIS: Funny. Of course, it would be funnier if the sandbags who pass for my classmates got your joke. Then you'd all share a big laugh.

MR. WYCOFF: You know, it's a small town we have here. You'd probably make friends quicker if you lightened up. Lost the ennui.

FRANCIS: *Leave it to Beaver.*

MR. WYCOFF: What?

FRANCIS: *(Stops holding his pose.) Leave . . . it . . . to . . . Beaver.* See? I know old TV shows too. You're a social studies teacher, not a guidance counselor.

MR. WYCOFF:	Fine.
FRANCIS:	(*Pause.*) I wasn't the one making the farting noises.
MR. WYCOFF:	I know you weren't.
FRANCIS:	Then why am I being detained?
MR. WYCOFF:	Am I keeping you? Are you supposed to meet your friends now? (*Pause.*) What do you do for fun?
FRANCIS:	Fun?
MR. WYCOFF:	Yeah, you know, football, playing records, the glee club. I collected stamps in high school.
FRANCIS:	Oh, fun!
MR. WYCOFF:	Who do you hang out with?
FRANCIS:	Sammy Torino. His clique.
MR. WYCOFF:	Really?
FRANCIS:	Sure. Like after school we usually get together. Well, not exactly "together." They'll walk about twenty paces behind me, and when they want my attention, a rock will whiz past my ear. Or sometimes they'll leave notes for me on my locker. Literally, on my locker. Which is really cool because they do it with ketchup.
MR. WYCOFF:	I get the picture.
FRANCIS:	And when I feel like chillin' cause I'm tired of hangin' with my boys, I'll head down to the volunteer fire department and listen to the noon whistle. I can't get enough of that noon whistle.
MR. WYCOFF:	You sound like someone else I know.
FRANCIS:	Yeah, who's that?

MR. WYCOFF:	My daughter.
FRANCIS:	Jamie Wycoff? The senior? President of the Enrichment Society? Student Council Secretary? Prom Committee Chairman? Loud hallway-laugher with a penchant for snug cardigans?
MR. WYCOFF:	I was talking about the younger Wycoff girl.
FRANCIS:	Oh, Deborah. A freshman and chubby. She doesn't seemed destined to follow in sis's footsteps.
MR. WYCOFF:	Well, that's the rub. I mean it's not a problem for us, not for Mrs. Wycoff and myself. It's Deborah . . . well, Jamie casts a long shadow. It's difficult for Deb. It doesn't help that her father's a teacher here.
FRANCIS:	Not even a popular one.
MR. WYCOFF:	So much for being a "Christian" Goth.
FRANCIS:	There are popular teachers and popular students and then there's the rest of us. Nobody's breaking down your classroom door or my coffin lid. (*Pause.*) My parents are the religious ones, not me. We've compromised. If I continue to go to church, I get to dress the way I want.
MR. WYCOFF:	My heart goes out to them.
FRANCIS:	My heart goes out to Deborah.
MR. WYCOFF:	You two should commiserate. (*Pause.*) Have you ever talked to her?
FRANCIS:	She's a freshman. (MR. WYCOFF *doesn't understand.*) I'm a sophomore.
MR. WYCOFF:	Right. That whole year difference in age. (*Pause.*) You might have a lot in common.
FRANCIS:	Is this a small town ritual? The lottery winner sacrifices his youngest daughter to the freak?

MR. WYCOFF: Who says you're a freak? You're a bright kid with a . . . a strong sense of style. That's not a crime.

FRANCIS: The eye makeup?

MR. WYCOFF: That might be a crime. (*Pause.*) Look, I think you're a compassionate guy with a . . .

FRANCIS: I am not compassionate. Compassion is a bourgeois construct. I'm the antithesis of compassionate.

MR. WYCOFF: Okay. (*Pause.*) Deborah thinks you're—and these are her words—"all that."

FRANCIS: She said that?

MR. WYCOFF: "All that." I wouldn't make it up.

FRANCIS: She told you this?

MR. WYCOFF: I overheard her on the phone.

FRANCIS: Uh-huh.

MR. WYCOFF: It was an accident . . .

FRANCIS: You were eavesdropping. It happens. (*Pause.*) So she didn't ask you to ask me to ask her out?

MR. WYCOFF: No.

FRANCIS: You're doing this as a concerned father? Does she know? I mean, did she see you by the phone? (*No response.*) You were listening on another extension!

MR. WYCOFF: (*Pause.*) Life at the Wycoff home hasn't been hunky-dory. Jamie has enough going on with being a senior and all that entails. But Deborah . . . well, it's a difficult age for girls.

FRANCIS: She wears a nose ring now.

MR. WYCOFF:	Add that to the wad of gum she's always chewing and the glum look on her face, and she looks like a calf being led to slaughter.
FRANCIS:	Plus the long eyelashes.
MR. WYCOFF:	What?
FRANCIS:	She has long eyelashes.
MR. WYCOFF:	Right.
FRANCIS:	Body piercing is the bomb.
MR. WYCOFF:	It looks painful. And if it isn't painful for her, it's painful for me.
FRANCIS:	Why did you let her do it?
MR. WYCOFF:	You of all people are asking me why? Look at you. Why don't your parents stop you? Stigmata tattoos? For Christ's sake, you look like a . . . a . . .
FRANCIS:	A person with a strong sense of style? (*Pause.*) Is your wife still staying at her mother's? (*Silence.*) You know, Mr. Wycoff, it's a small town we have here. (*Pause.*) The one perk of being dragged to church every Sunday.
MR. WYCOFF:	I didn't know my family was the sermon topic.
FRANCIS:	It's after the service, when we're bottlenecked on the stairs, waiting to shake the Most Reverend's hand. That's when the congregation starts speaking in tongues. Clicking mostly. "Tch, tch, tch. Poor Teddy Wycoff. And the children!"
MR. WYCOFF:	(*Pause.*) My wife suffers from chronic fatigue.
FRANCIS:	"Marital discontent" is what Mrs. Torino calls it. Not that I'm eavesdropping.
MR. WYCOFF:	Yeah, well, Sammy Torino is a bedwetter.
FRANCIS:	Really? Damn!

MR. WYCOFF: I'll deny saying that if you repeat it.

FRANCIS: Who would I tell? (*Pause.*) How do you—

MR. WYCOFF: And don't ask me how I know. (*Pause.*) My wife is tired. Christ, I'm tired. I'm tired of this town. This school. This classroom. The clothes I wear. I'm tired of the clothes the students wear. I'm tired of looking into their dead eyes. (*Pause.*) I can't help my wife. I'm simply too tired. Let her parents help her. (*Pause.*) Deborah used to cut my hair. The little I had left, no sense going to a barber. We'd make a game of it. Pretend I was at a barber shop. We'd make up gossip about the town. "Old man Lupinski's selling his mobile home for parts." Nonsense like that. She'd even pat my face with aftershave when it was over. Hell, now I'm lucky if she looks at me during dinner.

FRANCIS: It's just puberty.

MR. WYCOFF: No, it's something else. Jamie's always been her mother's child, but Deb, she enjoyed being with me. And that's something . . . I mean, you said it. The kids aren't knocking down the door. I'm not great with them. I know that. But Deb, man, I could really make her happy. You know, really make her laugh. (*Pause.*) She wants to stay with her mother. (*Pause.*) I thought if something was going right for her then . . . Jeez. This is pathetic. I'm sorry. (*Pause.*) You can take off.

FRANCIS: (*Long pause.*) I am a sophomore.

MR. WYCOFF: Yeah, I know. I'm very sorry. I shouldn't have . . . it's inappropriate . . .

FRANCIS: Deborah's only a freshman.

MR. WYCOFF: What?

FRANCIS: That one-year difference in age.

MR. WYCOFF: (*Pause.*) Oh, I see.

FRANCIS: And I'm mature.

MR. WYCOFF: So's she.

FRANCIS: Is Jamie seeing any—

MR. WYCOFF: She doesn't know you exist.

FRANCIS: I felt compelled to ask. Truth is, Deborah's much more my type.

MR. WYCOFF: The nose ring?

FRANCIS: The eyelashes. I have to give you props. I don't know how I'd feel about my daughter being attracted to a guy like me.

MR. WYCOFF: I don't know, I've seen you laugh at some of my jokes in class. Not that you're compassionate.

FRANCIS: The boy who laughs at your jokes gets a date with your daughter. Now that is pathetic, Mr. Wycoff.

                (FRANCIS *goes to exit.*)

MR. WYCOFF: Hey, Francis. (FRANCIS *stops.*) I really do like your cape.

                (FRANCIS *dramatically tosses the cape over his shoulder. They exchange a smile. FRANCIS exits. MR. WYCOFF's smile fades. The lights fade to black.*)

                                    END

Richard Keller's one-acts have been produced at numerous theatres in New York City and at the Actors Theatre of Louisville. He is a 2004 recipient of a New York State Foundation for the Arts Fellowship in playwriting and is a past recipient of a Creative Artist Grant from the Michigan Council for Arts and Cultural Affairs. Richard lives in Ithaca, New York, with his wife, Karen, and their daughter, Sasha.

Richard Keller

Attention

Holly Walter Kerby centers her play on the physical and external: setting, props, and other specific references to the world beyond the stage. Setting can, of course, generate action. The places where we must be create obvious pressures; those where we choose to be may act on us more subtly. Our own places are often an outgrowth of, or at least reflect, ourselves. *Attention* gives us both ends of a telephone conversation between Amber and David, who have reached a crucial point in their developing relationship. David, having assisted his brother Tim in relocating to another town, is calling Amber from the study in Tim's new home; Amber is in her own study, playing *The Sims,* a game that involves creating and building lives for computer-generated characters.

The settings, miles apart, underscore the distance in the relationship. David, inspired by the example of his brother's established family, is on the point of asking Amber to marry him; she, upset at his having excluded her from the move, is distracted by the game. She continues to play throughout their conversation, and notes that the game is "here when I need it." The play is full of "stuff" that helps to get what's inside the characters to emerge in dialogue and action, triggering memories, emotions, and conflicts, and revealing wants and needs. Ultimately, these elements complicate the play's resolution by suggesting that the distance between Amber and David may remain as an obstacle to their future happiness.

45

Holly Walter Kerby

Attention

CHARACTERS	AMBER: early twenties; an attractive, vivacious woman who has trouble sitting still.
	DAVID: early twenties; a kind, sincere, serious guy.
SETTING	DR—office chair, wastebasket, and computer desk laden with various components of a computer system and the litter of daily living.
	UL—cardboard boxes, some partially unpacked.

(*As lights rise we hear the opening music for the computer game* The Sims *and see* AMBER *at the computer, deeply engrossed in the game. A cell phone rings. She waits for three or four rings to look for it, find it, and answer it.*)

AMBER: (*Distracted.*) Hello?

DAVID: Hi.

AMBER: (*Surprised, but warm.*) Hi. Where are you?

DAVID: At my brother's house.

AMBER: In Beloit?

DAVID: Yeah. I'm in his study. Except there's just boxes now. We got most of the stuff moved in last night. Two loads.

AMBER: (*Tentative. Probing.*) I didn't expect to hear from you this weekend.

DAVID: Well. I've been thinking about things and a . . . how are you?

AMBER: (*Wistfully.*) Fine. I'm drowning my sorrows.

DAVID: (*Alarmed.*) You're drinking?

AMBER: No! I'm on the computer. Playing *The Sims*.

DAVID: I take it that's a game.

AMBER: Yeah. You create characters, make them a house, get them jobs. Build relationships. (*Pause.*) You wouldn't like it.

DAVID: It was nice of you to offer to help my brother move.

AMBER: You know how I feel. I'd like to—

DAVID: (*Interrupting.*) I feel bad I said no. But, I got nervous. I mean, they're my family.

AMBER:	I know. You explained. You're not ready.
DAVID:	But I have been thinking.
AMBER:	(*Pause.*) Go on.
DAVID:	Because. This morning Joan, that's Tim's wife, she made us breakfast.
AMBER:	Uh-huh.
DAVID:	Pancakes. But the kids, they ate like two bites and they were gone. They couldn't wait to try out their new backyard. Have I told you about Tim's kids?
AMBER:	Not much.

(AMBER *continues playing the game, working the mouse with her free hand. She becomes more absorbed as DAVID goes on in following speech.*)

DAVID:	Two girls. Leah and Grace. Tim and I went outside to see what they were up to and they're playing in the sandbox under this huge tree. They make us sand pancakes and we pretend to eat them. Tim asks me what's new. I tell him I've been dating this woman for a couple months and—

(*Computer emits the sound of a man whistling a tune. DAVID stops to listen.*)

DAVID:	Is there someone there with you?
AMBER:	Huh? Oh. That's Dirk.
DAVID:	Dirk?
AMBER:	He's my guy Sim. He's puttering around the house.
DAVID:	Are you still playing that game?
AMBER:	Just maintenance. If you don't stay on top of it, the characters get disgruntled.

DAVID: (*Disgruntled.*) But I'm talking.

AMBER: I'm listening. I can do two things at once.

DAVID: Well, that bugs me. I want you to listen, that's all. Not play a game.

AMBER: (*A little put out.*) OK. Fine. I'll pause it. But I was listening.

DAVID: Where was I?

AMBER: In the backyard, with your nieces.

DAVID: Talking with Tim. He asked me if I wanted to go to the hardware store to get stuff to ground the outlets in the study. For the computer. But we'd have to take the girls, so I said no—I'd hang out and watch them. Guess what they wanted to do as soon as he was gone?

AMBER: I don't know.

DAVID: Climb the tree.

AMBER: Ahh.

　　　　　　　　　(AMBER *sits still, listening, for a beat or so, but as* DAVID's *story continues, she starts swiveling her computer chair from side to side. At one point in her chair antics,* AMBER *spins all the way around. Another spin stops with her facing the monitor, and, without a thought, she un-pauses the game and begins to play. The intermittent muttering of* The Sims *characters is heard.*)

DAVID: I couldn't blame them. It's a beautiful tree. Nice low branches. They dragged their plastic picnic table over and stacked up sand pails to reach the lowest branch.

AMBER: Uh-huh.

DAVID: I said, you know, this isn't safe. But, tell you what. I'll help you out. So I boost them both onto the lowest branch which is about shoulder high. Leah starts climbing—which is pretty easy, the branches are nice and close. And Gracie, that's the four-year-old, she stands on the lowest branch singing the "Star Spangled Banner" at the top of her lungs.

(DAVID *pauses, but* AMBER *doesn't.*)

DAVID: I think this is pretty funny, until, all of a sudden, at the "land of the free," she jumps off the branch. No warning, nothing. Just leaps into thin air.

(Sims *shopping music plays.*)

AMBER: Humm.

DAVID: (*Listens.*) Amber? Are you still playing that game?

AMBER: What? Whoops. I guess I am.

DAVID: I asked you to stop!

AMBER: I know. I'm sorry. I'll pause it again. Can you actually hear it through the phone?

DAVID: Yes! But that's not what tipped me off.

AMBER: What do you mean?

DAVID: I'll call you when I get back.

AMBER: No, no. I said I was sorry. It's just that . . . I . . . must have . . .gone on autopilot. But I'm aware of it, now. So. It's under control.

DAVID: Are you sure?

AMBER: Positive. Go on with your story.

DAVID: Well. Gracie jumped out of the tree into thin air.

AMBER: My God.

DAVID: Lucky for her, I caught her. In my arms she sings, "And the home of the brave!" and starts laughing. I start to yell at her, but she's laughing so hard that after a while I start laughing, too.

AMBER: Smart kid.

DAVID: Then Leah's calling from up in the tree. I can't see her, so I step back, and I still can't see her, so I go way back, midway into their yard and there she is, way up near the top of the tree. It's like a hundred and fifty feet up. She yells, "I don't know how to come down!"

AMBER: Oh, no.

DAVID: Oh, yes. I swing up into the tree and start climbing as fast as I can, all the time saying things like, don't panic, I'm coming, whatever you do, don't jump. But then, two thirds of the way up, the branches get so thin they won't hold my weight. Gracie's below yelling, "Call the fire department! My sister's going to die!" I think, what the hell am I going to do? My brother's gone. I don't know where Joan is. I'm the fucking grownup here. Then I think, stay calm, work with the situation. I say to Leah, "It's OK. I'm going to teach you how to get down." She says she wants me to come up and carry her down. I say, "No. You're a big girl. You can come down yourself. Just listen and do what I say." And Amber, I do it, I talk her down from the tree. I was worried at first—she's not that great with right and left. But, she's really smart! Once she figured out what I was talking about, she climbed down like a pro, jumped from the bottom branch, and landed on her feet. Then she's telling us how brave she was and how she's going to climb an even bigger tree tomorrow. Then Gracie says—and this is the part I wanted to tell you—Grace says, "Uncle David, how come you're not a daddy?" And I think, where did this come from? Except that I did, sort of, save the day. I say, "Well . . . for one thing, I'm not married." Gracie says, "How come?" And Leah says, "He's not married because he hasn't found someone to love." And I think—yes, I have! (*Pause.*) I don't want ahead of myself here, talking about kids and stuff, but . . . well, I care about you in a way I only care about . . . family. Ummm. Know what I mean?

> (*At the start of* DAVID's *speech beginning, "Lucky for her, I caught her,"* AMBER *listens intently, making appropriate murmurs in response. Soon, however, she starts playing with the mouse and starts up the game.*

She catches herself, re-pauses, and sits on her hands. Then she resumes swiveling in the chair, forgets herself, and starts up the game again. When the sound of The Sims *television makes her realize what she is doing, she jumps to pause it again, and listens guiltily, to see if DAVID heard the game. He pauses, too, but then goes on. AMBER tries, unsuccessfully, to keep her eyes off the monitor and finally resorts to shielding her eyes from the monitor with one, then both hands. The computer continues to beckon her [This can be done with lights.] To resist, she rolls the chair UP, away from the computer and around DL and UR of the stage. As the allure of the computer grows stronger, she must go to more and more extreme measures to keep from getting "sucked" in [Think Lucille Ball]. At some point where she seems to have resisted or even broken the spell, she finds a hair on her sweater, picks it off, hunts for the wastebasket, and deposits the hair. Then, without a thought, she begins to play the game again. The* Sims *romantic music plays and she freezes, realizing she is playing again. She covers the mouthpiece of the phone with one hand and turns off the sound with the other. Now a decision—will she continue or stop? She gives in to the allure of the game, and quietly, covertly, begins to interact with the computer, covering the mouthpiece of the phone. Soon she is in a dream world, just her and* The Sims, *oblivious to whatever DAVID is saying.*)

DAVID: Amber? Amber! Are you there?!

AMBER: What? I'm listening.

DAVID: No, you're not. You're on that goddamn computer again.

AMBER: David. I'm sorry, but just before the last pause, their basement flooded, and then this neighbor wandered over, a guy she's been flirting with, and I wanted to see what would happen. I tried to ignore it, but I couldn't resist.

DAVID: See you later.

AMBER: No. God, David! Don't go. I'm just being honest. I want to listen, but I can't be by the computer and not play. It's too tempting.

DAVID: Turn it off.

AMBER: What?

DAVID: Turn off the computer. Then you won't be tempted.

AMBER: (*Pauses. This is a horrifying thought.*) But . . . I'll have to turn it on again once we're done talking.

DAVID: So? Turn it off now.

AMBER: That seems a bit extreme.

DAVID: Extreme? I'm pouring out my soul here, and you're playing your fucking game, not hearing a word I say.

AMBER: All right. I'll shut it down. Just let me save my people.

DAVID: No. Just turn it off.

AMBER: But I haven't saved in a while.

DAVID: I don't care.

AMBER: I've spent the whole morning with these characters.

DAVID: For Christ's sake, Amber. They're not real!

AMBER: (*Overlapping.*) I know that!

DAVID: It's a game!

AMBER: (*Overlapping.*) I know!

DAVID: A diversion!

AMBER: (*Overlapping.*) I know! But what's wrong with that? It's entertaining, and . . . (*Pointedly.*) it's here when I need it.

DAVID: (*Ouch.*) Listen. (*Pause.*) I know I let you down about this weekend.

AMBER: Then don't make me choose.

DAVID: You choose either way! If you can't listen, you choose the game. If you turn it off . . . Amber, I'm trying to tell you something. I need your attention. Is that too much to ask?

             (*She doesn't respond.*)

DAVID: Amber?

AMBER: I'm thinking! (*Pause of decision. Deep sigh.*) Shit.

             (AMBER *uses the mouse to exit the program and to shut down the computer. Then, still clutching the mouse.*)

             It's done.

DAVID: (*Surprised.*) You did it?

AMBER: Yes. You have my attention.

DAVID: Wow. I'm impressed.

AMBER: Great. Because now I feel anxious . . . and vulnerable. And needy.

DAVID: Oh.

AMBER: So. (*Pause.*) What was it you wanted to say?

DAVID: (*Nervous.*) Umm. Well, I a . . . was thinking and a . . .

AMBER: Spit it out!

DAVID: (*Quickly.*) I love you, too.

AMBER: What?

DAVID: You told me you loved me. I love you, too.

AMBER: (*Overjoyed.*) Really? Oh, my God.

DAVID: (*Happy.*) That's what I wanted to tell you.

AMBER: All this time?

DAVID: All this time.

AMBER: You wanted to tell me.

DAVID: Yes.

AMBER: (*Long pause.*) What took you so long?

(*The lights fade to black.*)

END

Holly Walter Kerby teaches chemistry and playwriting at Madison Area Technical College. *Attention* was written for Mercury Players' production of *Computers in Love* in January 2002. Kerby lives in Madison, Wisconsin, with her husband, two teenage daughters, and a retired greyhound.

Interpreting a Dream

Language is again the focus in this short play by Judy Klass. The setting is a high school principal's office in which Mr. Miller, the voice of authority, is unable to communicate with Ivania, a recent immigrant from a Spanish-speaking country, except through the agency of Ariel, a socially confident student who moves easily between English and Spanish. Miller's goal is clear: he must insist that Ivania adapt to her new surroundings and, most importantly, that she learn English. As he says, "'bilingual education' . . . means both languages, not just Spanish." Equally clear is the irony that neither Miller nor his guidance counselor can speak Spanish.

Klass dramatizes the situation sharply and effectively by her extensive use of Spanish. Those audience members who speak only English must share Miller's frustration and bafflement. They also see how the well-meaning Ariel struggles to be fair to both worlds in an ultimately doomed effort to bridge the gap. More importantly, they gain a real sense of the social and cultural alienation that drive Ivania farther into herself, into a dream of the homeland she has lost.

Judy Klass

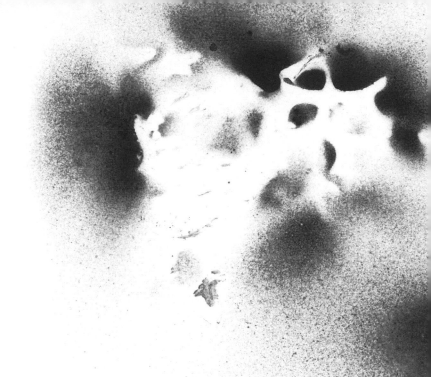

Interpreting a Dream

CHARACTERS   ARIEL: A confident, hip, high school senior, secure enough about her popularity to try to help a nerd in trouble. Her clothes and hair should reflect her level of cool.

IVANIA: A shy, sensitive girl, lost in a dreamworld. The same age as ARIEL, but appears younger. She wears a blouse with a Peter Pan collar, with brand X jeans or a simple, dark polyester skirt.

MR. MILLER: A high school principal, in his forties. Stuffy, though he sees himself as able to rap with kids and be one of the gang.

SETTING   MR. MILLER's office, the present—and then IVANIA's dream bedroom.

(*As the lights rise,* IVANIA *sits sullen, slumped in a chair in the principal's office.* ARIEL, *in the chair beside her, tries to cheer her up and reason with her.*)

ARIEL: So, listen, don't be scared or nothing like that. I'll try to do some damage control for you.

(IVANIA *does not respond.*)

Listen, I been meaning to tell you—if you want to go to the mall some time, together, that would be cool. We could go with Sandra and Elise, or whatever. I could just go with you. Pick out some new clothes. I'd be happy to do that.

(IVANIA *looks down at her clothes, then over at* ARIEL, *expressionless.*)

I'm not saying you have to spend a fortune, and buy all Calvin Klein and DKNY or whatever. *Oiste? No es necesario a comprar muchas cosas, es posible a llevar mucho que ya tu tienes . . .* I just mean, like, if you want to fit in more. Don't take it the wrong way.

(IVANIA *continues to glance around the room.*)

Que piensas?

IVANIA: (*Shrugs.*) *Nada.*

ARIEL: *Nada.* Great. *Espero que tu insanidad no me dañe. Mira, quiero ayudarte, pero tienes que intentar ayudarte tu mismo.* You gotta try to help yourself!

(IVANIA *again shrugs.*)

He's not such a bad guy. *No es mal hombre. El cree que un dialogo,* you know, a "dialogue" *puede resolver todo. Pero, la cosa es para parecer escuchar su consejo—y no a mostrar miedo!* Don't look like you're scared!

IVANIA: *No tengo miedo.*

ARIEL: (*Annoyed.*) *Y porque no?*

(MR. MILLER *enters. He gives the girls a big, reassuring smile, and moves to shake hands with both of them. IVANIA lets him lift her limp hand, but applies no pressure to his.*)

MR. MILLER: Hello, ladies. Thank you for waiting. (*He moves behind his desk, sits.*) And, Ariel, thank you for volunteering to help out here.

ARIEL: No problem, Mr. Miller. I'm glad to do it.

MR. MILLER: I think this is the third time we've had you in here interpreting for someone, is that right?

ARIEL: Fourth time.

MR. MILLER: Well. If this keeps up, you can go to work for the U.N. after college.

(ARIEL *smiles at his little joke.* IVANIA *remains expressionless.*)

You are planning to go to college, aren't you?

ARIEL: Yes, sir, I've applied to five schools where I maybe got a shot.

MR. MILLER: Well, that's terrific. You know, I've heard really wonderful things about you from Mrs. Caldicott. (*Clasps hands on desk. He pronounces the first syllable of "Ivania" the same as "eye."*) So. Does Ivania know—

IVANIA: (*Sharply corrects him, stressing the "ee" sound.*) Ivania.

MR. MILLER: (*Taken aback, pronounces it correctly.*) I'm sorry. Does Ivania know why she's been sent to my office?

ARIEL: (*To* IVANIA.) *Entiendes porqué estamos aquí?*

(IVANIA *shrugs.*)

MR. MILLER: We understand that she's having trouble adjusting, and that a new country can seem big and scary. We're not trying to gang up on her here. We want to try to

Judy Klass

63

help her, be her friend.

ARIEL: *El dice que es tu amigo, quiere ayudarte. Hazlo más facil!*

(IVANIA *shrugs*.)

MR. MILLER: Aha. Ariel, do you have any idea what's going on with her?

ARIEL: Oh, I don't know. I think she's just sad, she misses her country, maybe she misses her old friends.

MR. MILLER: Well, but she's been over here since the start of the year. And apparently she's making no effort to adjust or learn the language. Explain to her, please, that when we say "bilingual education" we do mean it. "Bilingual" means both languages, not just Spanish.

ARIEL: *Dice que "bilingual" significa ambos idiomas. Porque no puedes hablar inglés?*

IVANIA: *No me gusta.*

ARIEL: *Qué?*

IVANIA: *Es un idioma feo, un ruido, con sonidos como la ladrido de un perro. No tiene lógica ni ritmo. Es feo como este país es feo, y tosco . . . y cruel.*

MR. MILLER: What did she say?

ARIEL: (*Uncertain how much to tell him.*) Um, she says that English is very hard for her to learn, it's, uh, different from Spanish . . .

MR. MILLER: But did she just say we were being cruel to her?

ARIEL: Oh, no . . . she's saying that . . . she doesn't like English and the U.S. so much.

MR. MILLER: But she's here now. And frankly . . . I'll level with you Ariel. This is something I don't understand about a lot of our Hispanic students—and obviously you're an exception. If I go on a trip to visit a foreign country, I at least listen to Berlitz tapes. I mean, I would make an effort to learn the language, to at least say "How much does that cost?" Or "Where is a good hotel?" It's just polite. I wouldn't expect them to speak like me. And yet we have students here . . . and of course I don't mean you, your English is wonderful . . .

ARIEL: Well, I was born here. I'm an American.

MR. MILLER: Well, all right then, you see? But the ones who weren't born here, they're not just here on vacation. Most of them are planning to live out their lives here. And yet so many just won't make an effort. And I suppose, in their homes, in their neighborhoods, they don't have to. But what about when they get a job, out in the real world?

ARIEL: Plenty of jobs you don't need English for, Mr. Miller. I mean, you're making a really good point, don't get me wrong—

MR. MILLER: But earlier generations of immigrants, they learned the language. They had to.

ARIEL: Well, you know. First generation?

MR. MILLER: (*Annoyed at being challenged.*) First generation, second generation, they learned it. This is a nation of immigrants, yes. But in order to be united, we need to have one language in common, a *lingua franca*, a coin of the realm. The name for the United States in Latin is *e pluribus unum*, did you know that?

ARIEL: No, sir.

MR. MILLER: "Out of many, one." And the common language makes us one. That's what I don't understand about a student like this. Her attitude. What does she think about when the teachers are trying to help her with her English?

ARIEL: (*To* IVANIA.) *Qué pasa cuando las clases son en inglés? Porqué no lo aprendes?*

IVANIA: *Porqué no vale la pena. Generalmente, no estoy allí en el aula.*

ARIEL: (*Surprised.*) *Dondé estas?*

IVANIA: *Estoy en mi cuarto en mi casa. Mi casa de verdad, no ese pequeño apartamento feo donde vivimos ahora en esta ciudad sucia. En mi casa de verdad, en mi país, tengo una vista de los árboles alrededor del patio. Huelo las hojas y las flores, y siento el silencio y el viento. Escucho los discos de mi abuelita. Y . . . eso es todo.*

MR. MILLER: What did she say?

ARIEL: (*Again, trying to be diplomatic.*) She . . . gets distracted during class. She feels homesick, she misses her old house, the courtyard. Stuff like that.

MR. MILLER: Well, sure. I can understand that. But her parents decided to come here to build a better life, right? They wanted her to be an American. Doesn't she owe it to them to try?

ARIEL: (*To* IVANIA.) *Mira, si tus padres quieren vivir aquí, tu debes aceptar esta cultura, dice.*

IVANIA: No.

ARIEL: No?

IVANIA: *En mi propio país, por supuesto tuve mucho cariño y respeto de mis padres. Pero eso era antes de su traición a mí y a mí país. Allí tenían trabajos admirables, aquí son mugre. Ellos piensan que es un cambio bueno, yo no.*

ARIEL: Ay.

MR. MILLER: Well?

ARIEL: She's mad at her parents that they moved here. She doesn't—respect them so much anymore.

MR. MILLER: I see. So, she refuses to learn English in order to get back at them. Well, we all go through a phase when we're angry at our parents, when they make choices we don't understand. (*Smiling, affable.*) Tell her that the great writer Mark Twain used to fight with his father when he was growing up.

ARIEL: (*To* IVANIA.) *Habla de Mark Twain. Creo que va hacer un chiste.*

MR. MILLER: And he said, when I turned twenty-one, I was amazed to find that my father had suddenly become so much smarter!

(*He chuckles.* ARIEL *smiles, and urges* IVANIA.)

ARIEL: *Sí, lo hizo. Algo aburrido sobre el padre del escritor. Por lo menos, sonríe!*

(IVANIA *remains expressionless, staring at* MR. MILLER *without seeing him.*)

You know, I think she's a really messed-up person, with a lot on her mind. (*To* IVANIA.) *Mira, estas en un aprieto! El es el principal del colegio!*

IVANIA: (*Shrugs.*) *Y, pues?*

ARIEL: *Llamara a tus padres. Quieres eso?*

IVANIA: *No importa.*

ARIEL: Oh no?

IVANIA: *No. No creo en él. No creo en mis padres. No creo en tí. Todo esto es un sueño que no significa nada, mi vida real es en mi pueblo, en mi casa vendida, donde hay belleza y suavidad, donde las personas son gentiles y no son vulgares . . . todo esto no existe.*

MR. MILLER: What is she telling you?

ARIEL: (*Uncertain once more how to tell him.*) She says, um . . . we don't really exist.

MR. MILLER: (*Surprised.*) What?

ARIEL: She feels . . . she sees all this as a dream. She wants to be back in her country.

MR. MILLER: I see. (*Thoughtful.*) Perhaps the school counselor should have a talk with her. It's a shame that he really doesn't speak Spanish. We might need you to interpret for us again, and I don't want to keep pulling you out of class, so maybe we can arrange some kind of meeting after school. Do you play any team sport?

ARIEL: No, not right now. And I'm not doing any clubs.

(MEANWHILE: *from the moment* MR. MILLER *mentions the school counselor and he and* ARIEL *begin to talk, a* SPANISH BALLAD, *from the forties or fifties, begins to play. It should be a love song about loyalty, about not forgetting a loved one.* IVANIA *looks off to the side of the stage, previously in darkness, where a bed with a nicely patterned blanket is revealed. There is a potted plant on a table by the bed, and books in Spanish on the table and the bed. The other two do not see it.*)

MR. MILLER: So that might work out. I think I'd better have a meeting with her parents first. Again, it's so hard, when the parents don't speak English, to find out about a child's emotional state, what's going on in the home. I don't suppose you know the family?

ARIEL: No, I don't know them. You know, I see her around, we have homeroom together, and at lunch a couple times I invited her to come sit with me and my friends. But she just keeps to herself.

(*As the conversation in English continues, the music grows louder, drowning it out, and* IVANIA *rises and crosses to the bed. The others do not notice—*MR. MILLER *or* ARIEL *occasionally indicates* IVANIA's *seat, as if she's still in it.*)

MR. MILLER: Well, her parents really should get her some kind of professional help, but of course that costs money. There are some community counseling services in Spanish, though. I'll have to have my secretary look into it.

(*We can barely hear him by this point. As his conversation with* ARIEL *fades,* IVANIA *sits on the bed, and parts imaginary curtains as if looking out on a courtyard, and finally we see her smile and look happy. The* SPANISH BALLAD *swells, and the lights grow brighter over this area and go down over the principal's office—until they go off completely, all over the stage.*)

END

Eighteen of Judy Klass's one-act plays have
been produced, all over the country. Several
have appeared in small magazines; one is
published in the textbook *Access Literature*.
Her full-length plays *Damage Control* and
Transatlantic have been produced in New York
City, and she also co-wrote the Showtime
version of *In the Time of the Butterflies*.

Judy Klass

We All Give Thanks

Troy Tradup offers a mordantly funny take on family Thanksgivings featuring interruption—more properly disruption—of the holiday ritual idealized annually in scores of television movies and commercials.

As the middle-aged Abbott siblings—Garrett, Randall, and Jill—try to make the best of the holiday at the family home with their apparently Alzheimer's-afflicted parents and their "ancient" grandmother Nana Anna, they continually resort to irreverently humorous dialogue and action that mock the social codes to which most of us pay at least lip service. Tradup also gives this brief comedy substance by focusing on such objects as a defective television set, an anything-but-traditional meatloaf, and a typical array of Christmas decorations put to highly unusual—and hilarious—use.

Tradup's play, however, doesn't simply take the easy route of poking fun at an earlier generation's shallow pieties and pretensions. By the play's conclusion, we have learned that the Abbott siblings, too—particularly Jill—are dealing with their own intimations of mortality, that they care about each other and the rest of their family, and that the ancient Nana Anna, when roused, can give as good as she gets.

Troy Tradup

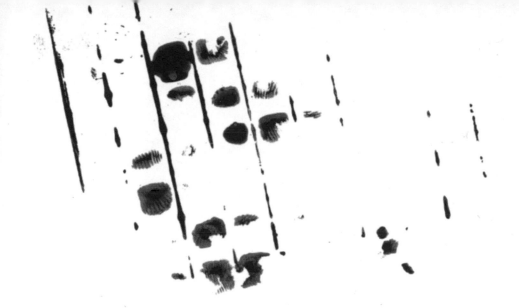

We All Give Thanks

CHARACTERS   GARRETT ABBOTT: 50.

RANDALL ABBOTT: his brother, 48.

JILL ABBOTT: their sister, 42.

NANA ANNA: their grandmother, ancient.

SETTING   The basement of the Abbott family home, late afternoon, Thanksgiving Day.

(*The basement of the Abbott house. There's a ratty old sofa, an old console TV, and a swiveling recliner currently turned away from us and facing the wall. At rise, GARRETT ABBOTT sits on the sofa nursing a drink. The TV is on, but it's just a greenish glow with no sound. After a moment, GARRETT's brother, RANDALL, tiptoes down the stairs. He doesn't notice GARRETT until—*)

GARRETT: So. What's the verdict?

(RANDALL *nearly tumbles down the last few stairs.*)

RANDALL: Jesus! I thought you were out in the garage or something.

GARRETT: Nope. Right here, the last hour.

RANDALL: Jesus.

GARRETT: So. What's happening with dinner? Is there going to be a dinner this year?

RANDALL: Good question. Jill just went into the kitchen and made a few nonspecific but very loud exclamations, and I made my escape down here. (*He notices GARRETT's drink.*) Got any more of that, by chance?

GARRETT: Chance has nothing to do with it.

(*He reaches behind the sofa and hauls up a bottle of Scotch.*)

RANDALL: You're the best big brother ever.

(*He finds a cup, pours a drink.*)

GARRETT: So. Nonspecific exclamations of what sort?

RANDALL: What do you mean?

GARRETT: Well . . . horror, outrage, awe and wonder at the magnificent feast about to be shoveled into our grumbling bellies?

RANDALL: Nonspecific. I think the definition is self-explanatory.

GARRETT: But not very helpful.

(RANDALL *sits on the sofa and squints at the TV screen.*)

RANDALL: Who's playing?

GARRETT: I don't know. Picture tube's shot, so both teams are sorta green-on-green and they're playing in a green stadium.

RANDALL: Who's winning?

GARRETT: The green team. I think.

(GARRETT *and* RANDALL's *sister,* JILL, *pounds down the stairs.*)

JILL: She didn't turn the oven on. She's been checking the bird for six hours, can't figure out why it's not getting done.

GARRETT: Meaning dinner is . . . when? Ten, eleven o'clock tonight?

RANDALL: My plane leaves at 10:45.

JILL: You just got in this morning and you're leaving tonight?

RANDALL: I have to work.

JILL: You're such a schmuck, Randall. (*To* GARRETT.) No, I tossed the turkey in the garbage and threw together a meatloaf. We'll eat in about an hour.

GARRETT: What'd you do with Mom?

JILL: Gave her a gin and tonic and a Seconal and told her to lay down on the couch until it was time to eat.

(*She grabs the Scotch and takes a big swig right from the bottle.*)

RANDALL: Man, they're getting old, aren't they?

GARRETT: Aren't we all?

RANDALL: You know what I mean. She didn't even turn the oven on?

JILL: That's nothing. Sometimes she'll turn the oven on but then forget to put anything in it. Or she'll go out to get the mail but forget to put any clothes on first.

RANDALL: Great.

JILL: Well, old Mr. Peterson across the street seems to like it. (*Beat.*) No. Yeah. She's old. Dad's old. I'm tired. We're gonna have to do something pretty soon here.

GARRETT: I told you a long time ago—we'll just put 'em in a home.

JILL: They were in their forties when you said that, Garrett. I don't think they would have been very cooperative.

GARRETT: Well, give 'em enough Seconal and gin . . .

RANDALL: We are not talking about this right now. I am not ready to put my parents in a home.

JILL: Then maybe you should try coming home for more than twelve hours at a stretch once in a while.

RANDALL: Sixteen hours, thank you very much. Jill, have you ever seen one of those places? What they do there?

JILL: (*To* GARRETT.) I'm going to kill him, you know. I'm going to kill him and bury him in the back yard.

GARRETT: (*To* RANDALL.) You forget, little brother . . . our lovely sister here not only watches over Mom and Dad for us on a daily basis, she also keeps semi-regular tabs on Nana Anna down there at the Sunnyside-Up Drool and Gruel Retirement Home, or whatever the hell they call it.

JILL:	Oh God, that reminds me. I put Nana Anna down for a nap right after we brought her home, and I haven't checked on her since. I'll be right back—

	(*She starts up the stairs.*)

GARRETT:	Hold on. I've got you covered there, Sis.

	(*He points to the recliner.*)

RANDALL:	Oh God.

	(JILL *carefully swivels the recliner around to reveal* NANA ANNA, *ancient and sound asleep, decorated right now with all of the Christmas decorations that Garrett could find. Tinsel, garland, ornaments, strings of popcorn and cranberries . . .*)

JILL:	Oh, Garrett. You didn't.

GARRETT:	Clearly, I did. Just like old times, eh? But wait—there's more. (*He picks up a garish tree-topper of some sort—a star, or perhaps an angel—and places it gently on* NANA ANNA's *head.*) There.

RANDALL:	We're all going to Hell for this, you know. Is she even breathing?

	(GARRETT *holds his glass close to* NANA ANNA's *face to check for respiration.*)

GARRETT:	Yep. Alive and well, pretty as a picture.

JILL:	Randall's right, though—as much as that pains me to say. We're definitely gonna burn for this.

GARRETT:	What? We do this every year.

RANDALL:	We did this once, when we were still in grade school. And it was Nana Anna's idea! We had permission!

GARRETT:	Well, she doesn't seem to be objecting too strenuously right now. I'd say permission is implied.

(*All three siblings stand and watch NANA ANNA sleep for a moment. As much as they try to fight it, RANDALL and JILL can't help but smile. JILL, in particular, has a devilish glint in her eye . . .*)

JILL: Wake her up. Make her do it.

RANDALL: Jill, don't encourage him.

GARRETT: Do what, little sister?

JILL: You know what. Wake her up. Make her do the song.

GARRETT: The song?

JILL: Garrett, I'm gonna pummel you severely about the head and shoulders.

GARRETT: All right, all right. (*He goes to NANA ANNA and shakes her very gently by the shoulder.*) Nana Anna. Nana Anna, wake up. We want to hear the song.

(*NANA ANNA opens one eye and tries to brush GARRETT's hand away. Her movement is somewhat limited by all of the Christmas decorations.*)

JILL: Please, Nana Anna. We want to hear the song.

NANA ANNA: (*Somewhat more awake now.*) Who are you people?

RANDALL: It's just us, Nana Anna.

JILL: Please sing the song for us, Nana Anna.

NANA ANNA: I don't know any songs. Who are you people?

GARRETT: You know who we are, Nana Anna. And you know exactly which song we're talking about. You don't fool me for a second.

(*NANA ANNA glares at him. Then she motions with her head toward the glass in GARRETT's hand.*)

NANA ANNA: All right, smarty pants. Give me a sip of that and I'll sing your damned song for you.

               (GARRETT *gives her a drink from his glass.*)

RANDALL: Should she really be having that?

JILL: She's a hundred and fifty years old. What difference could it possibly make?

NANA ANNA: I am not a day over a hundred and thirty, you little cretin. Now do you want to hear your song or not?

JILL: Yes, Nana Anna. Please.

GARRETT: Sing it, girl.

NANA ANNA: (*In a surprisingly clear voice.*) "Old Mrs. Bliss . . . she went to piiiiiiiiiick . . . some flowers. And in the grass . . . she wet her aaaaaaaaaaaankles . . . to her knees. And on the stoop . . . she took a pooooooooourple old bandana. And as a stunt . . . she touched her counnnnnnntry man at arms . . . "

               (NANA ANNA *instantly falls back to sleep. She snores once, loudly, and then just slumbers quietly.*)

GARRETT: Just like old times.

               (JILL's *wristwatch beeps several times. She removes a small pillbox from one of her pockets.*)

RANDALL: I can take those up for you. Are they Mom's or Dad's?

JILL: Well, actually . . .

               (*She takes out several pills and downs them with a swig of Scotch.*)

RANDALL: What are those for?

GARRETT: (*Overlapping.*) What are you taking there, kid?

JILL: Oh, it's nothing. It's stupid, really. Just this thing.

RANDALL: What thing?

JILL: Oh, it's just this . . . lump thing. This little lump.

RANDALL: A lump where?

JILL: What do you care? You're only here for sixteen hours, remember?

GARRETT: Jill.

(*She glares at him, takes another swig of Scotch. Then—*)

JILL: It's nothing. I was in the shower one day, and I found this lump. Now there are a couple more. But it's nothing. It's just stupid. Don't worry about it.

RANDALL: What do you mean, a couple more? Where?

JILL: Randall, where the hell do you think?

(*She goes to him and grabs his hand. She moves it up under her shirt and presses it against her breast.* RANDALL *fights her for a moment, and then—*)

RANDALL: Oh. Christ.

(JILL *lets go of his hand and he pulls it away as if he's just been burned.*)

JILL: That's enough now. We need to talk about Mom and Dad. We're going to need to move them somewhere.

GARRETT: When did you, uh . . .

JILL: Well, this is November. Six, seven months, I guess—

RANDALL: Seven months? Are you out of your mind? They need to cut those things out of you, Jill. You need chemo, radiation, something . . .

(*A long moment. Then—*)

JILL: Yes, well, that would be one approach.

RANDALL: One approach? What are you saying? You will have surgery, you will have chemo, and you will have radiation or whatever the hell else they need to do to fix this!

JILL: Randall, you have a plane to catch in just a few hours. Why don't you go and talk to Mom and Dad for a while before you have to leave? Don't worry about this other stuff. It's just really not that important.

RANDALL: Hey, I can't help it that I had to come in and leave again on the same day this year. I can't help it that I can't be here every day to help with Mom and Dad—or Nana Anna! I can't help it that—

GARRETT: You know, little brother, I don't think she's asking you to.

> (RANDALL *looks at* JILL. *She smiles softly and shakes her head gently: no.*)

RANDALL: Oh, Christ. Oh, God.

JILL: Randall, it's okay. It really is.

RANDALL: Oh, God. Oh, my God.

GARRETT: Hey, you know, we kind of lost track of what we were doing here.

RANDALL: Oh, for crying out loud, Garrett.

GARRETT: No, come on now. Just like old times, remember?

JILL: Just like old times.

GARRETT: Come on. That meatloaf's gonna be done soon, and there's something we need to practice before dinner. Don't want to disappoint Mom and Dad now. They'll be expecting us to remember it, you know.

JILL: He's right. They'll be expecting it.

GARRETT: Come on then. (RANDALL *and* JILL *join* GARRETT *near the sofa.* RANDALL *is a mess, but they all join hands,* JILL *in between her older brothers.*) Can you reach that light there, little brother? (RANDALL *reaches up with his free hand and pulls the chain to click off the overhead light. The pale green glow from the TV is the only illumination.*) Okay. Let's see if we remember. Just like the old days now. One . . . two . . .

GARRETT/
RANDALL/
JILL: (*Together.*) God is great, God is good, let us thank Him for our food. Amen.

(*A moment. Then—*)

RANDALL: That is the lamest prayer ever.

JILL: It's the only one I remember.

(GARRETT *plugs an extension cord into the wall.* NANA ANNA *is suddenly illuminated by several strands of brightly-colored Christmas lights wrapped all around her and the recliner.*)

GARRETT: Wait—there's more.

(*He does something to the extension cord, and the lights around* NANA ANNA *begin to twinkle on and off in the darkness.*

The three siblings move to the sofa and sit. They huddle close and pull a big quilt up to their chins. They sit for a time, just watching the beautiful blinking lights. The lights fade to black.)

END

Troy Tradup is the author of nine plays, including award-winners *The Desired Effect* and *Chuckling in Limbo*. His anthology contribution, *We All Give Thanks,* was a finalist for the 2003 Heideman Award, and his stage adaptation of *The Island of Dr. Moreau* was recently published by Playscripts, Inc. Troy's adaptation of Charles Dickens's *Hard Times* premiered in the Twin Cities.

Troy Tradup

Someday

This play, like *Attention*, emphasizes distance. In this case, however, dialogue itself becomes the vehicle by which Allison Williams shows how we may be "divided by a common language." In a workroom at the Ginza Vending Company in Tokyo, two women—Michiko and Nomi—put on new panties from a box, wear them for a short time, then remove them and place them in plastic bags to be sold as fetishes in vending machines. They speak in phonetic Japanese, translated into English by Interpreters 1 and 2. This, of course, places demands on the audience's attention. But the demands do not end there, for the interpreters further translate many of the English lines into second, more direct versions that Japanese politeness inhibits the women—who know each other only through their work—from expressing. Nomi's curiosity, however, ultimately breaks through the older Michiko's reserve, thereby interrupting the social ritual.

Again, the "stuff" of the play not only reinforces, but creates its essential action and resolution. The women are dressed normally from the waist up, yet are forced into uneasy intimacy from the waist down. And the double translation of their dialogue, which begins in verbal comedy, drives the play convincingly to Michiko's final moving revelation and the closing of the distance between both characters and audience.

Allison Williams

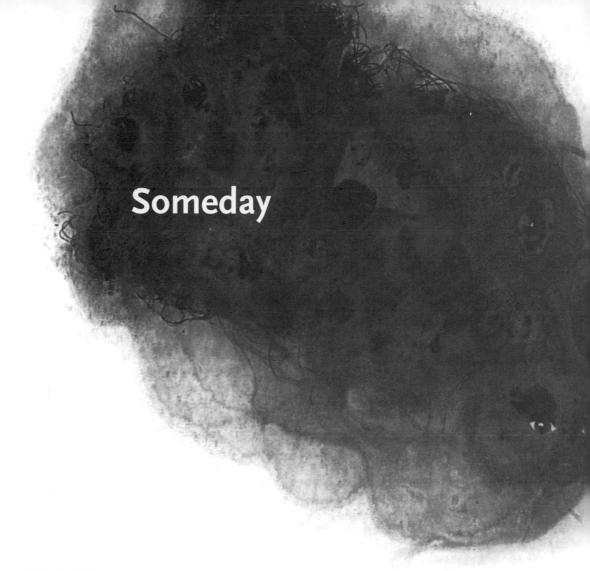

Someday

CHARACTERS	MICHIKO TAKASHI: a worker.
	NOMI CHIGURA: a worker.
	INTERPRETER 1: (represents Michiko), dressed in traditional Japanese attire.
	INTERPRETER 2: (represents Nomi), also in traditional attire.
SETTING	A room in a down-market office building on the edge of Toyama, the Pittsburgh of Japan. Today.
AUTHOR'S NOTE	Japanese translation by Jana Duchova. The lines translated from Japanese to English are literally translated. The Japanese has been written phonetically, and it is recommended that any production of this play consult with a native speaker for help with pronunciation.

(MICHIKO TAKASHI *and* NOMI CHIGURA *are sitting in their workroom. A table holds a stack of cardboard boxes. The top box is open, and girls' underwear spills out. The panties are all new, all white and pink cotton bikini-style. Some have pictures on them, Sailor Moon, kittens, etc. A second table holds a stack of small plastic bags with brightly printed labels, a stapler or heat-sealer for the bags, and a box marked "Ginza Vending Company" in English and Japanese into which completed bags are thrown.*

MICHIKO *and* NOMI *are dressed normally from the waist up, business blouses, everyday makeup, everyday hair. Each wears a pair of panties from the box. Each wears normal business shoes, pumps with a modest heel.* MICHIKO *is reading R.* NOMI *is sitting L.*

INTERPRETERS *enter from opposite sides, dressed in traditional kimonos. They bow to each other.* INTERPRETER 1 *looks for where she should go.* INTERPRETER 2 *surreptitiously indicates 1's place.*

INTERPRETER 1 *goes to DR.* INTERPRETER 2 *goes to DL. Together, they sink to kneeling in a formal posture.* INTERPRETER 1 *represents* MICHIKO. INTERPRETER 2 *represents* NOMI.

The interpreters have a screen that they can hold up or set down—perhaps two matte boards, or large fans, or even the sleeves of their kimonos. The screen covers NOMI *and* MICHIKO *from mid-calf to waist-high when it is up, and it's inconspicuous when down.*)

NOMI: *Sono hon te tomoshiroi ka?*

INTERPRETER 2: Is it good?

MICHIKO: Eh?

                    (INTERPRETER 1 *looks to* INTERPRETER 2, *who nods.*)

INTERPRETER 1: Mmm?

NOMI: *Omoshiroi ka to kiita.*

INTERPRETER 2: I said, is it good?

MICHIKO: *Nani ga omoshiroi no?*

INTERPRETER 1: Is what good?

NOMI: *Takashi-san no yondeiru hon.*

INTERPRETER 2: Your book, silly.

MICHIKO: *Maa ne.*

INTERPRETER 1: It's fine.

(*They sit.*)

NOMI: *Nan ni tsuite no hon?*

INTERPRETER 2: What is it about?

MICHIKO: Eh?

INTERPRETER 1: Mmmm?

NOMI: *Takashi-san no hon wa nani ni tsuite no hon?*

INTERPRETER 2: Your book. What is it about?

MICHIKO: *Jitsu wa—*

INTERPRETER 1: Well, it's—

(*A bell rings.* MICHIKO *and* NOMI *each stand up, go to the box of new panties and take one. The* INTERPRETERS *hold up a screen between them, which* MICHIKO *and* NOMI *step behind.* MICHIKO *and* NOMI *take off their panties, put on a new pair of panties, go to the table, put the old panties in bags, seal the bags neatly as if they are wrapping presents, carefully stack the bags in the 'completed' box. There is nothing sexual or coy about this—it's like watching them brush their teeth.*)

(MICHIKO *returns to her book.* NOMI *fidgets.*)

NOMI: *Tabako wo suitai naa.*

INTERPRETER 2: I wish I could have a cigarette.

MICHIKO: *Sore wa muri yo.*

INTERPRETER 1: Well, you can't.

NOMI: · *Nande?*

INTERPRETER 2: I don't see why not.

NOMI: *Datte kohkohsei de mo tabako wo suu no ja nai ka?*

INTERPRETER 2: Surely, some of the schoolgirls would smoke?

NOMI: *Atashi kohkohsei no toki sutta yo. Kouen no naka de kakurete . . .*

INTERPRETER 2: I smoked, when I was a schoolgirl. I remember, hiding in the park . . .

MICHIKO: Eh.

INTERPRETER 1: Mmmm.

(*They sit.*)

NOMI: *Nan no hon ka?*

INTERPRETER 2: What is it about?

MICHIKO: It's hard to say.

INTERPRETER 1: I just want to read.

NOMI: *Sono hon tte romanchikku ka?*

INTERPRETER 2:   Is it a romance?

MICHIKO: A little bit.

INTERPRETER 1:   It's not a romance.

NOMI: *Saikin no ka?*

INTERPRETER 2:   Is it a modern book?

MICHIKO: It's difficult to say.

INTERPRETER 1:   I don't want to talk, I want to read. Would you please shut up?

>   (NOMI *reacts as if* MICHIKO *has spoken the interpreted line.*)

NOMI: *Takashi-san gomen!*

INTERPRETER 2:   I'm sorry, Takashi-san.

>   (*A pause.*)

NOMI: (*Hopefully.*) *Koko ni kuru mae atashi nani wo yatta ka wakaru?*

INTERPRETER 2:   Do you know what I did before I came here?

MICHIKO: No, Chigura-san.

INTERPRETER 1:   Do I look like I care?

NOMI: I was a tea lady. Pushing a big cart around the office, getting steam in my eyes. I thought this job would be so much better, nothing to do but sit and talk.

INTERPRETER 2:   Why don't you talk to me?

MICHIKO: And you left that job?

INTERPRETER 1:   Why did you leave a respectable job in an office to come here?

NOMI: My feet were tired all the time.

INTERPRETER 2: The office men treated me like a servant. I couldn't stand the way they talked to me. Sometimes they didn't even use my name, they called out "Tea lady!" and I had to come running.

MICHIKO: Well, now you don't have to run.

INTERPRETER 1: Now you sit and pretend to be a schoolgirl in panties for vending machines. (*As self, not interpreting.*) What the—?

INTERPRETER 2: (*As self, not interpreting.*) In Japan, you can purchase many things from vending machines, among them beer, sake, the pornographic comic books called anime by American geeks, and individually wrapped used panties, purportedly worn by schoolgirls.

INTERPRETER 1: Whoa-kay. (*Interpreting.*) Now you sit and pretend to be a schoolgirl in panties for vending machines. Does that make you proud?

NOMI: One day, I just looked around, and thought, I must find another job!

INTERPRETER 2: I threw a pot of hot tea on the man who pinched me. He couldn't have sex for a month. The company hushed it up, but they would not give me a good reference to find another job.

> (*A bell rings. MICHIKO and NOMI each stand up, go to the box of new panties and take one. MICHIKO and NOMI each stand up, step behind the screen, take off their panties, put on a new pair of panties, put the old panties in bags, seal the bags, carefully place the bags in the 'completed' box, using exactly the same movements as before.*)

NOMI: Perhaps you had another job sometime?

INTERPRETER 2: What did you do before you came here?

MICHIKO: Not really.

INTERPRETER 1: It's none of your goddamn business.

NOMI: I don't mean to pry.

INTERPRETER 2:   Are you even human?

                     (*They sit.* MICHIKO *makes a movement towards her book.*)

NOMI: Takashi-san?

MICHIKO: Yes, Chigura-san?

INTERPRETER 1:   What now?

NOMI: Do you have . . . well, this is silly.

INTERPRETER 2:   I should never have tried to talk to you.

MICHIKO: Do I have . . . ?

INTERPRETER 1:   Since you can't seem to sit quietly, you might as well ask the question.

NOMI: (*Shyly.*) *Yume nanka aruno?*

INTERPRETER 2:   Do you have a dream?

                     (INTERPRETER 2 *holds up a yellow card with the character for 'dream' on
                     it.*)

INTERPRETER 2:   In Japanese, "a dream" signifies a desire or wish that the speaker believes will
                 never truly happen.

MICHIKO: Do you?

NOMI: I think that I would like to live in a house, on the edge of Tokyo, close enough
                 to town to come in on the train and shop, but far enough to have a garden, big
                 enough for a fountain and a tree and a little bench to sit on. And there, maybe I
                 would write a poem. (*A pause, but no* INTERPRETER.) It's silly.

INTERPRETER 2:   It's important.

MICHIKO: *Itsuka . . .*

INTERPRETER 1: Someday . . .

> (INTERPRETER 2 *holds up a yellow card with the character for 'someday'.*)

INTERPRETER 2: In Japanese, the word "someday" signifies something that the speaker knows will never truly happen.

> (*They sit.* NOMI *makes a little movement towards* MICHIKO *but checks it.*)

Ok, fair's fair—your turn.

MICHIKO: *Uchi no musuko wa hayaku shinjau no wo negau wa.*

INTERPRETER 1: I dream that my son will die.

NOMI: Takashi-san!

MICHIKO: *Itsuka okite kare no heya he ittara . . . nokku nashi ni doa wo akete . . . itsumo nokku nashi ni hairu no . . . nokku suru noni imi nai kara saa.*

INTERPRETER 1: I dream that one day I will wake up and go to his room. I will gently push open the door without knocking, I never knock, what would be the use?

MICHIKO: *Kare no beddo he chikazuitara sheetsu wo sawaru to . . . nanka kare no karada to te no aida de hasamatteite. Makura wa ne kare no tsuba de nureteiru saa.*

INTERPRETER 1: I go to his bedside and touch the sheet—it's caught between his arm and his body. The pillow is damp with saliva.

MICHIKO: *Jimejime shita nuno wo totte kare no hitai wo fuitara tsumetai da to ki ga tsukun darou naa. Atsukunai no yo, tohtoh tsumetakunatteiru . . .*

INTERPRETER 1: I take out the damp cloth and wipe his forehead, but instead of burning, today it's quite cool. Finally, it's cool.

MICHIKO: *Soshite kare no kao wo sheetsu de kabusete . . .*

INTERPRETER 1: And I cover his face with the sheet.

NOMI: Takashi-san—

MICHIKO: I am not finished. And I take the plastic shit-pot, and the plastic braces yellowed from sweat, and the box of diapers, and the feeding tube, and the towels that catch his spit and his tears and the food that falls from his mouth, and I pile them in his wheelchair. And I wheel the chair into the garden—I have a garden, Chigura-san, I live on the edge of town—and I pour oil from the car on top of everything, and I light a match. And it all goes up.

> (*The bell rings. MICHIKO stands up and follows the routine. NOMI lags a step behind, and she is still getting her panties on when MICHIKO slaps the timer. MICHIKO sits down. After NOMI puts her old panties in the box, she realizes she has her new panties on backwards. She steps between the interpreters and they put the screen back up while she takes them off again and puts them on again.*)

MICHIKO: *Taimaa ga naru mae ni kimi no nioi wo utsusu tame sukoshi jumpu shitegoran.*

INTERPRETER 1: You're going to have to jump up and down to get the smell on before the timer rings.

> (NOMI *jumps up and down. Then she sits.*)

NOMI: *Takashi-san, sore wa honto anata no yume ka?*

INTERPRETER 2: Takashi-san, is that . . . really . . . your dream?

MICHIKO: *Itsuka . . .*

INTERPRETER 1:   (*Very softly.*) Someday . . .

>   (INTERPRETER 2 *rises and crosses to* INTERPRETER 1, *kneels beside her,*
>   *and puts her hand on the other interpreter's shoulder. They look to each*
>   *other and at the card with the character for 'someday' on it. The lights fade*
>   *to black.*)

END

Allison Williams is a partner in the physical theatre company Commedia Zuppa and an actor, director, and aerialist. Her plays include *The Tale of Tsuru* (adapted from the Japanese), *Hamlette, Mmmbeth, Miss Kentucky,* and the radio plays *Dead Men Don't Carry Handbags, Dead Men Don't Jay Walk,* and *Scanners.* Her solo show, *True Story,* is currently touring.

Jana Duchova (translator) is a graduate of Charles University and lives in Prague. She is a writer, translator, and interpreter of Japanese and English, and spent nearly two years in Japan.

Dreidel Daze

Gaylord Brewer's *Dreidel Daze* places a man and his ten-year-old niece in a restaurant where, engaged in the ritual of a meal, they discuss the larger rituals of religion and culture. This piece demonstrates that the brevity of the ten-minute form can allow a writer to focus primarily on theme, a virtually anti-dramatic approach that in a longer piece runs the risk of making audiences restive or, worse still, making them head for the exits.

In this case, Brewer's well-drawn main characters, complemented by a chatty waitress, and his specific, humor-laced dialogue, move the play gracefully to its disarmingly ironic final plea on behalf of peace and understanding. The play also cleverly evokes the Passover feast or seder, with several allusions to The Story, to Uncle Charley's steak as "sacrificial," to dietary restrictions, and to other religions and cultures. By means of these allusions, Brewer wittily raises in our minds the actual Passover question, thereby dramatically having his feast and eating it, too.

Gaylord Brewer

Dreidal Daze

CHARACTERS   MAN: 30.

GIRL: 10.

WAITRESS.

SETTING   Restaurant.

(Seated at a table are MAN and GIRL. All in all, they get along and enjoy each other's company. As they fiddle with the condiments, WAITRESS enters with plates.)

WAITRESS: Prime rib, very rare, fries, hot.

MAN: Oh yes.

WAITRESS: Coming at you.

MAN: Is the steak nice and bloody? Sacrificial?

WAITRESS: The cow's still screaming. Hash browns, apple sauce, side of sour cream.

GIRL: Here.

MAN: The fries steamy hot?

WAITRESS: Cook burned himself gettin'm on the plate.

MAN: Beautiful.

WAITRESS: *(To* GIRL.) You sure that's all you want, honey? You don't want a hamburger? A salad? That ain't much of a meal.

GIRL: No thanks. This is good enough.

MAN: It's tradition.

GIRL: Sort of. This isn't really it.

MAN: *(To* WAITRESS.) Try it, Linda. Plenty of ketchup it's not bad.

WAITRESS: Hmm. Anything else now, Charley? Another beer?

MAN: Sure.

WAITRESS:	Okay.
	(She exits.)
MAN:	Alrighty. You were telling me The Story.
GIRL:	It's okay. You know the . . .
MAN:	*(As he rips into his food.)* Now c'mon. I love it, I just can't ever remember the damn thing. You know I love it.
GIRL:	Well, where was I?
MAN:	Judah . . . Judah. Hey. Was he the first Jew? Is that where it comes from? Jew. Judah.
GIRL:	Uh, no, Uncle Charley.
MAN:	Oh. Okay, I'm a dumbass. So: Judah, uh . . . Macabee, alright, and his clan of wandering indigents . . .
GIRL:	Brothers.
MAN:	His brothers. They ran the still.
GIRL:	Huh?
MAN:	I'm being silly. They're at war.
GIRL:	With the Philistines. Or the Syrians. I can't remember.
MAN:	And the brothers, they're hiding out in the castle . . .
GIRL:	The temple.
MAN:	What temple?

GIRL: The Old Temple.

MAN: Whoa. Their backs to the wall, like Helen Keller, like, like, no, like Anna . . . Christie, ah fuck, like . . . Anne Frank, the Macedonians are coming on, mean godless mothers, and no chance, no chance at all. "Have we been forsaken?" they ask themselves. They wring their hands. "Where is our Father?" "Has he turned away?" "Why must we suffer so?" "Are we not The Chosen?" Their very lives in peril . . . (WAITRESS *enters with the beer and a small basket* .) But no. Yahweh has not abandoned us. Shit no.

WAITRESS: I brought you more rolls, sugar.

MAN: Beautiful. Thank you.

GIRL: (*Perplexed, but amused*.) What are you talking about?

MAN: I'm talking salvation, kid. Standing up. Making it happen.

GIRL: That's not how it goes.

WAITRESS: (*Starting to leave*.) I'll check back with you . . .

MAN: Linda, wait. You got a minute?

WAITRESS: Sure.

MAN: Kid, the stage is yours.

GIRL: I can't.

MAN: You know you love it. You're a natural ham. No offense. C'mon, c'mon.

GIRL: Well, they're in the tem . . .

MAN: Stand up. I want my ticket price.

                (GIRL *stands, recites the following quickly but melodramatically, covering any minor omissions or revisions with a cheerleader's chutzpah*.)

GIRL: And Judah Macabee, and the brothers of Judah, so they withstood the attack of the Philistines, and they stayed in the temple, they kneeled in the, the temple, the Old Temple and they kneeled down. And they prayed. And the lamp, they had a lamp, and no oil, oil, oil, oh where was the oil?, they had oil enough only for a single night. But the Lord, the lamp, it burned, eight nights, brightly it burned for eight long nights, and because of this miracle the war was won. (*Pause. No one speaks.*) We won. The end.

MAN: Isn't she something? A scholar, a fireball, a fullback.

WAITRESS: I didn't know you had a daughter, Charley.

MAN: She's my niece. My brother's girl. His wife's Jewish.

WAITRESS: Well, she's cute.

MAN: Ethnically, not practicing. I think. We're Lutheran.

WAITRESS: Well that explains it.

GIRL: I'm sitting down now.

WAITRESS: Sit down, honey, you must be worn out. Eat your food.

MAN: Bravo. (*He applauds.*) You're Julie Christie and Anne Frank.

GIRL: Who's Julie Christie?

MAN: We're going all the way.

WAITRESS: I gotta get over there to that booth. Look at those three idiots in the jerseys, they're killing me. Think they're hot stuff. One question, honey: how come a lamp burning for eight days won the war?

(*Pause. GIRL eats.*)

GIRL: (*Giggling.*) I don't know.

WAITRESS: What about it, Charley?

MAN: Darlin', I haven't the foggiest.

WAITRESS: Then I guess it don't matter.

GIRL: But it gets me presents for eight days.

MAN: I need some of this action.

(MAN *and* GIRL *exchange a thumbs-up*.)

WAITRESS: Okay. You two doin' alright? I gotta get over there. Look at those clowns.

MAN: We're beautiful. So are you.

WAITRESS: Well personally, and no offense, I can't wait for Christmas. The people are pigs, but that's where the money is. I never made a nickel off Hanukkah or however you want to say it.

MAN: Amen.

WAITRESS: You need another beer?

MAN: Why not? And a shot of Jack to be festive.

WAITRESS: You bet.

(*She exits*.)

MAN: You were magnificent. A marvel. You are my favorite grandchild.

GIRL: I'm your niece, dummy.

MAN: Oh yes.

GIRL: Your only one.

MAN: It's coming back . . .

GIRL: You don't have any children, and no wife, and you drink.

MAN: (*Laughing.*) Wise man say: "Beware the one-eyed fish of God."

GIRL: My potatoes are cold and greasy.

MAN: Hold it right there, young lady: you're in the South now.

GIRL: So?

MAN: So your potatoes are what?

GIRL: (*Catching on.*) They're . . . they're . . . gggrr . . .

MAN: Mmmm?

GIRL: . . . REAZ-Y! They're greazy, greazy, greazy.

MAN: A prodigy.

GIRL: I can't eat them.

MAN: Try the ketchup.

GIRL: It's okay. I'm not hungry.

MAN: (*Still amused.*) We'll get you some ice cream on the way home, chock-full of luscious and healthful additives. Two of everything.

GIRL: Man, you're weird.

MAN: That notwithstanding, my svelte one, my darling, my protégé, have we a message for our friends even further south, along the coast and through the Congo, from Liberia to Nigeria?

GIRL: I know it.

MAN: And it is?

GIRL: Happy Kwanzaa.

MAN: With gusto?

GIRL: HAPPY KWANZAAAAA!!!

MAN: Booga booga. Remember: all cultures deserve our respect. Even the poor, barbaric, really shitty ones. It's a big world.

GIRL: I'll tell Mom and Dad.

MAN: Tell your friends, too.

(*Pause. Lights out.*)

END

Gaylord Brewer is a professor at Middle Tennessee State University, where he founded and edits the journal *Poems & Plays*. His recent books of poetry include *Barbaric Mercies* (Red Hen, 2003) and *Exit Pursued by a Bear* (Cherry Grove, 2004). *Dreidel Daze* is one of a series of shorts collectively titled *The Holidays Play*.

Diorama

In a short play, as in a short story, nothing can be extraneous; thus, titles take on significance almost too obvious to mention. The title of a play is the first part of the work of art the audience sees, and is often the writer's one comment upon it. Playwrights may begin with a title or they may find one within the play as they write. One way or another, the best title has an organic relationship to the play. Lewis Horton's *Diorama* is an excellent example of this organic, symbiotic relationship.

Horton's play works because its irony is in its characters. They exist in a complete world, a diorama, where they never wink at the audience about the absurdities of their dialogue or situation. In fact, the world of Billy and his parents is a frame for the world of the radio show, which is in turn a frame for the world of the Italian monk. The characters, whatever their playfulness, their incongruities, are not stereotypes. The play works because the playwright never lets the characters lose their straight faces.

The structure of the play is the diorama. The lines of the story go out and out—back and back—from the family to the radio show to the monk. However, as foreshadowed in the title, the lines of the drama are brought skillfully back with the final line of the play. The "tautology" circles back, revealing the structure in an absurd situation. Billy is tired, and we see why as the diorama begins again. One reason why the ending satisfies is that it has been there—albeit hidden—from the beginning.

Lewis Horton

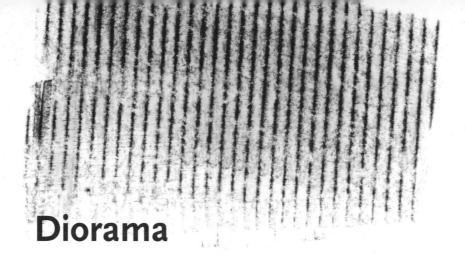

Diorama

CHARACTERS   FATHER ADAMSON.

MOTHER ADAMSON.

LITTLE BILLY ADAMSON.

HARTLY P. FULSOME: Announcer.

MIDGET: Voice in radio.

SETTING   The living room of the Adamson home, a modest tract house of the early 1950s. Furniture is arranged in a half-circle, facing a massive radio whose dark wooden cabinet might have been hewn from a Sequoia tree, or joined together with large segments of an abandoned canoe.

FATHER Adamson, seated on the mohair couch, is wearing a blue worsted suit and black bow tie, like the dull rubber ones used by the Highway Patrol. FATHER's thin moustache could be glued on.

MOTHER Adamson is seated at the other end of the sofa. A geranium stuck in her pillbox hat waggles as she looks at pictures in a huge book open on her lap. She is wearing a gray suit with large shoulder pads. The book in her lap is Audubon's *Birds of America*.

LITTLE BILLY is the same height as the radio or his parents sitting down. He wears a brown, double-breasted gabardine suit with a pink shirt, brown tie, oxfords, and a small fedora. He holds a thin stick at the top of which is a leather pennant with a message in yellow script: "MISSION SAN JOSE."

LITTLE BILLY: But, Dad, if the Padres were so learned, why didn't they build a castle, or a palace?

FATHER: Gosh darn it, Billy! Sorry Mother; pardon my French. That was a castle to those people. (FATHER *jabs the air with his pipe stem for emphasis.*)

LITTLE BILLY: Castle? That was one el dumpo. It ought to be against the law to charge people to see it. (*Billy shakes the pennant and yellow lettering falls like pollen onto the carpet.*)

FATHER: (*Chews for a moment on his pipe stem.*) Well, look at it this way: it wasn't exactly the Army Corps of Engineers helping them. Why, drawing something in the dirt with your big toe would be too complex. Before the Padres got there, those rascals used to lie down and cover themselves with mud just to keep warm.

LITTLE BILLY: I bet the Indians didn't paint the dumb pictures.

FATHER: Don't be too sure, Billy. They were taught many things.

LITTLE BILLY: Like what? (*Shakes the pennant and sneezes.*)

FATHER: Agricultural stuff. Home economics. Remember that stone bowl with the hole in the bottom? Some Indian sat there and ground corn nuts until he wore it out.

LITTLE BILLY: How long did that take?

MOTHER: What about that there cushion you're sitting on? You almost wore a hole in it. You don't find that monotonous?

FATHER: I'm talking about singlemindness. A one-track monotony. I could be sitting here listening to Mantovani or Spike Jones. I could look at pictures of Niagara Falls on the ViewMaster. With my spare hand or foot I could conduct the orchestra of St. Martin's in the Field.

LITTLE BILLY: So, how long did it take?

FATHER: Jeez, lifetimes. Grandma, Great-Grandma. Hundreds of years went by and the only thing left worth seeing is the hole. I suppose it kept the rascals out of trouble.

LITTLE BILLY: What kind of trouble, Dad?

MOTHER:

(*Slams her bird book shut with a tremendous clap, blowing half the lettering from BILLY's pennant onto his fedora. She slides the enormous book onto the coffee table and adjusts her geranium.*)

I thought we was going to listen to a radio program.

FATHER: We are, dear. Turn on the Lux Theater, Billy. (*Points at the radio with his pipe.*)

(*There are two big knobs on the face of the radio. BILLY turns the one marked "ON."*)

HARTLY P. FULSOME: Good eve-ven-ning, ladies and gentlemen, boys and girls! This is your announcer, Hartly P. Fulsome. Welcome to *The Lux Theater Hour.* Tonight's drama transports us back 900 years into the dim abscesses of history. To a cave on an Italian hillside where a simple monk will soon become Abbot of the magnificent monastery at Costello. Time has all but erased the memory of our hero. Only a small wooden plaque affixed to the side of the Lerici Linguisa Factory reminds today's stroller that here lived a man for all times. And now, a word from our sponsor.

(*MIDGET is sitting on a bar stool inside radio cabinet. Next to him is a shelf of candy boxes and altered popcorn boxes with the bottoms removed: Milk Duds, Flicks, Gum Drops, Jujubees, Dots, etc. A second shelf contains double boxes, taped end to end. Names are affixed to the boxes with strips of tape: Dorothy Gale, Don Winslow, Mrs. Miniver, Boston Blackie, Joan of Arc, Giapetto, Puck, Stephen Dedalus, Algonquin J. Calhoun, etc. Beneath the stool is a thick anthology,* World's Greatest Plot Outlines. *MIDGET speaks through a single Jujubee box.*)

MIDGET: Thank you, Hartly, and hello, folks. Mr. Old Gold here. Tonight, on this stage the world famous Old Gold Dancing Cigarette Packs will do a fabulous number for your delectation. Twenty gorgeous legs and a similar number of amazing feet.

(MIDGET *places a bent coat hanger around his neck. The front part of the hanger has been shaped so it holds the Jujubee box near his mouth, leaving* MIDGET's *arms free*)

And now, lovely ladies, uh one, and uh two . . . okay girls, hit it!

(*Sounds of tap dancing pour from the radio like hail against a cheap trailer. The tap dancing is produced by a series of spoons mounted back to back with rubber bands and fastened to a length of shower curtain rod. The contraption rests upon a piece of light gauge sheet metal. When* MIDGET *bangs the spoon handles with his forearm, they clatter against each other and the bottom spoons tap the metal sheet.*)

Okay, girls, let's bring it on home.

(*The tap dancing intensifies as* MIDGET *engages a second set of spoons with his other forearm.*)

And . . . and . . .

(*Several rubber bands break and spoons fall, bouncing on the bottom of the cabinet.*)

All right! That's it! The grand finale! You nailed it, girls. Wonderful! It's amazing how you can dance backward with your arms linked and still keep time with the leg kicks. I bet there's eye holes somewhere in those packs. Back to you, Hartly.

HARTLY P.
FULSOME: Thank you, Mr. Old Gold. And, hats off to the marvelous dancing cigarette packs. Let's return, 900 yesteryears, to that hillside in Italy, not far from where Percy Bysshe Shelley's heart was removed, in perfect condition I might add, from his cremated body and buried in a nearby wall. A simple, emaciated monk sits in a dreary cave. He is writing in a large book. It is difficult to know his emotions because his features are hidden by a cowl. Someday he will become the thirteenth Abbott of Costello. For now he is a lowly novice Capuccino, transcribing holy works.

(HARTLY *signals* MIDGET *who grabs a DfX6-Rbox. The Rbox consists of two empty cardboard toilet paper rolls scotch-taped together. Six holes are punched in the top. The sound effect resonates like someone speaking in a cave. Without holes, the device is identitied as DfX-Rbox and is useful for recreating voices in a submarine, e.g.,* Twenty Thousand Leagues Under the Sea.)

Scene 2

(*The Adamson family sits on a couch in their living room before the huge radio cabinet.* HARTLY P. FULSOME *stands in one corner of the room in front of a microphone. A robed, hooded monk sits at a stone desk writing in another corner of the room. Inside the radio* MIDGET *does a voice-over, reading aloud what the monk is writing.*)

MIDGET: (*As* MONK.) And so Roderigo, my dear brother, it is with a heavy heart I admit that you were correct: this place is the pastafazoolo. And I'm not even in the monastery. I've been farmed out to a cave. I guess there was no room at the Inn. Ha, ha. Remember when we lived at the Triunfunio della Rosa? We said no place could be colder, more drafty. We said that before either of us had lived in a wet cave. How I yearn for the della Rosa and our old blankie, the one somebody (who shall remain nameless) peed on every night. Yes, I miss that old urine-soaked rag. I remember Mama sitting in front of the cook pot, stitching our blankie together out of furry pelts. You immediately recognized the hides of our missing dogs. But, I never told you what was in the cook pot. Oh, for a bowl of dog stew and our old blankie. I'd be in Heaven.

Nowadays, I'm given a brick of cheese and when somebody thinks of it, a few breadsticks. Have you seen what happens to cheese left over night in a cave? Nibbled at by mysterious night crawlers, crapped on by bats and other winged creatures. Frozen at night; thawing out by noon the next day. There are things growing on my piece of cheese I could not describe with ladies present. We don't know when we are well off. Always wanting something more grand. Be careful what you wish for, Roderigo.

I'm currently engaged in making twelve copies of *The Rules of the Order of St. Bobbio*. The book is eight hundred and thirty-two pages. It took a long time just to copy the first large capital letter of the first word of Chapter One. The ink along with the cheese is frozen in the morning. By the time the sun gets to the rock I've set them on, it's mid-morning. The ink thaws first and I was able to complete the first letter when the cheese thawed and it was time for lunch. The letter wasn't complicated but the surrounding curlicues, embellishments, ivy, and doo-dads are time consuming. Having finished the letter, I wonder if I should start all twelve pages since I seem to have the knack of it. Or, plow ahead with the eight hundred and thirty-two pages before starting the second one?

I've been thumbing through *The Rule* and there are parts I find ridiculous. Some editing may be required. Certain crackpot sections will be eliminated. For example, St. Bob speculates on the origin of sex. Did sex originate in the Garden of Eden? Between Adam and Eve? Or later, after they were kicked out? What about the animals? Were they watching Adam and Eve in the Garden? Is that where they got the idea? What kind of controls were in place? If two elephants wanted to have sex in the Garden of Eden, who was going to stop them?

> (MIDGET *in radio sets down his DfX6-Rbox and picks up an inflated hot water bottle with a hair comb covered in wax paper mounted over the outlet. Loosening the stopper on the water bottle produces a noise like someone dragging pallets full of heavy equipment across a linoleum floor, or bull elephants in rut.*)

MIDGET: HHHRRRRRRRNNNNNNA! HHHRRRRRRRNNNNNNA!

> (MIDGET *puts down water bottle and resumes speaking through the DfX6-Rbox.*)

(*As* MONK.) I think you can see where this is going. Circular reasoning wrapped in a tautology, ending in a moot point. In a nutshell: who cares if the elephants were going at it in the Garden? Where Adam and Eve began playing hide-the-salami is nobody's business, except maybe God's.

MOTHER: What's with all this religion crap? (*Rises from the couch, switches off the radio, and sits down again.*) Are we fixing to change faiths?

LITTLE BILLY: Really, Mother. We can hardly change something that we don't possess.

MOTHER: Don't smart-mouth me, mister. I'll tan your butt. You know what I mean. Spending half the day at . . . what's it say on that stick? 'SS JOSE'? You didn't say you was going to see a Mexican boat. And now, we got to listen to the Rosencrucian Hour. I'd better not be missing Major Bowels.

LITTLE BILLY: (*Rises and moves toward the hallway.*) I think that I shall go to bed and call it a night.

MOTHER: (*Picks up a bag of yarn and begins knitting.*) Oh yeah! What for?

LITTLE BILLY: To sleep, perchance to hallucinate.

MOTHER: Well, try perchancing what your room would look like if it was picked up. (*She knits furiously at a large yellow sleeve.*)

LITTLE BILLY: I picked it up.

MOTHER: When would that be?

LITTLE BILLY: Last . . . week?

MOTHER: Your best gabardine suit is laying in there on the floor covered in sunflower seeds. After you wear a suit all day, it gets like a magnet and sucks up everything. You have to take the tweezers . . . are you listening to me?

LITTLE BILLY: Yes'm.

MOTHER: It's not enough just to beat the clothes against the wall. The husks won't fall off. It's like they're welded on. You have to take a pair of tweezers and pick each piece of crap off separately.

LITTLE BILLY: I won't do it again. I'm out of sunflower seeds.

MOTHER: What's that stuff on your hat?

(BILLY *removes his fedora and brushes at the yellow pollen from the pennant.*)

MOTHER: Don't be doing that on the goddam rug. Go do it over the toilet.

LITTLE BILLY: Fine. Goodnight! (*Waves his hat, creating a flurry of sparkles.*) Vio corn dios everybody!

FATHER: Goodnight, Billy. Sleep well. (*Salutes Billy with his pipe.*)

                 (MOTHER *throws yellow sleeve, yarn, knitting needles in a bag.*)

MOTHER: Okay, that's a wrap. Come on over here, Billy.

LITTLE BILLY: (*Puts on his fedora.*) I really am tired.

MOTHER: Hey, kid, we're all tired. Now, get over here. (*Slides the big book off the coffee table onto her lap.*)

                 (BILLY *stands at* FATHER's *end of the couch.*)

MOTHER: (*Opens big book.*) Hey, you ever see a picture of a brown-headed goat sucker?

LITTLE BILLY: I could use a new pennant.

FATHER: (*Clutches the bowl of his pipe and stabs tentatively at the air.*) I could use a new pipe.

MIDGET: (*Falsetto voice from the radio.*) I could use some new rubber bands.

MOTHER: I want the varmint in the radio to lay off the castanets. My ears are still ringing.

MIDGET: For your information . . .

MOTHER: Just can it, or I'll take this book and . . . (*Struggles to get off the couch but is restrained by* FATHER *and* LITTLE BILLY.)

FATHER: Now, dear.

LITTLE BILLY: Mother! You wouldn't hit a dwarf?

MOTHER: No, I wouldn't hit a dwarf. But this is a full-growed midget. (*Settles down on the couch and rearranges the geranium stuck in her pillbox hat.*) All right, places everyone. Altogether now: ready, steady, hit it!

LITTLE BILLY: But, Dad, if the Padres were so learned . . . .

(*The lights fade to black.*)

END

Lewis Horton's stories and essays have
appeared in several magazines, including
Cutbank, and three anthologies. A nonfiction
book, *Escape From Mexico,* came out in 2001,
an adventure which Rick DeMarinis describes
as "a hilarious tour of Hell." Lewis, born
in Detroit, Michigan, currently resides in
Sacramento, California.

Playtime

The strength of Kent R. Brown's *Playtime,* about an estranged mother and daughter living on the edge of violence and poverty, comes from its refusal to sentimentalize. Playwrights turn to sentimentality when they cannot find common ground with their characters, romanticizing an abused wife or a runaway child or a homeless man by implying that their outsider status gives them uncommon insight. But the characters remain generalizations and their creators' sentiments ring false. In this play, Brown works successfully with the universality of broken relationships. His characters are a mother and child whose uniqueness comes out in the "stuff"—the specifics of their relationship, of the daughter's friends, of the mother's life with an abusive man, of the clothing in the bag, of the unopened gift. In a short play, the audience doesn't need to know everything. Brown uses deftly-sketched details to suggest the reality of a rich life for his characters: Nicole's relationship with men; Maureen's visit to a doctor; their relationship with Farty Marty.

The characters' inability to approach each other emotionally gives rise to the play's complication. This alienation emerges not only through their dialogue, but from their placement on the stage. The playwright positions them at a physical distance from each other that stands for and emphasizes their emotional distance. This physical distance makes their one approach dramatically crucial and their final separation dramatically moving. In the short space of ten minutes, the audience comes to care about these characters as individuals, because the playwright cares enough to create them in detail, without succumbing to the laziness of sentimentality and stock response.

Kent R. Brown

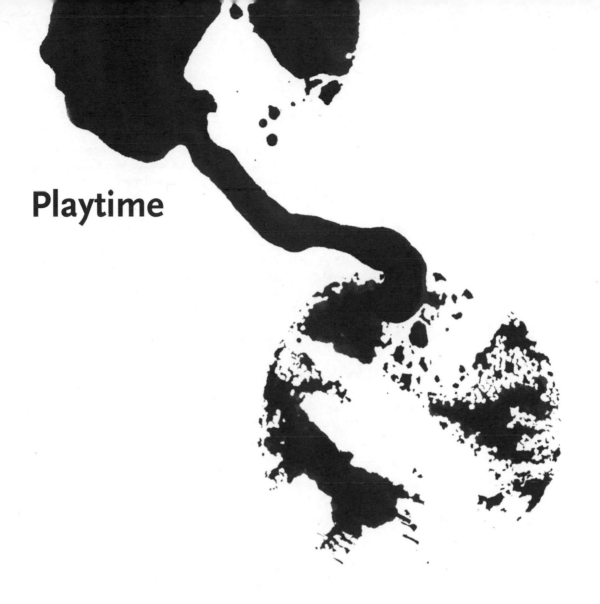

Playtime

CHARACTERS   MAUREEN: late 30s. Has led a hard life. Compassionate. Bitter. Needy. Dressed
in clothes purchased at Goodwill and church thrift shops.

NICOLE: early teens. Maureen's daughter. A runaway. A survivor. Also dressed by
Goodwill and hand-me-downs. Carries a knapsack.

SETTING   A playground park: teeter-totter, swings, benches, merry-go-round, trashcan—
whatever can be comfortably provided—the present, summer, bright moonlight,
warm breeze.

(*As the lights rise, we see* MAUREEN *sitting on a bench, a picnic basket by her side. On the ground is a large garbage bag stuffed with assorted items and pieces of clothing. For several moments,* MAUREEN *sits patiently on the bench. Then . . .*)

MAUREEN: Nicole, I'm not gonna sit here all night. Midnight is late in the day for me. I'm gonna pick my butt up off this bench, take this lovely picnic lunch I made you . . . and go. (*A beat.*) I've got good things in the bag, honey. (*A beat.*) Nicole . . . you there? Don't make me feel stupid.

(*After another moment,* MAUREEN *gathers up the garbage bag and the picnic basket. As she begins to leave,* NICOLE *enters. She is as far from* MAUREEN *as she can be.*)

NICOLE: What did you make? Did you bring me any books?

MAUREEN: You do this every time. You make me beg. You shouldn't do that, Nicole. I'm your mother. I don't have to be out here. I don't have to come.

NICOLE: Yes, you do.

MAUREEN: No, I don't!

NICOLE: Yes, you do!

(*A beat.* MAUREEN *returns to the bench, puts down the garbage bag and picnic lunch basket and sits.* NICOLE *doesn't move.*)

(*Continuing.*) Where'd you get the picnic basket? It's cool.

MAUREEN: First Baptist.

NICOLE: They're nice at First Baptist.

MAUREEN: The folks at First Baptist, they don't ask a lot of questions. They just give you stuff. You say a coupla prayers, makes 'em feel good. The ones at the Congregational Church, they talk to you so they can get to know you better. Hell, I don't want nobody to know me any better.

NICOLE: How are you feeling, Mama? You getting your beauty sleep?

MAUREEN: Do you want me to give all this stuff back? I could maybe sell it myself maybe and—

NICOLE: I cut my arm. Yesterday. I fell down some stairs, the ones up behind Pitkin Drugs? Out back? I fell down. See?

            (NICOLE *extends her arm to* MAUREEN, *who glances over.*)

MAUREEN: What were you doing on those stairs? Are you staying in those apartments there, Nicole? Those are terrible places, you know that?

NICOLE: I might not live, I might get blood poisoning. Randy Black did.

MAUREEN: I know Randy Black. He's a viper. A despicable human being. Nothing can kill Randy Black. And his mother's no better.

NICOLE: She's a real good cook. Randy got a chocolate pie from her three days ago. I had a piece for breakfast. Uuummm good!

            (*The tension between mother and daughter is palpable. This is a ritual they play out. To see who is the weakest, who wants the other the most.* MAUREEN *indicates the basket and the garbage bag.*)

MAUREEN: What do you want me to do with all this?

NICOLE: Just leave it on the bench. Step back. Over there.

            (NICOLE *points to a spot some distance from the bench.* MAUREEN *complies.*

            NOTE: *if the setting and props permit, the continuing action should integrate the playground equipment, positioning* NICOLE *on the bars, perhaps; or both could be seated on either end of a teeter-totter. It is important that* NICOLE *puts an obstacle between herself and* MAUREEN. *This is done out of habit. She behaves this way with anyone. She lives defensively.*)

(*Continuing.*) Don't move now. You move and I'm gone! I'm fast. I've got everything I need. Don't need you! You don't move! You don't touch me!

MAUREEN: I know the rules. I'm not movin'. 'Sides, you're too fast for me.

(NICOLE *crosses to the bench and begins to look through the items: sweaters, sweat shirts featuring a major university such as Michigan or Alabama, a few pairs of sweat pants, two pairs of sandals. The clothes are old, well-used.*)

I thought you could cut the sweats if you wanted. For shorts. For the rest of the summer . . . maybe keep one for the fall? The sweat shirts should fit. Got those for seventy-five cents each.

NICOLE: That's a good price. (*She holds up one of the sweat shirts.*) Hey, look at me! I'm going to Michigan [*or appropriate school*]. Gonna get me some learnin', right, Mama?

MAUREEN: Got to finish high school first.

NICOLE: Nope. Don't have to. I'm already too smart for my own good, that's what you said.

MAUREEN: You have everything you need? Where are you stayin' now? In case I have to contact you.

(MAUREEN *takes one step toward* NICOLE *who retreats quickly. She is highly accomplished in the art of disengagement.*)

NICOLE: You do this every time! Every time! You get me lookin' one way and come at me from the other! I can't trust you.

MAUREEN: I just want to . . . Come here. Just let me hold your hand.

NICOLE: No.

MAUREEN: Please?

NICOLE: Don't beg! Begging is weak. Begging is dirty. Begging means you don't have enough. "We don't beg in this household, Nicole!" That's what you always told me. Did you bring any pop?

MAUREEN: It's in the basket.

NICOLE: All right.

(MAUREEN *moves slowly to the picnic basket and removes the contents.*)

MAUREEN: I made you some chicken salad. No onions. And two peanut butter and jelly sandwiches.

NICOLE: I don't like grape. I hate grape. I'll scrape the grape off, you know that.

MAUREEN: (*Laughing.*) Don't get your panties in an uproar. I didn't do you any grape.

NICOLE: What kind?

MAUREEN: Guess.

NICOLE: I'm not a little girl anymore, Mama. I wash my face every day. I even know how to get a ride on the road. I know how to keep drivers happy.

MAUREEN: Don't tell me such stuff. You lie! I don't wanna know. (*She steps back from the bench so* NICOLE *can approach safely.*) Eat this nice picnic lunch I fixed you.

NICOLE: (*Moving to the picnic basket and begins to eat. She is ravenous.*) You want to know, Mama. Every mama wants to know. "Don't let 'em touch you, sweetie. Look both ways before you cross the street. Don't get in an elevator alone with a man. Don't look a man in the eyes, he'll think you're interested in him." Well, I do look 'em in the eyes, Mama. My hormones are raging! They're smelly and stinky, Mama, and they burp a lot. But they feel good. Real good. (*Sees a can of pop.*) Strawberry, thanks.

MAUREEN: You finished shockin' me now? Ready for some apples? Granny Smiths, and three hard-boiled eggs, a jar of olives and two bananas.

NICOLE: Got 'em. Right here.

             (NICOLE *"fires" the bananas at MAUREEN as if they were pistols.*)

MAUREEN: And some Twinkies. (*A beat.*) Happy birthday, sweetie.

NICOLE: It's not my birthday, Mama. You know that. You gettin' old in the head?

MAUREEN: (*A beat.*) You ever going to come back home?

NICOLE: (*Talking with her mouth full while keeping one eye on* MAUREEN.) Did you bring me any books? And magazines? Who's hot 'n who's not? Got to keep up. Gonna be an *American Idol* some day. Famous. Real famous. Famous for something . . . just don't know what it is yet. But I'm not gonna sit around here talkin' to you all night, that's for sure. I got things to do, people to see.

MAUREEN: I forgot the books.

NICOLE: You can bring 'em next time. Books on the Romans and the Vikings! None of that Young Miss stuff. Give me war, death, sex, and destruction! I wanna be just like a big person.

MAUREEN: (*A beat.*) I like your hair. You look good.

NICOLE: Amber cut it for me. She cuts mine, I cut hers. She's nice. She's my new best friend. I've got a lot of friends, Mama. Can't keep 'em all straight. You want a banana? Here.

             (NICOLE *places a banana on the ground half way between herself and* MAUREEN, *then steps back.*)

MAUREEN: Where are you sleeping, Nicole? I won't tell the police. (*Beat.*) I won't tell Marty.

NICOLE: Don't you mention his name! (*She viciously stomps on the banana.*) Farty Marty! Farty Marty! Does he know you're out here? Did you take two buses like I told you? Is he out there in the dark (*Calling out.*) You out there, Farty Marty? (*She pulls a knife from her pocket.*) I got me a knife. Wanna see it, wanna see it? You come at me and I'll slice you in half!

MAUREEN: (*A beat.*) Do I know Amber? (*A beat.*) Do you always have a knife, sweetie? That's dangerous.

NICOLE: I suspect you don't know my friends, Mama. And of course I have a knife, you think I'm stupid? On the streets and no knife? It's dangerous out here, Mama. Don't you watch television?

MAUREEN: Where did you meet Amber?

>   (NICOLE *continues looking through the garbage bag, pulling out numerous items and flinging them over the bench, on the grass, anywhere. She also remains alert to her mother and to her surroundings.*)

NICOLE: At the tennis club, where I meet all my friends. Out and around, Mama. Shawna, and Dougie, and Raphael. I like Raphael a lot. He's my new best boyfriend. Bobby could be—I love Bobby's hair, Mama—but I don't like his laugh. Laughs real high up, like a girl. (*She takes out a bunny doll that has seen its day.*) Hey, Roscoe, what's happenin', bunny boy? Let's see what Mama put in my goody bag, OK? Hey, you got me some pajamas, Mama! Thanks. (*She steps into her bottom pajamas.*) I can trade these with Amber. She's got two belts I want. And some suspenders. Suspenders are cool. (*She reaches into the bag and pulls out a box wrapped in birthday paper appropriate for a young child. A gaudy outsized bow flops over the edges.*) It's not my birthday, Mama. I told you that.

>   (NICOLE *places the package on the bench.*)

MAUREEN: You still leavin' next month?

NICOLE: Frank and Billy and Sarah Lynne and little Roscoe here and me and Jeffrey are thinkin' maybe we'll go to Los Angeles. Walk along Hollywood Boulevard. Go to Universal Studios. Get discovered. Get me a great tan. On the beach. Naked! Fall in love with a movie star. Just your everyday run-of-the-mill American dream. (*A beat.*) What's in this package, Mama?

MAUREEN: I don't want you leavin'. It's not good to be out and around at your age.

NICOLE: Of course it's not good, Mama. I'm still a punk kid. But it's all a part of life, right? That's how we learn what you can take and what you can't. Like you and Farty Marty. You keep takin' what Farty Marty keeps throwin' your way and you keep comin' back for more. Why do you do that, Mama?

MAUREEN: You lost a little weight, maybe, since last month? You look good.

NICOLE: You been to the dentist like I told you to? Did Doctor Johnson say, "Looks like a broken jaw to me, Maureen. That sure must hurt."

MAUREEN: There are things you don't understand!

NICOLE: And I bet you said, "No, Dr. Johnson, I just ran into a tree playin' hide 'n seek with my baby girl." (*With passion.*) You're too old to be playin' hide 'n seek, Mama. And the dentist knows it. I'm not your baby girl any more! You see me standin' here? Do I look like a baby girl to you?

MAUREEN: He doesn't mean it, Nicole.

NICOLE: How can he not mean it, Mama? He walks over to you and smashes his fist into your face! Did he think he was goin' out to the kitchen to take out the trash on his way to the bathroom to brush his teeth, and you just happened to stand in front of him with a big smile on your face?

MAUREEN: I hit back.

            (NICOLE *is suddenly very tired. And frightened. And very much the little girl. She begins to put items back into the garbage bag.*)

NICOLE: I know, Mama. You hit him good. Both of you are real good hitters. I've been watchin' for a long time. Both of you gonna get in the hall of fame. I'm proud of you. You can take a hit and keep on tickin'. That's an old commercial, Mama. About a watch. They were doin' golden oldie commercials on television this week.

MAUREEN: Where do you watch television?

NICOLE: In the woods, Mama. In the trees with the other monkeys!

MAUREEN: Where are you living, Nicole?

NICOLE: No one else reads but me, Mama. They just sit around watchin' TV and snortin' crap and—

MAUREEN: (*Overlapping.*) Nicole, you answer me this instant!

NICOLE: —sayin' how they're so smart and everyone else is so dumb and how they should be makin' a lot of money but the system wants to keep 'em down! I gotta get me away from here!

MAUREEN: (*Sitting on the edge of the bench.*) Oh, baby, don't—

NICOLE: All I do is the cooking, Mama. Anybody mess with me and I'll put do-do in their hamburgers. (*A beat.*) I gotta go. You follow me . . . I'll never come here again. You got Farty Marty in a car out there somewhere? He follows me, I'll kill him. You know I will.

                        (NICOLE *continues to shove everything back into the garbage bag*)

MAUREEN: You don't do things with men, do you, sweetie?

NICOLE: Blah, blah, blah.

MAUREEN: You can't make it easy for men.

NICOLE: Time to go, Mama. I heard this song before. Thanks for all this stuff.

MAUREEN: Most men are nice enough. Your daddy was. He was nice. But some men are mean, not right in their hearts.

NICOLE: Amber says you're scared you won't know who you are if you don't have a man in your life. She watches Oprah. Why don't you leave? Just leave. When he's out drunk, you get his keys and you start driving. Drive until the road stops, Mama. Then get out of the car and start walkin' 'til you drop. Then start crawlin' 'til you can't crawl any more. (NICOLE *is exhausted. She sits on the other end of the bench, an apple in her lap.*) You ready to do that and I'll go with you anywhere. Just like Thelma and Louise, only we'd be Maureen and Nicole! But we'd make it, right, Mama?

MAUREEN: (*A beat.*) I think I'm going to kill him, Nicole.

NICOLE: (*Having heard it all before.*) Hey, there's an idea. You'll need some energy. Want a bite of my apple?

MAUREEN: I've thought about it. I've done it in my head. If I don't . . . stop him for good . . . he'll come after me.

NICOLE: Walk out. Slam the door!

MAUREEN: You walk away, he wins! I won't let him win! He just sits and laughs at me. "You leavin' me again, Maureen?" He knows I'll come back. 'Cause that's what we do. We fight. We yell. We scream. That's what keeps me going! I'm gonna get him, Nicole, for all the things he's done to me. (*A beat.*) And to you.

NICOLE: You know he's never touched me, Mama. This is just about you and Marty. And you must like it, Mama. And that's . . . not good, I don't think.

MAUREEN: I'll fix my famous potato salad and we'll sit down and have a talk. Just like families do. All three of us. Turn off the television, pull up our chairs. And be civilized. And if it starts up again—and he hasn't been drinking, Nicole, not for a week now . . . almost a week, I think . . . coupla days now—but if it starts up again then you and me will take his keys and open the door and we'll . . . we'll just . . . leave. Marty'll understand. Will you come back?

NICOLE: What's in the box, Mama?

MAUREEN: (*A beat.*) When he's sleeping . . .

NICOLE: Where'd you get the ribbon?

MAUREEN: I'll just get the frying pan from the kitchen . . .

NICOLE: My birthday isn't until next month, Mama.

MAUREEN: Then he won't come after us. 'Cause he'll be dead.

(NICOLE *steps behind* MAUREEN *and fixes her hair. She touches her mother lovingly.*)

NICOLE: You talk that every time I come out here! You've killed Farty Marty a thousand times. I've got to fix dinner, clean out the trailer and do everyone's laundry and then I have to read my books and learn new vocabulary words because I don't want to sound like trash any more and then pillage—that's one of my new words—pillage a few morsels—that's another one—from the grocery stores to hold up my end of the trailer commune thing. And all you got to do is kill Farty Marty. Does that seem fair to you?

MAUREEN: I won't be here for your birthday next month, baby.

NICOLE: 'Course you will. It's my birthday. (*A beat.*) Mama? Has anything happened?

MAUREEN: Just blowing off a little steam, sweetheart. Just talking to Doctor Nicole. You're a good listener.

Kent R. Brown

137

(MAUREEN *reaches her hand up and touches* NICOLE's *hand. Then she brings* NICOLE's *hand to her lips, then to her cheek.*)

NICOLE: (*A beat.*) You need a haircut, Mama. Bad. Maybe I'll get you a coupon for your birthday. Would you like that? Mama, let go. Next month you can do my hair, OK? (*A beat.*) Let go of my hand, Mama. (NICOLE *tries to pull her hand away.* MAUREEN *holds on tight.*) Let go, Mama! Let go! (MAUREEN *releases* NICOLE's *hand.* NICOLE *stands back.*) You gonna be here next month?

MAUREEN: (*Rising from the bench.*) Take the basket with you, OK? Happy birthday, baby.

NICOLE: I'll leave a note. Tell you where to meet me, OK? OK?

MAUREEN: I got to go now, baby. You be good.

(MAUREEN *exits. The birthday package is left unopened on the bench. For a moment,* NICOLE *is motionless. Then she calls off as the lights begin to fade.*)

NICOLE: Mama? Come back here! Where you goin'? Mama? You comin' back? Mama? I don't want you to leave. Come back here right now . . . or I'll leave you, Mama. You know I will. Mama?

(*The lights fade to black.*)

END

Kent R. Brown is a playwright, director and
editor who lives in Fairfield, Connecticut with
his wife Gayle. His works, including *Hope 'n
Mercy, The Phoenix Dimension, Valentines and
Killer Chili,* and *The Seduction of Chaos* among
others, are published by Dramatic Publishing.

For information concerning production rights
to *Playtime,* contact Dramatic Publishing
at 1-800-448-7469 or log on to
dramaticpublishing.com

Driver's Ed.

One good place to begin a play is with a character's need to tell a story to another. Another good place to begin a play is with one character's need to teach a second something the first character feels is important. Steven Schutzman has used both of these plot devices in *Driver's Ed.*

The teacher, Michael, is all philosophy—clever interesting philosophy supported by real examples from his real life, but philosophy nevertheless. The student, Patricia, not only wants to tell her own story about the death of her father, but also wants the teacher to face—or acknowledge—the dishonesty of his story. The characters circle each other with their respective lessons and stories before they begin the ritual of learning to drive with the actual physical ritual of circling the car. Here the physical action that ends the play mirrors the dialogue and the conflict that have grown out of the individual needs of the two characters: Patricia's need to tell her story and Michael's need to teach.

Steven Schutzman

Driver's Ed.

CHARACTERS   MICHAEL: 42.

PATRICIA: 17.

(MICHAEL *and* PATRICIA *enter and move toward car.*)

MICHAEL: I like teaching teenagers to drive. Especially girls. Because girls need it more, in general. Don't get mad. I'll say stuff you won't like but it'll make you a better driver in the long run, better than any boy. The truth is that girls start at a disadvantage. Because you don't ride bikes wildly in the streets. Because you don't make cars the enemy of your ball games in the streets. That could be good; to think of traffic as the enemy. It could make boys cautious but boys like to turn everything into a fight. They attack.

PATRICIA: Because boys are idiots.

MICHAEL: Boys attack the exterior. Girls defend the interior. A girl is less likely to know about traffic and how fast it can come on. Because you haven't paid attention. Because you sit sunk in your body in the haze of morning carpools and afternoon carpools resisting entrance by grown-up questions. While a girl may pay attention to her appearance, to the exterior of her vehicle, she is also deeply caught in the interior of her vehicle. Unlike boys who simply attack, there is this separation.

PATRICIA: You are so surreal. Everybody's talking about the poetic things you say. It must be depressing for you to have to teach driver's ed. in this school.

MICHAEL: I like teaching teenage girls to drive. Because you are not by nature attracted to machines and how they work. Because of your stillness on the interior you are not connected to the speed of your vehicle. But we can use your natural defense of your interior as an asset in driving. Now that I have your attention, the first thing we're going to do is walk around the car.

PATRICIA: I know, three times. I also know other things about you.

(*Pause.* PATRICIA *smiles.*)

I know you're going to teach me to feel safe behind the wheel. Because of you the world will be a safer place. I already feel safe with you.

MICHAEL: All right then.

PATRICIA: I know you're old enough to be my father. When my Dad was alive and couldn't sleep, he'd go down to the basement with milk and Oreos, wrap himself up in his old sleeping bag and listen to the Beatles. I could hear the music way up on the second floor through the air conditioning ducts. This is not surreal. This is real life. It was my job to wake Dad in the morning. He was like a six-year-old kid then. All milky and warm.

(*Pause.*)

MICHAEL: You have to listen now.

PATRICIA: I love the Beatles.

MICHAEL: The first lesson is just you listening. No driving at all.

PATRICIA: I know. Boys live by conquest and occupying an interior other than their own, that's a direct quote from you.

MICHAEL: Who told you that?

PATRICIA: One of the idiot boys. I'm a virgin. I resist conquest. I'd never let that idiot put his idiot hands on me.

MICHAEL: As I said, we can use your natural defense of the interior as an asset in driving. The first thing we're going to do is walk around the car.

PATRICIA: I know, three times.

MICHAEL: We're going circle the exterior of the vehicle three times before we occupy the interior.

PATRICIA: I know. The whole junior class knows this drill.

MICHAEL: I'm glad it made an impression.

PATRICIA: It did. Because of the idiot boys. The girls have health together and the boys driver's ed. Then the boys have health together and the girls driver's ed. You know what health really is? Sex education, so we have it separate from the boys, and this idiot boy said you learn more sex in driver's ed. than you ever do in health. I never saw eyes as blue as yours.

MICHAEL: If you learn today's lesson, it could save your life. I'm going to try to burn it into your brain so that every time you drive you'll remember what I said. You will touch the exterior of your vehicle before getting in and when you slide behind the wheel you will think of yourself as occupying the interior of the exterior of your vehicle. The exterior and interior will merge in your mind so you'll never forget how you're speeding along, never forget and believe in the illusion that you are sitting still. As opposed to other times, when you are driving the exterior and interior must be one and the same.

PATRICIA: I already know how to drive.

MICHAEL: I hate that teenage arrogance but in driving too much arrogance is better than no arrogance at all. Now walk with me around the exterior of the . . .

PATRICIA: You are famous in this school.

MICHAEL: Because of the idiot boys?

PATRICIA: What would you do if I came on to you right now?

MICHAEL: What?

PATRICIA: Came on. To you. Right now. Offered myself to you.

MICHAEL: I'm your teacher and I'm married.

PATRICIA: No you're not. I followed you walking home on Tuesday. You have no car. Whoever heard of a driving instructor without his own car? You live in a studio apartment past the green from here. You have no wife but wear a wedding ring like I wear lip and tongue rings, to keep the faint of heart away. I am not faint of heart.

MICHAEL: I'm separated.

PATRICIA: I was going to secretly tape record you today but decided it'd be a sucky thing to do. I thought I could use the interior-exterior rap for the school literary magazine. My life is completely fucked-up and my fucked-up mind gives me this irresistible energy. I'm a genius, the editor of the magazine and the main writer. I'd be careful if I were you because talking like you do could get you into trouble around here. This is the suburbs, not the city.

MICHAEL: I'll watch my step. Now let's walk.

PATRICIA: If you had to give up one of your senses which one would be first? Could you make a list of the order in which you'd give them up? Where would touch be on the list, before or after seeing? Would you rather be blind and have feeling when someone touches you, or see and have no feeling at all?

MICHAEL: I'll have to think about that.

PATRICIA: It's a question game I made up. I think it can teach you a lot about a person. You're not like a teacher at all. I'm speeding on the exterior but the interior of my vehicle is peaceful and still. Do you find that attractive?

MICHAEL: It's not an asset in driving.

PATRICIA: I have the highest grade point average in my class. I make my own clothes and could play the flute professionally. It's something to fall back on, my mother says. I also sing and dance. Last year, I was the star of the school musical. I have never failed at anything. All the boys are idiots. When I sleep down in the basement, I can hear my mother and her boyfriend Donny through the air conditioner ducts. Donny has a silver Jaguar. He let me drive it once in the parking lot of the old fairgrounds. My mother waited only seven months before she'd let Donny sleep over. Do you think that's enough time? I don't. After my father died, I used to see his ghost sitting on my windowsill and his ghost seemed happy and that made me happy. Ghosts can't talk and they can't hear you talk. It's not like *Hamlet* at all. Ghosts just want to be in the room with you. They just want you to see them. I filled a whole composition book the night I first saw Dad again. My hand couldn't stop. Whenever I read it over it makes me cry. I will be reading it over my whole life. 'Let me introduce you to who I was and let who I am now express the terrible surprise of what has happened to me.' How could a twelve-year-old girl write that? I'm a virgin. I have my father's eyes. For more than a year afterward, every night at six o'clock the dog would sit by the door and wait for Dad. My brother who's in college now thought it was the sequence of cars coming home to the neighborhood, every car but Dad's, so it fooled the dog. The dog has lived in that house all his life and so have I. He will be famous one day, my brother not the dog. I started sleeping in the basement when my mother started letting Donny stay over, for privacy, but when their lovemaking noises come through the ducts I can't help but listen. If I asked, would you kiss me just once?

MICHAEL: No.

PATRICIA: Dad was supposed to teach me how to drive, not you.

(*Pause.*)

How come you don't have a car? If they let you teach driver's ed. without a car, would they let you teach sex education without a wife?

MICHAEL: I have a wife.

PATRICIA: You have no wife. I found out you wrote a book of poems and I took it out of the library. I read half of it last night and it's really far out. I have it here in my backpack.

MICHAEL: Thanks. That's nice. It's in the library. I never thought . . .

PATRICIA: Tonight, will you think of me reading your book in bed?

MICHAEL: Yes.

PATRICIA: To see and not feel would be horrible. I'd much rather be blind and feel on the inside, wouldn't you?

MICHAEL: Yes I would. But don't try driving that way.

PATRICIA: Don't worry. I won't.

MICHAEL: I'm sorry about your father.

PATRICIA: That's all right. No problem. Now you may teach me how to drive.

(MICHAEL *and* PATRICIA *begin to walk around the car. The lights fade to black.*)

END

Over the past six years, more than thirty productions of Mr. Schutzman's one-acts have been mounted in theatres across the country. His play *Tree Man* won 1st prize in the First Stage L.A. One-Act Contest/2004. Recently published one-acts include *Blue and Darker Blue* and *Where Things Are* in *Alaska Quarterly Review*, and *The Bank* in *Post Road*. *Driver's Ed.* is available in acting script form from Brooklyn Publishing (brookpub.com).

Steven Schutzman

The Nancy

We meet Bethany Gibson's characters, Eve and Alyssa, in an upscale coffee shop, where they sit across a table from each other. In David Mamet's *Glengarry Glen Ross,* the three first-act scenes are similarly all "sits," two-person encounters in which one character wants something from the other and negotiates to obtain it. In *The Nancy* the object of negotiation—represented by "a markedly empty chair between them" (pun certainly intended)—is Mark, Eve's new husband and Alyssa's old friend.

Each of Mamet's brilliant scenes illustrates a sales approach that reflects the main character's level of self-confidence: the desperate Levine oscillates between pleas and demands, punctuated by insults; the cynical Moss establishes common interests, then proceeds to intimidation and blackmail; the glib and confident Roma works almost entirely by indirection, so much so that Mamet closes the scene even before the "pitch" is complete. In Gibson's brief and funny play, Eve—neither desperate nor quite sure of herself—chooses the middle route, beginning with the "parable" of Nancy, but finally draws the line she hopes will establish clearly that her claim on Mark supersedes Alyssa's. The women's tentative acceptance of this "deal" is comically undermined in the play's final moments by their simultaneous and identical greeting to the never-quite-seen Mark.

153

Bethany Gibson

The Nancy

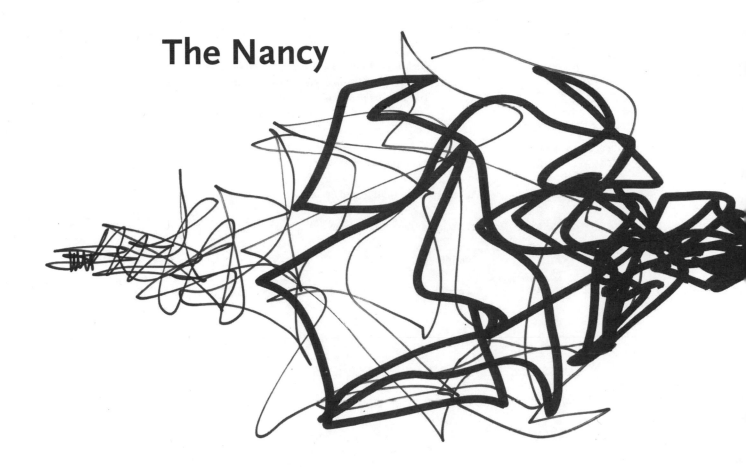

CHARACTERS   EVE: mid-twenties, business casual-attired and high-strung.

ALYSSA: mid-twenties, wears glasses and a smirk.

SETTING   A coffee shop attempting to attract the upwardly mobile crowd, the present.

(*Lights up. A table is C where* EVE *and* ALYSSA *sit with a markedly empty chair between them. There are napkins and three coffee cups on the table. There is a palpable uncomfortable silence as the two women avoid eye contact.* ALYSSA *occupies herself with her coffee drink while* EVE *picks up her purse, considers it for a moment and puts it back down again. The silence continues a few more moments until* EVE *sucks in a deep breath and turns to address* ALYSSA.)

EVE: I've always been intimidated by you.

ALYSSA: (*Looks up quickly.*) Excuse me?

EVE: You. Intimidate. Me.

ALYSSA: (*Scoffs.*) Sure. You don't even know me. (*Beat.*) But I'm beginning to think you're weird.

EVE: I know.

ALYSSA: That you're weird? Good for you.

EVE: No. I know. About you.

ALYSSA: Yes, this is all very ominous. (*Brief pause.*) You seem to have something to say to me, so will you just speed through all the creepy talk and get there?

EVE: You're my Nancy.

ALYSSA: (*Speaking slowly, as if to a two-year-old.*) My name is Alyssa.

EVE: (*Annoyed.*) I know.

ALYSSA: (*Still speaking slowly.*) And you're Eve.

EVE: (*Bitingly sarcastic.*) Is that my name? Thanks.

ALYSSA: Hey. Just trying to help.

EVE: (*Ignoring her.*) So. My old boss. She was a paranoid psychotic, basically. A crazy-ass bitch, if you will.

ALYSSA: (*Acting bored as she lifts the lid off her cup.*) Yes, but was she a good boss?

EVE: She was fired. So not really. Anyway, now that she's no longer my boss and way out of the picture, some of the seemingly insane things she did back then are starting to make perfect sense to me now. And I didn't realize it then, because . . . well, she was a crazy-ass bitch, but . . . I don't know . . .

> (EVE is *lost in thought for a moment.* ALYSSA *watches briefly, then shakes her head dismissively.*)

ALYSSA: (*Rattling her nearly empty coffee cup.*) If you're on a story break, do I have time to get a refill?

EVE: (*Without hesitation.*) No. (ALYSSA *frowns, but* EVE *has caught her train of thought and continues.*) When my boss met the man who would be her husband, they didn't waste any time. After four months they were engaged, and, in four more, married.

ALYSSA: Kinda like you and Mark.

EVE: I suppose. Except I'm not a crazy-ass bitch. (ALYSSA *considers saying something, but wisely keeps her mouth shut.* EVE *catches her nonetheless.*) Yeah. That would've been an easy one. But you left it. (EVE *pauses, calculating.*) I wonder why that is . . . ?

ALYSSA: Consider it a wedding present.

EVE: But you got us that decorative pillow thing. I just sent the thank you.

ALYSSA: I'm the soul of generosity, what can I say?

EVE: (*Smiles blandly.*) Sure. (*Beat.*) So, my boss's husband has a best friend. Her name was Nancy.

ALYSSA: I was wondering when you'd get to the Nancy.

EVE: Well, I'm there. So listen.

ALYSSA: Since I don't have anywhere to be right away . . .

EVE: He and Nancy went way back. Had the shared history thing going for them, which irked my boss to no end. And any time he'd had girl problems—if he had a crush on someone or if he was unhappy in a relationship, whatever—Nancy was the one he'd run to.

ALYSSA: Okay, he had a thing on the side with Nancy? I don't see how—

EVE: (*Cutting her off.*) It was never a physical thing. I guess he just wasn't attracted to her in that way. At all. (ALYSSA *winces.*) Theirs was a mental connection. Which, in a lot of ways, is more intense than a physical one. (EVE *has* ALYSSA's *full attention.*) But the connection had . . . (*Beat.*) waned (*Beatlet.*) in the time that he and my boss had been together. See, my boss, despite being a—

ALYSSA: Lemme guess. Crazy-ass bitch?

EVE: Well, yeah. Despite that, she met her husband's needs in every way. Mentally, emotionally, and . . . physically. You get the idea. So he didn't need to talk to Nancy all the time. They were still friends, sure. And even though they didn't talk that much anymore, the connection was still there. They had a rapport. A very familiar, comfortable rapport. And when my boss saw this . . . rapport . . . first-hand, she felt threatened.

(EVE *pauses again, considering her next words carefully.*)

ALYSSA: Yeah? And?

EVE: I think the incident happened at their engagement party. Nancy had brought a cake and my boss offered to help her with it, but Nancy walked right past her and navigated her way around the kitchen just as if she'd always been there. As if she belonged there—and my boss didn't. My boss took offense. She talked to her husband, though I guess he was her fiancé then. He talked to Nancy and she claimed my boss was trying to sabotage their friendship. So the husband's in the middle of the two most important women in his life and, of course, they make him choose. And, of course, he chooses his wife. Nancy was pretty much ex-communicated after that. It became more trouble than it was worth for the husband to keep the relationship intact. That was the end of Nancy.

(ALYSSA *waits for her to continue, but* EVE *does not.*)

ALYSSA: What? (*Beat.*) What am I supposed to get out of that little story? Are you trying to tell me I can't be friends with Mark?

EVE: No. I never said that.

ALYSSA: You damn well implied it.

EVE: I don't think so. I didn't really understand what my boss was going through then because I had never loved anyone. Now I do.

ALYSSA: You can't tell me to get out of his life.

EVE: I would never. He derives pleasure from your company. I can't deny him that. (*Beat.*) I just want you to know that I could.

ALYSSA: You are seriously messed up. (*To no one in particular.*) How does Mark keep ending up with these psychos? (*Beat.*) And where is Mark, anyway? He's been in the bathroom awhile.

EVE: I told him to give us ten minutes. (*She smiles.*) So I could get to know you better.

ALYSSA: Which you haven't done. You don't know anything about me.

EVE: I know enough.

ALYSSA: If you knew me at all, you'd know that I'm no threat to you. Mark and I are just friends. Nothing more. So you have no reason to be pulling the crazy jealous girlfriend—

EVE: (*Quick to correct.*) Wife.

ALYSSA: Fine! The crazy jealous wife routine. (*Beat.*) You're making way too much of this.

EVE: You're right. I tend to do that. And I know that I can't fully understand your relationship because I've never had a close guy friend. Neither did my boss, for that matter. Well, she did. But he was gay. So it was different. Kind of. (*Short pause.*) What I mean is, if I had had a heterosexual guy for a best friend when I was single, you better believe I would have thought about it. (*Beat.*) And you're telling me that you never once thought about it. Never in your life did you ever even think that maybe, just maybe, you and Mark might end up together someday? Admit it. (ALYSSA *is silent.*) I don't get it. (*Beat.*) See, I may not have been around as long as you have, but I love Mark. More than you can ever imagine. I want him so much that I just don't understand how someone like you . . . or any girl, really . . . (*Short pause.*) Doesn't.

ALYSSA: I don't owe you anything. Except maybe a decorative pillow—and you've already got it.

EVE: Have it your way. I know enough, anyway. I'll go and find Mark.

(EVE *stands up and prepares to exit, but stops at* ALYSSA's *words.*)

ALYSSA: (*Looking into her coffee cup.*) I just always liked to know that he was an option. (*Beat.*) But now he's not.

EVE: (*Sitting down again.*) Damn right he's not.

ALYSSA: He never really made a big deal about any of the other girls. Until you.

EVE: Well, I am way cuter than any of them. Including you. (ALYSSA *gives her a much deserved glare.*) What? Mark said.

ALYSSA: Even if it were true, isn't that the kind of thing he'd have to say to his wife?

EVE: He assured me it was true. And I trust him implicitly. You, however, I'll be keeping my eye on.

ALYSSA: Can't say I'm surprised. But for someone who claims to trust her husband, you sure don't act like it.

EVE: Oh, I do trust Mark. More than anyone. But other women? You've got to be
                kidding.

ALYSSA: (*Conceding, but only slightly.*) Maybe.

                        (*A few moments pass in a slightly less uncomfortable silence.*)

EVE: You know, I hate to point this out, but we have a lot in common.

ALYSSA: But even if we do—

EVE: We could never be friends.

ALYSSA: (*Nodding.*) Of course not.

EVE: It just wouldn't work. Especially, if you realize that the qualities we share are very
                likely the things that attracted Mark to me in the first place.

                        (EVE *shudders visibly.*)

ALYSSA: But guys tend to think that if they just leave two women alone for ten minutes,
                they'll automatically become the best of friends.

EVE: (*Smirks.*) Or they'll start making out.

ALYSSA: But things aren't that simple. (*Beat.*) And you're really not my type.

EVE: Right back at you.

                        (EVE *folds and unfolds a napkin while* ALYSSA *drains the rest of her
                        coffee.*)

ALYSSA: (*Setting down her cup.*) You are a crazy-ass bitch.

EVE: (*Shrugs.*) Maybe.

ALYSSA: But I do believe you love Mark and you'll be good to him. He deserves his
                happiness. And if you're what makes him happy, then . . . well . . . (*She struggles
                to reach a grand conclusion of some sort, but settles for a shrug.*) Okay?

EVE: Thanks for the enthusiasm. (*Beat.*) If you so much as touched his hair, my first instinct would be to take you out to the parking lot and beat your ass. But I love him. More than anyone or anything. More than I resent you, even. And that's a lot. Because you're so important to him, you have my word that I won't beat your ass. (*She pauses for a moment, but can't stop herself.*) But . . . please . . . don't touch his hair. Especially in a familiar manner.

ALYSSA: I'll try and restrain myself. But not because I'm worried about you beating my ass. I could totally take you.

EVE: Yeah, probably. (*Beat.*) Do you want another coffee or something?

ALYSSA: Only if you're paying.

EVE: Why not? (*Reaches for her purse.*) Damn. I think I left my wallet in the car. (*Animatedly digging through the contents of her purse.*) Wait. I have Mark's credit card.

              (*She triumphantly slaps it down on the table.*)

ALYSSA: (*Peering at the card.*) Is that . . . ?

EVE: Darth Vader? Yes.

ALYSSA: (*Bursting into laughter.*) He's such a dork.

EVE: (*Joining in, in spite of herself.*) He is. But he's my dork. And you know what's even funnier? (*She picks up the credit card.*) He got me one with my name on it. (EVE and ALYSSA *continue laughing until* EVE *suddenly looks up.*) Mark's headed this way.

ALYSSA: (*She is not laughing now.*) Crap! He'll think we've bonded!

EVE: (*Devilish grin.*) Let him think it.

ALYSSA: Fine. Just don't start making out with me.

EVE: I'll try and restrain myself.

ALYSSA: (*Under her breath.*) Here he comes.

(*They both look off, toward the unseen* MARK.)

EVE and ALYSSA: (*In perfect unison.*) Hi, honey.

(EVE *and* ALYSSA *sharply swivel their necks and lock glares as the lights fade to black.*)

END

Bethany Gibson lives in Kalamazoo, Michigan, where she earned her MFA from Western Michigan University. She's had productions with the Paw Paw Village Players and All Ears Theatre and, most recently, was a semi-finalist in Lamia *Ink's* international one-page play competition. Currently, Gibson is at work on several projects—including a collaboration with her fellow playwright (and husband), Nick Gauthier.

Bethany Gibson

Bump

In *Bump,* Maryann Lesert provides a lesson in the power of crosstalk. The two characters, Him and Her, have come to a point in their marriage where they feel they are traveling down a long dark road like the one they are actually on at four in the morning. They have run over something headless and limbless and white, perhaps a dog, perhaps a body, perhaps nothing at all. As their late night discussion in the middle of the road comes close to the main issues of their marriage, they stop responding directly to each other:

HIM: . . . We're going to trash this trip . . . and get a divorce over the Meat Puppets and your inability to drive worth a shit at night?

HER: Honesty's working for you now, isn't it?

HIM: Well?

HER: The Meat Puppets are cross-dressers. I saw a new video and the lead singer was wearing a black and pink teddy with fishnet hose.

The obliquity of the dialogue reflects the characters' hesitation or inability to face each other and confront together the issues that threaten their relationship.

The playwright also uses repetition effectively to give weight and meaning to the dialogue. For example, the title of the play—*Bump*—is a simple noun, standing for no more than a real bump in a real road. But by the time we have heard the word used over and over, the bump may well signify a horribly mutilated body. Is there a dead dog or dead person behind them? Is the bump merely a bump in the road of their marriage or the horribly mutilated end of their relationship? As in many successful plays, the question—both dramatically and thematically— becomes more important than the answer.

Maryann Lesert

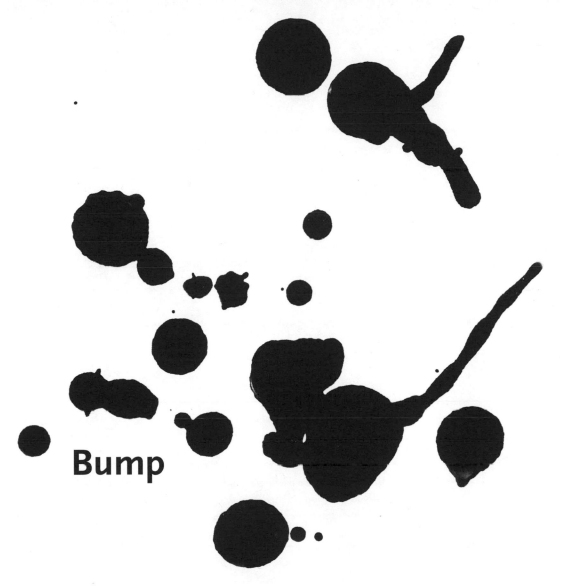

Bump

CHARACTERS   HER: Married woman.

HIM: Married man.

SETTING   A married couple—HIM and HER—are driving across the interstate on their way to the airport when they hit something in the road. She pulls the car over and an argument ensues. Was it a bump (Jimmy Hoffa's torso), or a ka-bump (a dog with legs)? In the process of yelling at each other, they realize the trip they were going to take, a late-night flight to New York City to rekindle passions of the past, is not going to work.

(*Loud* MUSIC, *punk-rockish with a fast, hard beat, blares until the lights go up. The play begins with* HIM *bending under the "car,"* HER *pacing nervously.*)

HER: I tried to miss it, but this fog, it's like rain. I couldn't see, and—that music! It's nerve-racking. No matter how many times I ask, you never turn it down. (*She pauses, thinking.*) It was so white.

HIM: Ahh. Dog.

HER: I don't know. There was something about it.

HIM: A white-haired dog. We need to go, we'll miss the flight.

HER: I didn't see any legs.

HIM: You can't see dog-legs when you run over a dog doing seventy miles an hour.

HER: But it was just one bump. A big bump. Bump.

HIM: I heard ka-bump.

HER: How could you have heard a thing with the Meat Puppets blaring? I can't believe I let you talk me into this. This four A.M. stuff was hazardous back then, too, don't you remember?

HIM: I thought you liked them.

HER: Liked what? Not being able to see the cement divider until you're almost on top of it?

HIM: The Meat Puppets. The resurgence of punk. The anti-hair bands of the eighties.

HER: You can't see a thing either, you just pretend to be able to. (*Pause.*) It looked like a human torso.

HIM: It was not a human torso.

HER: How would you know? You weren't even looking. You were doing that ridiculous Dah, duh-duh, Dah, duh-duh, Dah, duh-duh drum thing.

HIM: I heard it. Ka-bump. It was a dog. A big white dog. Or tan, or yellow, or a deer. Everything looks white in the headlights.

HER: There was no head.

HIM: There was too.

HER: See? You're pretending now. As if I'm stupid enough to fall for it.

HIM: I saw it long before you did.

HER: Then why didn't you say anything?

HIM: What was I supposed to say? Look out for that-KA-Bump!

HER: I didn't have time.

HIM: You had plenty of time. You just can't see worth a shit at night.

HER: Then why am I driving?

HIM: Because you won't let me. You never let me.

HER: You're a grown man.

HIM: Yeah, you'd think so.

HER: You cannot blame me for everything you're feeling.

HIM: It was a fricking dog! It's probably been dead for a month and no one's bothered to drag it away. Did you happen to notice it was near the divider wall? Where we should not have been, by the way.

HER: Oh my god! It was a body! Someone was trying to cross the road and got hit. And, oh god, I hit them again. We have to go back. What if they got hit by a truck and their arms and legs have been getting run over all night long?

HIM:	You can't kill an armless, no-legged torso that's been run over all night.
HER:	I feel sick.
HIM:	You've got to be kidding. It was a dog! I am absolutely, positively—
HER:	It's only a few miles back. We can make it.
HIM:	Not with you driving.
HER:	Why do you always have to be so negative?
HIM:	I'm being realistic.
HER:	Realistic? You call what you've been, realistic? You can't stand your job. You can't stand the laundry. The economy's crumbling and we're all stuck. I can't believe you actually booked us on a four A.M. flight. All you do now is come home at night and fall asleep in a chair (*She mimics his gaping-mouthed snoring.*) while I pack! You haven't gotten through the end of a movie in years. You know what that is?! That is apathetic, pessimistic, narcissistic, but not—Nay, I say not!—realistic.
HIM:	(*Deliberately objective.*) Ka—over his long white body. Bump—over his legs. Actually, it was more like a Ka—bump-bump.
HER:	Hah! That's where I've got you! It's that same Meat Puppets beat. The same beat that's in every single song you play. Dah, duh-duh. Dah, duh-duh. Over and over. Dah, duh-duh. Dah, duh-duh. You couldn't have heard a thing, and there were no legs.
HIM:	There were too.
HER:	I keep imagining something.
HIM:	A peaceful car ride? Yeah. Where are those days, huh?
HER:	Jimmy Hoffa. I keep seeing Jimmy Hoffa, laying in the road, dumped out in a thick chunk.

HIM:	Two decades later. What do you think they did, froze him just for tonight? Ah! We can't even get to Detroit Metro without tearing into each other. Who needs the mob?
HER:	I know.
HIM:	Come on. (*He motions to the car.*) Come on. But you better kick this mother out after we go back and verify that it was, indeed, a dog. A dog isn't going to be a pretty sight either.
HER:	Nothing's pretty anymore. What are we going to do?
HIM:	Go back.
HER:	Counseling?
HIM:	We'll go back.
HER:	No.
HIM:	We're going back.
HER:	No. We can't. We can't go back and rekindle something that was so raw and fun and young. We were so young, and so . . . un-worried. (*Pause.*) It did look an awful lot like a human torso.
HIM:	We're going back.
HER:	Don't do that. Just because I'm saying bump, don't you start saying bump. That's just what those trips were all about, and you're doing it again. Whatever I wanted to do, you'd seize on it, make it yours. I wanted to dare myself into those Soho Dungeon bars, so . . . you did too. I wanted to stop and watch the sidewalk pastels, so . . . you did too. It was always your old, red Horizon, your flip-book maps, your Meat Puppets blaring. That's the thing about men. They'll do whatever it takes to get laid, but when that wears off, there goes the friendship. Why don't you know when you're faking us out?
HIM:	I was young and I was trying to get laid.

HER:	Exactly. Exactly! And now that we're stuck together, what's the harm in admitting it, right?
HIM:	Right. Now I'm an old guy and I'm still trying to get laid.
	(*Silence.*)
HIM:	Let's go.
HER:	No.
HIM:	Come on.
HER:	No.
HIM:	It could have been Jimmy Hoffa's torso, or some poor college kid hitch-hiking, and he got caught alongside the divider and tried to cross, but ended up getting hit by a semi, and his arms and legs were blasted off. Could have been.
HER:	If we hit a torso, we would have gone flying, wouldn't we?
HIM:	Probably.
HER:	The Meat Puppets are all cross-dressers, you know.
HIM:	They are not. They're an anthem. Don't you remember some of those crazy, underground music stores?
HER:	Don't try to steer me.
HIM:	(*Sighing.*) We're not going, are we?
HER:	Like Frodo Baggins said, at the end of the journey, when you realize some old wounds go too deep, you can't go back.
HIM:	(*Quoting Tolkien.*) "For some the Shire is saved, but not for me."
HER:	Then again, Frodo was nothing more than a big-eyed emotional munchkin.

Bump

HIM:	He was a Hobbit.
HER:	Why do you have to take things so literally? I was referring to his lack of emotional development.
HIM:	Frodo was way developed.
HER:	Yeah? Well, all I'm saying is Frodo never got married. Tolkien married poor Sam right off, but never Frodo. No, because Frodo had other things to do, and marriage is all about resignation. Like Sam said, "Well, I'm back."
HIM:	What is that supposed to mean?
HER:	I don't know. Call it a joke.
HIM:	First of all, Frodo was not emotionally arrested. He had plenty of well-developed friendships. Satisfying, respectful friendships. And I don't wonder why his friends were all male. And if those college trips were all about me, that's because you made them that way. You said we should take my car because your car might break down, but your car was in better shape than mine. You just didn't want your car to ruin everything. Let my car break down, and then you could blame it on me. And so what if I wasn't into the art galleries. I went along with whatever you wanted because that's what friends do for each other. And I loved those underground music stores, even that Lurch guy with the giant safety pin pierced through his cheek. I loved that guy. And if you hated the Meat Puppets, then you shouldn't have sat there, nodding along. (*He mimics.*) Talk about fake. And. As I recall, you were pretty damned ready to get laid. So, so, go back! Go back! Because I am not going to be the reason you didn't.
HER:	This is why Frodo never got married.
HIM:	Smart Hobbit. (*Pause.*) Great. We're going to trash this trip, and what—what?— get a divorce over the Meat Puppets and your inability to drive worth a shit at night?
HER:	Honesty's working for you now, isn't it?
HIM:	Well?

HER: The Meat Puppets are too cross-dressers. I saw a new video and the lead singer was wearing a black and pink teddy with fishnet hose.

HIM: You shouldn't take things so literally.

HER: How could I not with his junk all wrapped in silk? (*Pause.*) Oh, for the want of spontaneity!

HIM: There is nothing spontaneous about us anymore. Except combustion. We were made for it.

HER: It did look like a torso.

HIM: I know.

HER: Now you're just saying that to make up.

HIM: Hey. I can always believe.

HER: Liar.

HIM: Not lying.

HER: You lie like a dog.

HIM: Fine. I'm a dog.

HER: You are. You're a dog.

HIM: I am. I'm a dog.

(*Silence.*)

HER: Bump. (*He remains silent, though wanting to dispute.*) It was just a bump.

HIM: That's why the adventure always worked. No time for the small stuff. How is anyone supposed to survive decades of this small stuff? (*He waits, but she doesn't reply.*) Remember being in that one bar, and we realized the shackles hanging from the bathroom walls were real?

HER: They may have been real. That was enough.

HIM: That was enough, wasn't it? (*Pause.*) Ah, what the hell.

HER: What the hell. Let's kick this mother out.

HIM: The trip?

HER: So what if we don't make the flight? We'll just keep going.

HIM: To where? Toledo?

HER: Why not? Hey, check it out (*Noticing a "sign."*), we're near the racetrack. We could pick up a pair of gearheads and do some swinging.

HIM: You can almost understand, can't you?

            (*Silence.*)

HER: No.

HIM: I knew that.

            (MUSIC *returns, fast and hard, as they exit. The lights fade to black.*)

                                    END

Maryann Lesert's play productions include *Superwoman, The Music In The Mess,* and *Natural Causes,* a finalist for the 2001 Princess Grace Foundation's National Playwright's Fellowship. Maryann completed her first novel while earning her MFA from Spalding University in Louisville. Currently, she teaches English at Grand Rapids Community College.

In Ruth Reichl's Restaurant Review

An issue of *The New York Times* and the culinary lure of *Moules Marinieres* play central parts in this play, in which Myra and Sy both make comically unsettling discoveries about each other over post-breakfast coffee in the kitchen of their Westchester County home.

As in much comedy, particularly farce, improbable coincidence also plays its part here. Myra reads a review by Ruth Reichl—the real *Times* food critic from the 1990s—that praises the mussels at a Manhattan restaurant, *Les Moules en Folie* (literally, "the mussels of madness"), taking her back twelve years to Sy's mad passion for the mussels—and for Myra—at a seaside bistro in the French resort of Honfleur. In another coincidence, Ruth Reichl has apparently dined at the same bistro. Sy, however, seems strangely reluctant when Myra proposes an excursion to the bistro's Manhattan counterpart. From here on, coincidences begin to accumulate, as when Myra spots Sy—with another woman—in a photograph accompanying the review.

What follows is a sequence of devices—quizzing or grilling, deception, fancy footwork to avoid exposure—that form the staples of stage farce. Steve Feffer's clever dialogue and comic invention provoke both laughter and empathy as we see Sy struggle and fail to avoid the inevitable. And in a particularly satisfying conclusion, the pattern of coincidences that skewered Sy like a mussel on a fork effect a reversal that winkles Myra out of her own protective shell.

Steve Feffer

In Ruth Reichl's Restaurant Review

CHARACTERS   MYRA: a woman, forties.

SY: a man, forties.

SETTING   A kitchen in Westchester County, New York during the mid-1990s, when Ruth Reichl was the restaurant critic for *The New York Times*.

for Laura

184

(AT RISE: *A Friday morning in a kitchen in Westchester County, New York. A couple is reading* The New York Times *at breakfast.* SY *is reading the sports section and* MYRA *is reading Ruth Reichl's restaurant review in the "Weekend" section. They both wear very smart suits. They have eaten lightly and only their coffee remains.*)

MYRA: I don't believe it! After all these years! Listen to what Ruth Reichl has written this morning in her restaurant review: "The mussels *marinieres* at *Les Moules en Folie* on New York's Upper East Side are as delectable as those I once found and have forever treasured at a seaside table in Honfleur on the Brittany coast of France."

SY: Hmm.

MYRA: "Hmm?" You were so enamored with the *moules marinieres* in Honfleur that you proclaimed to the whole seaside porch that if you ever found a restaurant in New York that served the *moules marinieres* like *L'Anchorage,* you'd dine there every day.

SY: That was twelve years ago.

MYRA: And for twelve years, everywhere we've traveled, you've looked for such a *moules marinieres.*

SY: My tastes have changed.

MYRA: Every time we're in a French restaurant, you ask the maitre d' if he knows of the *moules marinieres* they make in Honfleur at the seaside bistro called *L'Anchorage.*

SY: I like to seem informed about food.

MYRA: You ask anyone who is French.

SY: I don't know anyone who's French.

MYRA: Millie's French teacher?

SY: I thought a little small talk would help Millie pass the class.

MYRA: (*Returning to the review*.) Oh, my God, listen to this: "Each mussel seems seasoned to perfection with the crash of the salty sea spray so unique to Honfleur." I'm calling them right now for a reservation.

(MYRA *picks up her cell phone*.)

SY: You know I can't eat *moules marinieres* anymore. Twelve years ago in Honfleur I didn't know what my cholesterol was.

MYRA: One bowl of the mussels isn't going to kill you. I mean, imagine: Listen to Ruth Reichl: "The room transports one's senses back to that seaside town, as if on an Honfleur sea breeze." And, look, look at this picture. It could very well be that restaurant in Honfleur where you said—over a mammoth wooden bowl of the *moules*—Myra, I don't know if I've ever been more in love with you. That day the *moules marinieres* had a dramatic effect on you.

SY: And it will again. Ask Dr. Marx.

MYRA: (*Pause, as she begins to look closely at the picture accompanying the review*.) Huh? (MYRA *looks again*.) In the picture . . .

SY: Sea breezes, yes . . .

MYRA: . . .There's a man at one of the tables that looks like you.

SY: (*Taking the newspaper*.) Where?

MYRA: At that right front table.

(SY *takes a long look*.)

SY: He looks nothing like me.

MYRA: The resemblance is uncanny.

SY: That man is ten to fifteen years younger than me.

MYRA:	You could be twins.
SY:	Those photos are so misleading. You always say you're disappointed in how the restaurants' interiors compare to the pictures.
MYRA:	The interiors, yes, but not the patrons.
SY:	Well, I have a very common look, sorry to disappoint you. (*Quickly.*) If you're done with the "Weekend" section may I have it?

(*He tries to take it back from her.*)

MYRA:	I'm not done with the review.
SY:	How can you not be done? You've read about the *moules marinieres* and the sea breezes. What did Ruth Reichl write? A shellfish version of *Moby Dick*?
MYRA:	I haven't read about the desserts.
SY:	Will have you have room after the mussels?
MYRA:	According to Ruth Reichl I should make room, "if for no other reason than to prolong the experience of being in *Les Moules en Folie.*" (MYRA *pauses.*) Oh my!
SY:	Some desserts.
MYRA:	That's your tie.
SY:	What?
MYRA:	The man that looks like you is wearing the tie Millie bought you when you were promoted to Vice President. It's the Jerry Garcia Grateful Dead tie that she said would keep you from being "sucked into the corporate cesspool."
SY:	Do you think that Jerry Garcia only sold one tie? I mean, how do you think he got sucked into the corporate cesspool?
MYRA:	And the suit jacket . . . That's one of your suit jackets . . .

SY: No, that's one of Moe Ginsburg's suit jackets. The same warehouse suit jacket that every other New York Jew wears.

MYRA: Well this New York Jew is you at *Les Moules en Folie*. You are being transported on sea breezes back to the seaside of Honfleur with—what looks to be—another woman.

SY: I have never been to *Les Moules en Folie*.

MYRA: Would you like me to call down Millie? Would you like me to ask if this is her father?

SY: I see her so little, I'm not sure it would prove anything.

MYRA: Who is she? With who are you enjoying the *moules marinieres* that you have craved for a dozen years?

SY: It's not me . . .

MYRA: Millie!

SY: (*Beat.*) Wait. Yes. Yes, it's me. But it's not what it looks like. It's a business lunch. I merely felt guilty that I had dined on the *moules marinieres* with someone that is not you, when I should only be opening the delicate shells in your presence. But it was a very important client from out of town, who heard about *Les Moules en Folie* and I couldn't possibly say no.

MYRA: Then why didn't you say this before?

SY: I just told you. *Moules marinieres* is our dish. It was wrong of me. I'm sorry. Why don't you call right now for reservations? No, better yet. I'll call. And fuck my cholesterol. Let us have the *moules* for an appetizer, main course, and dessert. (*He takes out his cell phone.*) What is that number?

MYRA: This business associate . . .

SY: Ms. Claude, I believe her name is. Claude. Clyde. Whatever. What's the number?

MYRA:	What particular business requires you to hold her hand?
SY:	I never held her hand!
MYRA:	There behind the wooden bowl of discarded shells—the wooden bowl so like that which held our wantonly discarded cockles in Honfleur—isn't that your hand upon hers?
SY:	It appears to be some shells that have missed the bowl.
MYRA:	An extremity.
SY:	An exoskeleton.
MYRA:	A caress.
SY:	A crustacean.
MYRA:	A moment.
SY:	A mollusk.
MYRA:	Millie!
SY:	Let me see. (*He takes a quick look at the picture.*) Oh, yes, yes, now I remember. Miss Claude was in need of some assurance that the deal we were proceeding with was the right one, and I gave her a mollifying clasp, as I do in that type of business situation.
MYRA:	Why make this anymore painful than your meal of *moules marinieres* has already made it? Please, Sy, who?
SY:	I'm surprised Ruth Reichl doesn't tell you in her review.
MYRA:	With who were you immoral with the *moules* and besieged by the sea breezes if not me?

SY: Can't you tell?

MYRA: She's obscured by the flower arrangement—the flower arrangement that Ruth
             Reichl writes "is composed only of varieties that grow wild in the floral patches of
             the Honfleur dunes."

SY: Yes, and to think it'd be me who would be obscured by that damn "floral patch"
             if I didn't ask our waiter to move them because of my allergies.

MYRA: Who, Sy?

SY: Nicole.

MYRA: Nicole who?

SY: Millie's French teacher. When I asked her about a restaurant in New York that
             served the *moules marinieres* like I ate a dozen years ago in Honfleur, she didn't
             mock my memories like so many French foodies. She said, "Oh, you must've
             heard of *Les Moules en Folie*. It just opened and it is all the buzz of New York's
             Francophile-shellfish-loving community." And we've been going every Friday
             since.

MYRA: Every Friday?

SY: It's nothing physical—I assure you. We were just eating mussels.

MYRA: Just eating mussels? I've never seen you more physically alive than the afternoon
             we ate the *moules marinieres* in Honfleur. The cracking, the dipping, the dunking,
             the slurping, the ecstasy. Bowl after bowl. You ate them so fast, I saw sparks fly
             as the shells rubbed together. And then when the mussels were gone. You didn't
             stop. You attacked the *marinieres* with a loaf of bread. And then when the bread
             was gone, you lifted the wooden bowl like a holy chalice and held it to your lips.

SY: I'll call Nicole right now and tell her it's over. And we'll find Millie another French
             teacher. One that keeps kosher . . .

MYRA: Look at yourself in that picture, Sy. You haven't looked like that in twelve years.

You haven't looked at me like that in twelve years.

SY: I was looking at the mussels. I swear. (MYRA *picks up her cell phone.*) You're not still calling for a reservation, I hope?

MYRA: I'm calling my lawyer.

SY: Because of one seafood inspired indiscretion?

MYRA: Oh, if it was anything else but *moules marinieres,* Honfleur and sea breezes, I might be able to one day forgive you, but from the moment you opened that first shell and dipped into the *marinieres* broth, you must've know you were breaking open my heart and scooping out what was left of my love.

SY: Yes, yes, I know, because from the moment I first tasted the forbidden mussels with Nicole, it was if I had climbed out of the icy Honfleur sea, reborn like the first air-breathing creature.

MYRA: This is going to be messier than the *marinieres.* I suggest you call your lawyer.

SY: And not just in regards to us. I believe I may have an invasion of privacy suit against Ruth Reichl and her goddamn restaurant review.

(MYRA begins to dial. SY returns to the sports pages.)

MYRA: Martin Eliasberg, please. Myra Hirschberg. Yes, I'll hold . . .

SY: (*Pause.* SY *looks closely at the sports page for a beat.*) Yesterday, were you wearing that Jerry Garcia scarf that Millie gave you when you were made a partner at your firm?

MYRA: (*Still holding.*) Of course. There was the first fall nip in the air . . . Why?

SY: There's a picture here in the sports section of Mike Stanley leaning over the railing and into the stands at Yankee Stadium to catch a foul ball and his glove is over the head of a woman that looks remarkably like you . . . And a man that appears to be . . .

(*Beat, as SY struggles to discern who is in the picture.*)

MYRA: The chef at *Les Moules en Folie.*

(*Blackout.*)

END

Steve Feffer's plays have been produced by
theatres that include the O'Neill National
Playwrights Conference, Ensemble Studio
Theatre (New York), and Stages Repertory
Theatre (Houston). They are published
by Faber and Faber, Applause Books, and
Dramatists Play Service. Steve is an Assistant
Professor of English at Western Michigan
University.

Dada on Rails

Christopher Farran's *Dada on Rails* is a dramatic speculation on how a young Romanian named Sami Rosenstock transformed himself into Tristan Tzara, founder of the Dadaist movement in the early twentieth century. The transformation takes place appropriately on a train traveling from Romania to Zurich. Research can be a siren that compels a playwright to look for more and more information about a historical character instead of writing the play. But research is essential to the feel of truth in a drama, especially in such a short play. Tzara's betrayal of his father, the description of the Hungarian cavalry in the rain, the fate of Daphne, the sister Sami left behind—all are details that provide authenticity and substance.

One actor plays all the roles, a highly theatrical device pleasingly appropriate to its subject. The set is minimal—only chairs representing a train. The actor boards with a valise from which he pulls the costumes he will wear to represent the characters in his story. At one point, he represents both himself and his father, merely by the removal and replacement of an old-fashioned mortarboard. At another point he simply dons a black mask and becomes a bomb-throwing terrorist. Another stage device that adds to the theatricality of the play is the use of sound effects: the explosion of the terrorist's bomb; a piano playing; the train's whistle; a faint violin solo in a cabaret. The sounds create a rich yet simple setting for the action. And the play, itself, evokes its subject with great economy, like a Picasso sketch.

Christopher Farran

Dada on Rails

CHARACTERS   SAMI ROSENSTOCK.

SETTING   At CS, twelve chairs are set in rows of two with a narrow aisle between them, to simulate the seats in a train carriage. At SR is a lectern with a reading lamp on it.

TIME   May 1916.

(*A shrill train whistle, European style, sounds.*)

(SAMI ROSENSTOCK *stands in the aisle with a large valise in one hand, rocking slightly with the motion of the train. He's a slender young man of 19, his hair parted in the middle, almost foppishly overdressed. In his other hand he holds a train ticket and he's looking from the ticket to the chairs in order to find his correct seat.*)

SAMI: Who should I say I am? When I boarded the train before dawn yesterday, my papers said I was Sami Rosenstock, citizen of Roumania. Tonight I will meet the artists of the Cabaret Voltaire in Zurich . . . But who am I now? And what is notable about me?

(*The shrill train whistle sounds.*)

(SAMI *sits in a chair, rocking with the motion of the train, and looks to his right, out the window of the railroad car.*)

SAMI: The war was out there in the dark. The rail carriage was jammed with smelly people carrying their belongings in bundles on their laps. At dawn at the Tisza River we were stopped by a vast gray column of refugees; a squirming, organic mass like maggots boring through a dead host.

(*He pulls a small package from the valise, unwraps it, and begins to eat.*)

SAMI: Guilt and the sight of them made me hungry, and I ate the biscuits my sister Daphne had prepared.

(*He stands and opens the valise wider.*)

SAMI: There is another hunger, of course. In addition to sex. Ambition is an appetite that Daphne's biscuits won't satisfy. In Moinesti I was a math student, small and ugly and effeminate, the natural prey of the rough boys. But now as the train picked up speed into Hungary, I could try on the fantasies of my childhood.

(*He pulls an old bowler hat out of the valise and blocks out the crown with his fist so it looks like a cowboy hat.*)

SAMI: Who should I say I am? A wild west cowboy in America, shooting savages and buffalo and elk . . . ?

(He poses with one foot up on a chair, his fist on his hip, chin out, squinting across a distant prairie. He takes off his hat and stuffs it back into the valise.)

SAMI: The train is a cocoon for me; I could enter it as a timid little caterpillar and come out of it in Zurich as . . .

(He rummages in the valise again and pulls a black mask over his eyes and slaps a cloth workers' cap on his head.)

SAMI: A bomb-throwing anarchist, perhaps; why not? Responsible to a higher ideal that no one can quite articulate, but we know it must be pure and noble.

(He pretends to strike a match, touching it to a fuse; he tosses the bomb. A muffled explosion sounds. He cringes at the blast; then throws aside the eye-mask.)

SAMI: Brothers! We said the barracks, not the convent!

(He stuffs the anarchist get-up back into the valise.)

SAMI: I have experience in this field, too. I've already killed off my father, the dear anonymous headmaster of Latin; and that shivering sailor, who would have died anyway. They should be grateful; I made them martyrs. Not my intention, of course.

(From the valise he pulls a black academic robe and puts it on, with an old-fashioned mortarboard. He dons a monocle and raps the back of one of the wooden chairs with an ancient textbook.)

SAMI: *(As his father.)* Come, come, fellows. This is simple Latin. Can no one give me the answer? Sami, tell your classmates, please.

(He takes off the mortarboard, leaving the academic robe on. He looks bored and embarrassed as he answers.)

SAMI: *The Metamorphosis, Father. Ovid's Metamorphosis.*

         (*He puts the mortarboard on again.*)

SAMI: (*As his father.*) Precisely. You may sit down.

         (SAMI *sits in one of the train chairs, pulling off the robe and the
         mortarboard.*)

SAMI: And thank you, Father, for giving the rough boys a reason to beat me all the
         harder. Suffering will make me saintly.

         (*He pulls a handkerchief from the pocket of his coat and mimes wiping the
         condensation from the window on his right.*)

SAMI: In the mountains near the Austrian border it began to rain; a real downpour,
         a deluge. Out there in the rain stood the Hungarian cavalry, rank upon rank of
         steaming horses and men in their greatcoats, still as gravestones, as the water
         poured off their helmets and boots and moustaches.

         (*He pretends to salute them with a sword.*)

SAMI: I salute you, gentlemen. By now in Moinesti, the Death's Head Hussars have
         raped my sister Daphne; and would gladly have buggered me as well had I not
         put my own safety first.

         (*He stands and opens the valise again, throwing a paint-spattered smock
         over his shoulders and a floppy beret on his head.*)

SAMI: When the war ends I might go on to Paris, and become a world-famous painter.

         (*He mimics painting at an easel.*)

SAMI: I shall do nudes. Men, women, little boys . . .

         (*With his thumb and forefinger he squints at an imaginary model,
         measuring a tiny penis.*)

SAMI: . . . little girls, retired officers of the Russian artillery, angry poets from Finland who've been intimate with reindeer, Corsicans and Berbers; or . . .

           (*He takes off the smock and beret and puts on a pair of eyeglasses on a ribbon.*)

SAMI: Why don't I sail to New York and become an acclaimed actor and lecturer?

           (*He crosses to the lectern and turns on the reading lamp, pulling a folded paper from an inside pocket of his coat. He stands at the lectern and reads to the audience formally.*)

SAMI: When I was nine years old, a coal miner, whose son had always thrown lumps of coal at me, brought to our door a gaunt, barefoot fellow who needed a meal and a quiet place to avoid the police. Daphne and I were sent from the room as the adults negotiated in whispers. But we knew who it was. A month earlier, the Tsar's battleship *Potemkin* had been scuttled in the harbor at Constanza. The haunted figure was one of the Black Sea mutineers, the revolutionary sailors who had captured the Potemkin and bombarded the Tsar's garrison at Odessa.

           (*He puts on the academic robe and mortarboard of his father and stands behind one of the chairs with the Latin text in his hand.*)

SAMI: (*As his father.*) The reader of Ovid will see that time and again the metamorphosis is used as a means of escape; and indeed Ovid himself was exiled from Rome to save his life.

           (*He removes the mortarboard and puts down the book.*)

SAMI: The metamorphosis as escape? But if I change, will I know when to stop?

           (*He returns to the lectern and reads from his paper to the audience.*)

SAMI: When the rough boys taunted me I could escape into my fantasies. But when they taunted him, I was wounded twice.

           (*He steps away from the lectern and shouts offstage.*)

SAMI: You stupid boys! You think he's just a timid old schoolmarm, do you? Well let me tell you the truth!

(*He steps behind the lectern, to read from his paper.*)

SAMI: I knew I should have shut up, but I was too full of pride. At last I was going to set them in their place.

(*He shouts offstage.*)

SAMI: Do you know whom he's helped? Do you know who's our guest in the attic?

(*There's a heavy pounding at a wooden door. BAM! BAM! BAM!*)

SAMI: The soldiers came at night, with their bayonets and knee-high boots, and went directly to the attic. The feverish sailor lacked the strength to resist; but they took my father, too, before he could find his slippers. The soldiers hit him with the butts of their rifles, breaking his glasses. It took two minutes. They never even glanced at me and Daphne.

For nearly ten years Daphne and I were wards of the headmaster of my father's school. Professor Artioli and his aristocratic wife Elena provided us with pallets to sleep on, and rabbit and beet stew every day.

(*A piano tinkles lightly in the background.*)

SAMI: At age fourteen and sixteen, I was the court poet, the musician, the bard of the headmaster's dinners. I could play the piano and the violin. I could imitate the Prussian duelists.

(*With exaggerated movements he lampoons a swordsman.*)

SAMI: *En garde!*

(*The Sound of adult laughter.*)

SAMI: Daphne played the piano to my recitals of the Latin tragedies.

(*The piano becomes* profundo.)

SAMI: 'But you shall never bring him back
           With prayers and weeping
           From the common marsh of Death;
           But in that helpless grief you waste away;
           Your evils are unsolved in those tears.'

                (*Polite applause.*)

SAMI: And once a year for six years, Professor Artioli would deliver us a letter from our
           father.

                (*He unfolds another stiff and wrinkled sheet of paper and reads from it at
                the lectern.*)

SAMI: 'My beloved children, stay together at all costs and protect each other. In my
           present condition, I have been moved from the farm to the hospital laundry . . .'

                (*He folds the letter and addresses the audience.*)

SAMI: What present condition?

                (*He turns off the light at the lectern and returns to his seat in the rail
                coach, rocking with the motion of the train as he looks out the window on
                his right.*)

SAMI: So who am I now? Sami Rosenstock? The artists in Zurich will laugh at me just
           like the rough boys in Moinesti. And oh God, what if they're right?

                (*From his coat pocket he pulls the folded papers and a pen.*)

SAMI: As we passed Salzberg I played with names. Tara was the ancient Roumanian
           name for 'country'; perhaps I could use that. And I recalled that when Daphne
           went into the sanatorium—the fever and cough took her there for the first time
           at age fifteen—she took with her the book of her dreamy dreams: *Tristan and
           Iseult.*

                (*He gazes out the train window.*)

SAMI: Tristan and Tara.

(*He shrugs, shaking his head.*)

SAMI: In rural Hungary the churches were pagan and Catholic, smelling of blood. As we rounded Lake Bodensee into Switzerland, they were Lutheran, as smug as judges. Did they judge me? I wondered. Because Daphne needed chivalry and I left her instead with pneumonia.

  (*The shrill train whistle sounds again, then a rapid bell, as a train would use entering a terminal.* SAMI *stands and carries the valise downstage and opens it.*)

SAMI: Why do our parents embarrass us so? I betrayed him by trying to make him a hero—that was my need, not his—and years later when the war came and he was gone, I fairly sprinted to the train station.

  (*He fumbles in his pocket and holds out a wad of paper money.*)

SAMI: One fare to Zurich, please! Hurry!

  (*From the open valise he pulls out gray gloves and a top hat, and a formal cape. He begins putting them on.*)

SAMI: Why? Because among the taunts of the rough boys, he made sure he was teaching me. He bought my ticket to Zurich, with his lessons. He understood the day would come, and he beseeched Sami to protect his sister.

  (*He calls offstage.*)

SAMI: It's too late, Father! You taught me *The Metamorphosis*. Sami Rosenstock is dead!

  (*From the valise he pulls a small paper bag, hefting it once or twice.*)

SAMI: I knew the chameleon—to survive—could change its color to suit its surroundings. But does the chameleon then remember its first color?

  (*The lights dim on the train and the valise.* SAMI *holds tightly to the paper bag.*)

SAMI: Daphne gave me this, too; a talisman, she said, a charm for the journey, a charge to admit no regrets, a reminder never to look back.

           (*He reaches into the paper bag and pulls out a large rock: a glistening black lump of coal.*)

SAMI: So what should I do now with my guilt? Turn it into poetry, perhaps. Poetry is the respectable way to turn guilt into profit. Thus so, I can hold my own tonight among the artists at the Cabaret Voltaire.

           (*A faint violin solo plays, and the subdued murmur of voices. SAMI returns the lump of coal to the paper bag. He's in a softer light now, nodding discreetly as he greets poets and artists.*)

SAMI: Ah, Marcel Duchamp, what an honor.
           And Andre Breton, my pleasure, sir.
           Max Ernst, my sister and I adore your work!
           My name? How good of you to ask.

           (*Holding the paper bag and its lump of coal carefully behind his back, he draws a printed calling card from his coat and extends it to them.*)

SAMI: At your service, gentlemen.

           (*But he pulls the card back and reads it aloud himself.*)

SAMI: Tristan . . . Tzara!

           (*He sweeps aside his cape, removes his hat, and bows low with a melodramatic flourish. The violin solo again. The lights fade to black.*)

END

Christopher Farran was born in New York, grew
up in Winston-Salem, North Carolina, and
now lives in Nashville, Tennessee. He has two
children's books published by HarperCollins,
a parenting book published by Scribner's, and
an adult mystery published by Salvo Press. His
short fiction has appeared in two anthologies
and he's had nonfiction in magazines such as
Parents, Road & Track, and others.

SECTION TWO: LONGER ONE-ACTS

LONGER ONE-ACT PLAYS

If the ten-minute one-acts in the previous section may be compared to short stories in their subtlety and intensity of focus, the longer one-acts in this section, two or three of which might constitute a full evening of theatre, resemble the novella, allowing the playwright to deal with complications of greater magnitude and scope with correspondingly greater length and complexity of structure.

Ten-minute plays often deal with no more than two or three characters and are likely to observe Aristotle's three unities—of time, place, and action—with the play's events unfolding continuously in one temporal and physical setting. Of the fourteen plays in Section One, all conform to this general observation with only slight variation in three plays as regards the number of characters.

Of the twelve plays in Section Two, however, half feature more than three characters and more than one physical and/or temporal setting. Such structural complexity also allows playwrights to exploit more fully what Aristotle identifies as discovery (or revelation) and reversal, with correspondingly greater use of such devices as plants, pointers, connections, subplots, and the like (see *Appendices* for further discussion).

When playwrights work in longer forms, they must concern themselves with more than the question of "Why today?" and the thematic question of what the play means (or what idea animates it). Greater length makes crucial the dramatic question, which focuses on action, e.g., will this sequence of events end well or badly for the characters? This question speaks to how a play engages an audience's attention.

We believe you'll find that the plays here gathered certainly do attend to their dramatic questions and that they demonstrate the power—in common parlance—"to keep butts on seats."

Last Call

Constance Alexander's *Last Call* focuses on the widow and family of a man killed in the terrorist attacks of 9/11. The play avoids the easy sentiment that could be connected with this topic and looks at the lives of these survivors with a realistic and unblinking eye.

Alexander makes clever use of the physical. The set described at the opening of the play represents the chaos in the lives of this family. However, in line with the playwriting axiom that if there is a gun on the table it must be used before the end of the play, all the physical things onstage play an important part in the plot and character development. Newspapers lie in a heap, still in their wrappers; we learn that Shea, the mother and widow, will not allow them to be removed from their plastic sleeves. There are baskets of clean and dirty laundry; we learn that Shea has finally washed her dead husband's soccer shirt that their son believed still smelled like his father. The calendar date is wrong; the children remind their mother that their father insisted it be kept up to date. There are stacks of unopened mail; in the third scene we learn that opening a piece of mail provided Shea with final proof that her husband had betrayed her with another woman whom he chose to call instead of Shea before he died. Each physical detail of the set has an organic part in driving the action of the play and helping the audience to understand the characters.

Another effective use of the physical is the answering machine that still plays the dead husband and father's voice message. We hear him in the play's opening moments and over and over throughout the action. We also hear on the machine the voice of the final agent of change, a reporter who ultimately and thoughtlessly helps Shea to change the message, marking the end of the emotional paralysis caused by her husband's death.

Constance Alexander

Last Call

CHARACTERS   SHEA BARTON-BRINK: 38. Mother of three. Married to Guy Brink, college
sweetheart, for fifteen years. English instructor, part-time, at nearby university.
Prides herself on being in control, organized. Feels ashamed of herself when
she is not.

GUY BRINK/VOICE 1: 39. Married to Shea. Father of Bart, Anna and Baby.
Full-time bond trader and New York commuter. Upwardly mobile in his job.
Spends many hours away from home for his work, but consoles himself in
knowing that his mother and father take up some of the slack caused by his
frequent absences from home. Weekend jock.

BART BRINK: 10. At the stage where he goes back and forth between being a
little boy and a bully to his sister, to being a jock like his dad. Sometimes gets
angry when he's expected to be more of a grown-up than a little boy. And vice
versa.

ANNA BRINK: 8. Daddy's little girl. Tender-hearted, easily wounded by her big
brother. Feels somewhat displaced by the attention the baby gets. Gets attention
herself by being a good big sister.

BABY: 6 months. Only seen from the back in the high chair.

MYRA LEV: 42. Well-meaning, self-appointed neighborhood watch. Her husband,
Jerry, commutes with Guy every day. Her son, Aaron, former neighborhood
cry-baby, is a senior at Harvard.

ELLEN GUILFOYLE, 28. Reporter, *Middletown Times*.

VOICE 2/ELECTRONIC.

SETTING   November 15, 2001. Suburban New Jersey. Home of the Brink family.

(*As the lights rise, we see* SHEA BARTON-BRINK *in the kitchen, spooning baby food into the six-month-old. The room is in disarray. A pile of newspapers still in plastic wrappers is on the floor. There is a stack of clean, folded laundry, but dirty clothes spew from a variety of plastic baskets. Piles of unopened mail are on the counter. A calendar on the wall displays the date 10-28-01, even though it is 11-15-01.* SHEA *babbles to the baby in a comforting manner, but periodically yells upstairs to the kids. She is doing all the things an earnest suburban mother does at this hour, yet it is clear she is stressed and trying to keep herself together.*)

SHEA: Yes. (*To* BABY, *clapping hands.*) That's good. Num, num. Yay. See. Yay! Is that a toothie down there? Yay. (*Calling out.*) You two about ready up there?

BART: (*OS.*) I can't find my soccer shirt. Mom! I can't find it!

SHEA: (*Searching through the stack of folded laundry.*) Oh, God. (*Calling upstairs.*) It's down here! Don't worry. It's okay. (*She pulls out a neatly folded shirt and scrunches it up and throws it in the basket with the dirty clothes. Then she calls to the kids again.*) Six minutes to the bus.

  (*Phone rings.* SHEA *continues to feed the* BABY *while the answering machine picks up.*)

VOICE 1/
GUY BRINK: You have reached the Brink of Disaster. Home of Shea Barton-Brink and Guy Brink. You know the drill. (*Beep.*)

ELLEN
GUILFOYLE: (*Voice.*) This is Ellen Guilfoyle. *Middletown Times.* It's eleven-fifteen-oh-one—8:07. Trying to get in touch with Mrs. Brink.

  (*During the rest of* ELLEN's *message,* SHEA's *lines overlap with* ELLEN's.)

SHEA: (*Still feeding the* BABY.) I hate that. It says Shea Barton-Brink.

ELLEN: Could she please call me back? I'm trying to set up an interview. I talked to her in-laws way back, oh, ten-seventeen, I think. Oh-one. I need to talk to Mrs. Brink so I can have the piece ready for Sunday.

SHEA: A newspaper reporter for God's sakes, and she screws up my last name. (To BABY.) Isn't that silly? Daddy says right on our tape Shea Barton-Brink. Da-da. Can you say Da-da?

ELLEN: Call me. Toll free. One, eight-seven-seven, seven-seven-seven-seven.

SHEA: "Call me. Toll free." Sounds like a robot. I guess if you're a reporter you don't have to say things like "Please," or "I'm sorry." Say Da-da.

ELLEN: I'll be out your way later. If I don't hear from you, I'll give you another call. Nice day.

SHEA: Same to you. I'll have a peachy-keen day, Ms. Guilfoyle. (*To* BABY.) Da-da. (*She leans over and punches the answering machine button so the pick-up message is heard again.*) Da-da.

VOICE 1/
GUY BRINK: You have reached the Brink of Disaster. Home of Shea Barton-Brink and Guy Brink. You know the drill. (*Beep.*)

SHEA: (*Punching the button to silence the machine and calling upstairs.*) Kids. Anna. Come on down. The bus'll be here before you know it. (*Sings to* BABY.) She's daddy's little girl. Da-da.

                        (BART *enters carrying the newspaper, pulling it out of the plastic bag.*)

BART: Who was on the phone?

SHEA: Give me that, please. Here. No one. I asked you not to take it out of the plastic bag. I'll take it.

BART: I heard it ring. I hate it when you treat me like a baby.

SHEA: Wrong number. Bart, will you go out and bring the garbage cans in? If Myra Lev does it for us she'll be on the doorstep an hour from now and inviting herself in for a cup of coffee. I can't take another day. Please, honey. For Daddy.

BART: You let the machine pick up on Grandma again.

SHEA: I didn't. (*To the* BABY) There. What a good baby. (*To* BART) I only let the machine pick up when I'm taking care of the baby. You don't think I'd do that to Grandma on purpose?

>   (ANNA *enters. She holds an armful of sheets and a blanket. She is on the verge of tears.*)

ANNA: It happened again. I'm sorry, Mommy.

SHEA: Come here, honey. Don't worry. You can put them right here. (*Motions to dirty laundry.*) That's my girl. I'm doing another load of wash this morning. I promise.

BART: She let the machine pick up again.

ANNA: What if it was Daddy?

SHEA: Daddy is not going to call. We all wish he would, but . . . I'm sorry.

BART: Daddy says you're never supposed to let the machine answer when you can get it. You could lose the biggest deal of your life. And you're supposed to keep the calendar on the right date too. What if you forget something important because you don't know what day it is?

>   (*He rips off pages of the calendar to get it to the right date.*)

SHEA: Year's right anyway. Two-thousand and one.

ANNA: Daddy's on the machine. I like to hear him.

SHEA: Me too.

BART: It's not really Daddy. She is such a baby. You're gonna have to buy her diapers. Do they make Pampers for second graders?

SHEA: She'll be okay, honey.

ANNA: Mommy is gonna make me a copy of the tape. I can listen to it whenever I want.

SHEA: Here. Feed the baby and I'll comb your hair. That's right. That's good. What a good girl. Bart, honey. Could you be just a little nicer to your sister? Please. If Myra Lev sees those garbage cans out there, she'll think we've taken cyanide with our corn flakes or something. Oh, God. Don't tell anyone I said that.

BART: (*Sniffing soccer shirt.*) You washed it. You washed it!

SHEA: Hold still now. What?

BART: (*Fighting tears.*) You washed my shirt.

SHEA: I did not.

BART: You did so. (*Sniffs the shirt again.*). Look! I told you to leave it alone. It's mine. Daddy said.

SHEA: It must have gotten mixed up with the laundry. I'm sorry. It wasn't on purpose.

BART: You get everything mixed up. Grampa said.

SHEA: Grampa says a lot of things but he's not always right. Now, don't go and tell him I said that. It'll be okay.

BART: I hate it. Everything's a mess.

SHEA: I know. I'm trying really hard but it's not working out so well some days. Like today. We have to work together. Like Daddy always says. Teamwork.

(BART *exits.*)

ANNA: Grampa said he was gonna pick me up after school and we'll go to Bart's soccer game together. I'm gonna cheer.

(*She practices being a cheerleader.*)

SHEA: Grandma said she'd take the baby all day. I could pick you up from school and we could go shopping. Let Bart have some special time with Grampa.

(BART *enters.*)

BART: The garbage cans were already in. I hate it when she comes to my games. She thinks she's a cheerleader.

ANNA: I'm hungry, Mommy.

(SHEA *goes through the cabinets.*)

BART: Pop-Tarts again?

SHEA: There are juice boxes in the fridge. And—um, here are those power bars. You know, the ones that are supposed to—

BART: (*Interrupting.*)—be for camping. Daddy said we're supposed to save them.

SHEA: I'll try to go grocery shopping this morning. I promise. I'll buy more. It's just been so hard going out.

BART: We have to go to school every day.

SHEA: I know. I'm sorry. I'll do better.

BART: I hate you.

ANNA: I'm not hungry. Let's keep them like Daddy said.

(*Sound of school bus.*)

SHEA: Come on. Take one. You know what Daddy says about going off without breakfast. Most important meal of the day. Hurry up or you'll miss the bus. Here. Go. Anna! I'll pick you up after school.

BART: I'm telling Grampa and Grandma.

ANNA: I don't wanna go shopping. I'm going with Grampa too. I'll be a cheerleader for Bart's team.

BART: Can't you do something with her? She's such a pain.

SHEA: Go on now. You don't want to miss the bus.

(*The kids exit.*)

(*Calling after them.*) I love you. I love you! I'm sorry about the shirt, Bart. (*To the* BABY.) Good baby. (*Imitating* ANNA.) I'm going with Grampa too. (*In her own voice.*) I wanna go with Daddy. Da-da. Can you say Da-da? Can you? Can you? (*She swoops down and hugs the* BABY.) Say it. Da-da. Da-da.

Scene 2

(*Later that morning. Still in the kitchen. The high chair is empty. The dishwasher is going, and so are the washer and dryer. A stack of opened mail is on the table.* SHEA *is crying. At rise, the sound of the doorbell.* SHEA *ignores it at first. After a few seconds of knocking, she tries to straighten herself up a little. She takes several short breaths, in and out, in and out, and then runs in place before she goes to the door.*)

SHEA: (*Answering the door as if she is out of breath.*) Sorry, Myra. I was upstairs. Just finished—um, vacuuming. Dust. Makes my allergies . . . (*Makes a show of blowing her nose.*)

MYRA: The baby can sleep through all this and the vacuum too?

SHEA: Well, not exactly but—

MYRA: I was awake at six. I brought the garbage cans in. Thought it might help out. When I drove Jerry to the train, we saw Bart come out and get the paper. He waved when we beeped. Smiled. No braces for that kid. He looks just like Guy.

You look like you could use a cup of coffee. So the baby's still sleeping? What did you do, give her a sleeping pill?

SHEA: Why would you—? I would never give the baby—I'm the one who needs sleeping pills. Coffee. Let's see. (*She looks through the cabinets.*)

MYRA: Don't worry about it.

SHEA: I have a tea bag. Here. Sleepytime.

MYRA: You're still not sleeping?

SHEA: Neither is the baby. I think she's starting to teethe.

MYRA: It's kind of early, isn't it? Where is she?

SHEA: She'd never sleep through all this.

MYRA: Did you, um, take her to day care?

SHEA: I can't seem to make myself get out of the house. The thought of going to the grocery store, or even to the park with the baby just—

MYRA: I saw both kids get on the school bus, and about fifteen minutes ago you pulled Guy's car out of the garage into the driveway. You didn't put the baby out there and then get distracted doing something else, did you?

SHEA: What?

MYRA: You going in to class today?

SHEA: No. I've got laundry to do. Grocery lists. Bills. (*A beat.*) I thought I should start up the little car. It's been weeks—

MYRA: So where's—what happened to—

SHEA: —The baby? I thought I told you. I'm staying home with her a little longer. Extending my leave for the semester. My mother-in-law took her for the day.

MYRA: So Molly's got her. Must've come when I was in the shower. That's nice. You can have some time to yourself.

SHEA: I have plenty of that already. (A *buzzer sounds*.) There's the dryer.

MYRA: Why don't I stay? Maybe help you get things straightened up before the kids—

SHEA: They're not coming home till after dinner. (*Imitating* ANNA.) I'm going with Grandpa. (*In a normal voice*.) Bart said he hated me this morning. I washed his soccer shirt.

MYRA: They all say that. He didn't mean it.

SHEA: He did this time. It's his lucky shirt. Guy's shirt, really. He spilled a cup of coffee on it Labor Day, when they went sailing. Bart won't let me wash it. Says it smells just like Daddy. And Anna wet the bed again.

MYRA: She'll grow out of it.

SHEA: She grew out of it when she was three.

MYRA: So she'll grow out of it again. Kids are resilient. Here. Let me fold some clothes. Busy hands, happy hands. Sometimes kids regress. My Aaron started sucking his thumb when he got bit by that damn dog down the street.

SHEA: Bitten.

MYRA: What?

SHEA: Bitten by that adorable toy poodle down the street that wouldn't hurt a fly.

MYRA: Right. Bitten, schmitten. I forgot, English professor. Aaron did not tease that dog, by the way. I know that's what all the kids say, but Aaron never did such a thing.

SHEA: It's so stupid. I can't stop saying stupid things. I feel stupid. I probably look stupid.

> (*The phone rings. Shea motions to* MYRA *that she isn't going to answer it.*)

VOICE 1/
GUY BRINK: You have reached the Brink of Disaster. Home of Shea Barton-Brink and Guy Brink. You know the drill. (*Beep.*)

ELLEN
GUILFOYLE: (*Voice, OS.*) Ellen Guilfoyle again, Mrs. Brink. It's still eleven-fifteen-oh-one. If you're there, please pick up. I'm on my cell phone heading out your way.

SHEA: (*Leaning over and hitting the silence button.*) Blah, blah, blah.

MYRA: It's not a bill collector, I hope.

SHEA: I'm not talking to her until she gets my name right. Guy says it right there on the tape. Plain as day. Shea Barton-Brink and Guy Brink.

MYRA: It's that reporter. Who's doing the stories.

SHEA: The very same. (*Imitating* ELLEN.) "I'm on my cell phone. My precious cell phone." I hate those damn things.

MYRA: Jerry says he's got no one to talk to on the train anymore, so he's been reading those stories every morning. They break his heart. You're not reading them?

SHEA: I can't. But I'm saving them. (*A beat.*) I think I'll make each one of the kids a memory quilt. I read that somewhere. You know, bits of material from special clothes. That may be the only way to pry that soccer shirt out of Bart's hands before it disintegrates.

MYRA: I'll help. Jerry and I can help. And when Aaron comes home for Thanksgiving he will too. We'd love to. It's important. The kids will have these things when they're older, so they can understand.

SHEA: When I'm older, do you think I'll understand?

MYRA: Is there anything I can do to help you feel better?

SHEA: The baby said Da-da this morning.

CLOWNY: (*Holds out the spoon to* RALPH.) Hey. Smell this.

RALPH: What is it?

CLOWNY: Smell it. (RALPH *chuckles self-consciously, shakes his head*.) Come on. Just smell it.

RALPH: I'd rather not.

> (*Beat.* CLOWNY *shrugs. But he keeps staring at* RALPH, *who becomes increasingly uncomfortable*.)

CLOWNY: Sooooo . . . You're the new guy.

RALPH: Ralph Mutter. (*Holds out his hand;* CLOWNY *gives it the hairy eyeball*.) Is there going to be . . . ? (RALPH *looks around the room*.)

CLOWNY: Mutter.

RALPH: It's German. Is there going to be another desk?

CLOWNY: Negative.

RALPH: So . . . We have to share this little table?

CLOWNY: Affirmative.

RALPH: Wow. (CLOWNY *looks at him*.) I mean, this is a pretty roomy office. And. I mean, there are two of us. (CLOWNY *is eating peas again. One at a time.* RALPH *watches with a kind of fascination*.) It just seems like it might be a little cramped. Both of us. At this dinky little table. You know?

CLOWNY: (*The spoon*.) I want you to smell this.

RALPH: I don't think so.

> (*Beat*.)

CLOWNY: Would you smell it if it weren't mine?

RALPH:	It is yours. You were eating off it.
CLOWNY:	So it's personal.
RALPH:	No . . .
CLOWNY:	Roger that, Mutter. No problem. How about that Cyn, uh? Something, huh?
RALPH:	She seems like a real nice girl.
CLOWNY:	Oooooh, yeah, babeeeee. She's nice all right.

(RALPH *chuckles a little, shakes his head confused*.)

RALPH:	So what do you think? Should we get started?

(CLOWNY *appraises* RALPH *through slitted eyes and finally nods*.)

CLOWNY:	Ever done this before?
RALPH:	I have six years' experience.

(*Beat*.)

CLOWNY:	Read or mark?
RALPH:	I prefer to mark. But I'll read if you want me to.
CLOWNY:	(*Holding out the spoon*.) We-e-e-ell . . . I could let you mark.
RALPH:	I'll read. (CLOWNY *shrugs. Puts the spoon into the can of peas and sets it aside. Picks up a sheaf of manuscript and hands it to* RALPH.) Okay. Just let me know if the pace is good for you. (CLOWNY *picks up a pen and sheaf of galleys.* RALPH *begins to read aloud*—CLOWNY *follows along squinting nearsightedly at the other copy*.) "Cap C Chapter cap O One. Initial caps The First Day."
CLOWNY:	Endmark?

RALPH:	No.
CLOWNY:	No endmark.
RALPH:	It's a chapter title. No endmark.
CLOWNY:	Gotcha.
RALPH:	Display cap *I*.
CLOWNY:	Drop?
RALPH:	Yes. Sorry. Drop. Display cap *I*. "It was a Friday morning, period . . . "
CLOWNY:	Cap *F* Friday?
RALPH:	Of course.
CLOWNY:	What do you mean by that?
RALPH:	It's a proper noun. I figure it goes without saying.
CLOWNY:	It's not our job to figure.
RALPH:	Fine.
CLOWNY:	You can't take anything for granted.
RALPH:	Sorry. Cap *F* Friday.
CLOWNY:	Initial cap, not all caps.
RALPH:	That's right. May I go on? (CLOWNY *nods*.) "It was a cap *F* Friday morning, period. He remembered that much, period."
CLOWNY:	Point. Not period.
RALPH:	You say point here?

CLOWNY:	That's what I'm telling you.
RALPH:	No problem. All set? (CLOWNY *nods*.) "That is, comma, when he thought about it at all, comma, he remembered that it had been a cap *F* Friday, point.". . . Am I going too fast?
CLOWNY:	Read back.
RALPH:	"It was a Friday morning. He remembered that. That is, when he thought about it at all, he remembered that it had been a Friday."
CLOWNY:	"Am I going too fast?"
RALPH:	What?
CLOWNY:	I don't show that here.
RALPH:	I was asking you about my reading rate.
CLOWNY:	Full stop.
RALPH:	Really? That's so . . . I don't know . . . British. Or something. (CLOWNY *just stares at him*.) Fine. Full stop. Am I going too fast for you?
CLOWNY:	No.
RALPH:	Fine. Anything else? (CLOWNY *mumbles something under his breath*.) What?
CLOWNY:	Enunciate.
RALPH:	Oh! Sorry.
CLOWNY:	Try not to mutter . . . Mutter.

(*Beat. They stare at one another with open hostility now.*)

RALPH:	Shall. I. Begin?

CLOWNY:	Sometime today? (*More eye contact.* RALPH *breaks it, takes a deep breath, and is about to go back to reading.*) And don't say "comma." Just say "com."
RALPH:	New paragraph.
CLOWNY:	Just "graph" Is fine.
RALPH:	"Graph. Cap *H* How had he fallen into this miserable corner of hell, question mark. How had it all started, question mark."
CLOWNY:	Query.
RALPH:	All right. And while we're stopped. For future reference, is an exclamation point a bang or an ex?
CLOWNY:	A bang of course.
RALPH:	Of course. (*Continuing to read.*) "Cap *W* Was it when he had first laid eyes on cap *T* The cap *C* Clown that the back of his neck had begun to prickle, com, and that cold ball of fear had begun to form in the pit of his gut, query." (*Beat.* CLOWNY *looks up expectantly.* RALPH *continues.*) "Or was it the moment when cap *T* The cap *W* Woman had stepped into the office, query." (CYN *enters and takes a pose.*) "Graph. Open double quote cap *E* Excuse me, com, close double quote she had said, com, leaning her weight on one foot, point."
CYN:	Excuse me.
CLOWNY:	*W-E-I-G-H-T?*
RALPH:	(*To* CYN.) Oh! Hey there!
CLOWNY:	Full stop?
CYN:	How are you two coming along in here?
RALPH:	Oh. Good, good.
CLOWNY:	Full stop?

CYN: That's great. Dave showing you the ropes and all?

RALPH: Full stop, Dave. (*To* CYN.) Oh, he's showing me, all right.

CYN: I figured. Dave's the best proofreader we've got. Aren't you, Dave?

RALPH: You mean he *was* the best proofreader you've got. Ha ha. (*He gives* CLOWNY *a comradely punch on the arm.*)

CYN: Oh, yes. Dave's the company comma wrangler of choice. Who needs spellchecker when there's Dave, that's the motto around here. (*She reaches over and ruffles* CLOWNY's *wig. He puts up with it.*) That's why every day's casual Friday for Dave. (CYN *and* RALPH *laugh.*) Dave's a perfectionist. Aren't you, Dave?

              (CLOWNY *picks up the spoon again. He moves the can of peas closer and again eats one pea at a time.*)

RALPH: Actually. I'm a bit of a perfectionist too. In fact, if I have one shortcoming as an employee, I'd have to say that's it—

CYN: So are you reading anything, ya know, interesting?

RALPH: Oh, well. I can't really read this stuff for enjoyment. Got a job to do. You know.

CYN: Wow. Soldier on. (*She and* CLOWNY *chuckle at this.*) Anyhow. If you need anything . . .

RALPH: Great. Thanks.

              (CYN *exits.* CLOWNY *and* RALPH *watch her out. Beat.*)

CLOWNY: (*Holding up the spoon.*) Hey. Smell this a sec.

RALPH: Just grab your galleys, Dave.

              (CLOWNY *puts the spoon in the peas and picks up the galleys. He wipes his mouth on the back of one of the galley sheets.* RALPH *starts to protest but decides against it.* CLOWNY *picks up his pen.*)

Read back.

CLOWNY: (*Reading it back.*) "Graph. Open double quote Cap E excuse me com close double quote she had said com leaning her wait—*W-A-I-T*—on one foot, point."

RALPH: Wait, no.

CLOWNY: What?

RALPH: Weight. *W-E-I-G-H-T*. Come on, Dave—

CLOWNY: We spell out homonyms here.

RALPH: Gimme a break.

CLOWNY: You're in my house now, Mutter. Their, there, they're. Two, too, to. Where, wear. Weight, wait. The English language is a bugger. You ought to know that with six years' experience.

RALPH: This is all about the spoon, isn't it? (*Setting down his pen.*) I'm not some rookie, you know. I worked for a law firm before this. I was the lead reader for Chapley, Chapley, and Herringbone. I had a ninety-nine point nine percent accuracy rate.

CLOWNY: So what happened to the other point one percent, friend?

            (*Beat.*)

RALPH: (*Turns to the manuscript again. Frostily.*) "Graph. Cap I I checked her out, com, you bet I did, point. Cap S She was one—that's *O-N-E*, not *W-O-N*—cool costumer, point."

CLOWNY: Hold please. Costumer?

RALPH: Customer.

CLOWNY: You said costumer.

RALPH: Yes. Sorry.

CLOWNY:	No problem.
RALPH:	"Cap *L* Long legs, com, short tight skirt, com, and an ass like two duck eggs in a napkin, point." . . . What the hell is this?
CLOWNY:	Read back.
RALPH:	What is this we're reading?
CLOWNY:	*A Private Affair.* W.D.B. Klaunschpiegel.
RALPH:	I was hired for K-12! Lit and comprehension.
CLOWNY:	Yes, Mutter?
RALPH:	"Two duck eggs in a napkin . . . " What does that even mean?
CLOWNY:	You're wasting time, Mutter.
RALPH:	This isn't the real copy.
CLOWNY:	Picture a cloth napkin. And gently cupped within that napkin—
RALPH:	Where is the real copy?
CLOWNY:	Read back.
RALPH:	I demand to see the real copy.

(CLOWNY *gives him a long look. Then, slowly, he takes the spoon from the can of peas, sticks it in his mouth, pulls it out again, and holds it out toward* RALPH. RALPH *bolts up from the table breathing hard. Beat.* CLOWNY *puts the spoon back in the can and begins to count something on the galley proofs.*)

CLOWNY:	One . . . two . . . three . . . four . . . five . . . six . . .
RALPH:	We have a job to do here, Dave.

CLOWNY:	Ten. Ten sentences, Mutter. That's what we've done so far. Ten.
RALPH:	That's because you—
CLOWNY:	And some of those are fragments.
RALPH:	This is not K-12.
CLOWNY:	You're not a literary critic, Mutter.
RALPH:	What?
CLOWNY:	You're a proofreader.
RALPH:	Yes! I came here to read proof! Teacher's guides. Pupil editions. Blackline masters. True and false. Multiple choice. Fill in the blanks, short essay! Maybe some ancillary materials and answer keys!
CLOWNY:	You're going to have to step it up. What is this? Remedial reading? Slow Talkers of America? Special ed?
RALPH:	I asked you about the rate!
CLOWNY:	Are you special ed?
RALPH:	Now look, Dave—
CLOWNY:	Because I'm growing hair during the pauses.
	(RALPH *slams himself back into the chair and picks up the manuscript. He begins reading faster. As he does, CYN enters, hands on hips. She takes a pose.*)
RALPH:	"Cap *L* Long legs—
CLOWNY:	I see. Are we starting?

RALPH: Oh, we're starting all right. "Cap *L* Long legs, com, short tight skirt, com, and an ass like two duck eggs in a napkin, point. High, com, pert tits and a face like an angel. Graph. Cap *I* In short, com, she was just the kind of woman who considered it her personal mission to topple kings, em dash, and any little schmucks like me who got in her way, point. Cap *I* I gave her the once, hyph, over, point." (*He notices* CYN, *stammers a little.*) "Cap *S* She wanted something all right, point. Cap *S* She put her hands on her hips . . . and said in a throaty whisper, com, open double quote—"

CYN: Is everything all right in here? I thought I heard a noise.

(*Incredulous,* RALPH *looks from the manuscript, to* CYN, *and back to the manuscript.*)

CLOWNY: (*Reading from the galleys.*) "Cap *T* That voice, ellips. Cap *L* Like honey dripping from a spoon, point. Cap *A* A voice that could make a man change his life, com, his destiny, com, just like that, com, and drop everything, point." (RALPH *rises, backs away from the desk, and accidentally drops the sheaf of papers on the floor.*) "Open double quote—"

CYN: (*Bending to pick up the papers as* RALPH *stares at her ass.*) Here.

CLOWNY: "Comma, close double quote, she murmured, point. Open double quote—"

CYN: Let me help you with that.

CLOWNY: "Point, close double quote. Graph. Open double quote, cap *N* No, com, close double quote, I muttered"—that's all lowercase muttered, by the way, Mutter—"as I backed up against the wall—"

RALPH: (*Backing up.*) Stop it.

CLOWNY: "Cap I knew—*K-N-E-W*—I was in too—*T-O-O*—deep. I was thrashing around on a storm, hyph, swept sea—that's *S-E-A*. My head was swimming, point. Sweat ran into my eyes, point. Blinking, com, I gauged the distance to the door, point."

CYN: (*To* RALPH.) Are you all right? What's the matter?

CLOWNY: Mutter? Am I going too fast for you?

CYN: Are you all right?

CLOWNY: Am I going too fast for you, Mutter?

CYN: What's the matter?

CLOWNY: Mutter?

CYN: Are you all right?

CLOWNY: Query. Close quote.

RALPH: Stop!

> (*Beat.*)

CLOWNY: (*Softly, pointing his pen at RALPH like a gun.*) Bang.

> (*After a stricken moment, RALPH's eyes dart to the briefcase. CLOWNY zones in on the case at the same time. Beat. RALPH makes a lunge for it. At the last second CLOWNY snatches it away. RALPH stands there panting.*)

RALPH: Give. Me. That.

> (*CLOWNY sets the briefcase on the floor away from RALPH. RALPH tries several times to get past CLOWNY, but the big shoes always head him off at the pass. CYN is still on the floor trying to collect up the scattered papers. Finally, CLOWNY picks up the can of peas, with the spoon sticking out of it. Very slowly he holds it out to RALPH. Beat. RALPH shakes his head vehemently. CLOWNY moves the briefcase farther away with his big shoe. Finally, RALPH reaches out and takes the spoon. With a shaking hand he raises it to his nose and gives it a small, extremely tentative sniff. CLOWNY gestures. RALPH takes a longer, deeper whiff. CYN has collected all the papers now and stands up. RALPH begins to hyperventilate on the spoon. After a few moments of this, CLOWNY rises, disgusted, and with some difficulty manhandles the spoon away from RALPH, who continues to stand there gasping.*)

CYN: Are you all right?

CLOWNY: (*Handing* RALPH *the briefcase and the coffee cup.*) What's the matter? (RALPH *begins to stagger off.*) Mutter! Think fast!

(CLOWNY *wings the pen at* RALPH, *who ducks and scurries off. Beat.* CYN *straightens the stack of papers and puts it down on the desk.* CLOWNY *takes the hankie from his sleeve again. Blows on the spoon, then polishes it with the hankie. He studies his reflection in the spoon, then blots his forehead with the hankie.*)

CYN: Dave, com, Dave, com, Dave . . . Never happy. Never satisfied.

CLOWNY: Let me tell you a little something about this business I'm in, kid. It's a vocation as old as the printed word itself. (*He rises and slowly, with dignity, climbs onto the chair and then onto the desk. He stands there, a pen in one hand, a spoon in the other.*) It's a solitary undertaking. Exacting. Painstaking. And, com, hell yes, com, sometimes maybe even a little lonely. But that's what it takes to get the job done right. People ask me why I do it. "Klaunschpiegel," they say. "Why would a fella such as yourself settle for such a long wistful sigh of a job?" And I answer them this way: "Because I was given a gift. An inborn skill at finding fault." When I spot a typo, a broken letter, a misplaced modifier, a wrong font . . . am I happy? No! I'm disgusted. I want to vomit. Sometimes I do vomit. But even then, even in the very moment of that vomiting, I know that it is up to me—and me alone—to fix that error. (*Beat.*) It's not merely a responsibility and a duty, semicolon, it's a calling. There's no "we" in proofreader. The proofreader rides alone. He's a hired gun, bang. He's a maverick, bang. And if, com, now and then, com, there's a bit of blood on his saddle, ellips . . . that's just the price he's got to pay. (*A beat; then* CLOWNY *climbs rather gracelessly down from the desk and drops into his chair.*) Now if you'll excuse me . . . I have work to do, point. (CYN *shrugs, exits.* CLOWNY *sticks the spoon back into the can of peas, compulsively straightens both stacks of paper and picks up his pen. After a moment, he stares out front and recites with great feeling.*) "Cap C Chapter cap O One. . . Initial caps The First Day . . . Drop. Display cap I It was a cap F Friday morning, point. He remembered that much, point. That is, com, when he thought about it at all, com, he remembered that it had been a cap F Friday, point." (*Beat.*) "Graph. Cap W Was it when he had first laid eyes on cap T The cap C Clown that the back of his neck had begun to prickle, com, and that cold ball of fear had begun to form in the pit of his gut, query."

(*Blackout.*)

END

Lisa Dillman's plays have been produced at such venues as Steppenwolf Theatre, American Theatre Company, and the O'Neill Playwrights Conference. She has received fellowships from the Illinois Arts Council, Ragdale, Millay Colony, Blue Mountain Center, and the William Inge Foundation. Her work is published by Dramatic Publishing, Heinemann, and Smith & Kraus.

Lisa Dillman

Unwholesome

Unwholesome is a tour de force that compresses into one act technical elements
and a satisfyingly-realized story that could easily sustain a full-length play. The
two characters, a nun and a young man, share a doomed obsession with each
other that spans nearly a decade-and-a-half and began when Charles was a
fourteen-year-old student in Marita's parochial school classroom. The ascetically
simple setting—a table, two chairs, two telephones, and a crucifix—belies the
play's complex structure while hinting at its elemental emotional intensity.

The playwright sketches the unconsummated relationship with great economy,
moving fluidly among times and settings. Byers skillfully weaves flashbacks
incorporating monologues and telephone conversations (both one-sided and
two-sided) with present-day dialogue to dramatize the characters' yearning for
each other and the obstacles that separate them. Charles and Marita's climactic
face to face confrontation centers on a thoroughly credible and tragically ironic
revelation that underscores with finality the unbridgeable gulf between them.

Joe Byers

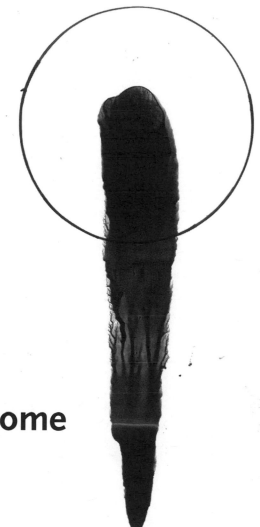

Unwholesome

CHARACTERS   MARITA: 42.

CHARLES: 28.

SETTING   A table. Two straight-backed chairs. Two telephones. A crucifix.

TIME   1972-1986.

(*Lights up on* MARITA, *a woman of early middle age, on her knees. She wears a simple, modest dress and no makeup. Her hair is cut short and simply styled.*)

MARITA: Take it.

I can't live this. I can't end it. Take it.

For his sake, take it? He's worse off than I am. He has his whole life . . .

Take it. I'm caught. I'm slipping. I'm weaker every day. Please? There's hardly any time. (*Pause.*)

Then give me strength. Help me choose.

(*Lights up on* CHARLES, *a young man, dressed in his Sunday best, such as it is, on the telephone. If he is aroused, he seems not to be aware of it. He certainly is not masturbating.*)

CHARLES: I see you. Sleeping. Eating. I see you in the chapel, praying. I see you go to the bathroom. That's all right. That's part of it, too.

He lets me see. God does. You are so precious to God, you know. Right after the Blessed Mother. He gave you to me, to protect. And I will. I'll stay right by you. No one will touch you. Ever. Not even when you're dead. I will stay here to the end. And after the end, when you're safe in the ground. That's why I'm younger than you, you know. God made sure I am. So I could see you safe and dead.

MARITA: (*Rising from her knees and moving to the table.*) I was horrified at myself. I hadn't felt anything like that for anyone, for years—not since I was his age, practically. We let them train that out of us, let them kill it. We helped them. I did. And I thought it was good and dead—(*She sits at the table.*) Till Charles McGonigle's eighth-grade year.

CHARLES: (*Moving to join* MARITA.) Before I say anything else, I wanna say thank you.

MARITA: What for?

CHARLES: For asking me here. After everything. All the things that happened.

MARITA: Let's just focus on now.

CHARLES: (*After a pause.*) I'm glad you're not afraid of me. You shouldn't be.

MARITA: I am. Afraid of you.

CHARLES: I don't want that. I never did.

MARITA: But you'll settle for it—if you can't get anything else from me.

CHARLES: How can you even think that? How can I make you—

MARITA: You move away from me. Do it, or I'll call the custodian. He's right outside that door.

CHARLES: But I would never—

MARITA: Then why did you say you would?

CHARLES: I didn't.

MARITA: You did.

CHARLES: Didn't mean it.

MARITA: How was I supposed to know that?

CHARLES: I was just was a kid.

MARITA: I see.

CHARLES: If you had just listened to me—like you're listening now—

MARITA: Yes. I'm listening. What did you have to say to me?

(CHARLES *hesitates, does not answer. A beat. He moves aside and picks up his telephone.*)

CHARLES: I will slap your face so hard I'll knock you on the floor and knock the sauce right out of you, take you by your hair and drag you out to the schoolyard—at recess. Right in front of everybody, so they all can see you, what you really are, what I found out you are. I might even have to make you strip.

You'd do it all right, or else I'd give you another slap, slap and just keep slapping, till you did exactly what I told you to and stripped completely nude—so all of them could see. I wouldn't care how cold it was. You would have to kneel down on the pavement, and maybe it would cut your knees and you would bleed like Jesus did when He fell down with the Cross on His shoulder.

Shut up! Shut up and take it! Jesus took it! So can you! Shut up—or this time when I hit you it will not be just your face and just my hand: I will take the biggest fattest stick there is and whale on you until I break it. I won't care how much you cry—or bleed.

MARITA: He was a quiet kid.

CHARLES: 'Cause it'll all be your fault.

MARITA: (*Rising.*) Kind of goofy—but sweet.

CHARLES: 'Cause you wouldn't do what I said, and wouldn't listen.

MARITA: (*Moving aside.*) Lanky. Blond. Fuzzy blond on his upper lip. Never been kissed. Wanting to be kissed.

I wanted to kiss.

Right from the very first moment I saw him, I wanted to see him all the time. And not just his face. Not just his lips.

I'd give seatwork to the class, just to keep them busy, just so I could watch him without them noticing, without him noticing. Some days they did seatwork all day long.

One day I was watching him and . . . he got an erection. He was just sitting there doing his seatwork, and then . . .

I was spell-bound. I had never . . . not in my entire life. I just turned to water. All the breath went out of me, and all the blood.

He wasn't doing his seatwork now. He was watching me, watching me watching him, with his legs still spread wide open. He seemed not to be aware that . . . he was excited. It was like he was sleeping with his eyes open, and his eyes were fixed on me. I couldn't look away from him. I felt like he was up inside me, wringing me, like I was a sponge.

And then I was wet between my legs. I was afraid to stand up and go to the blackboard to teach the lesson. Afraid it would show. And ashamed.

No matter how I prayed for God to cool me after that, I was only hotter every time I saw him—which was every day. Every time I thought of him—and I thought of him all the time—I thought . . . unwholesome things, things I still can't even say out loud. (*She turns to* CHARLES.) He must have known. He was always looking at me now. (*She returns to her seat at the table*.) The phone calls started later that year.

CHARLES: (*Moving to join* MARITA.) I'm gonna take you away from here. I have a place. We'll be all alone there. I've been getting it ready. I've got everything you'll need. You don't have to bring a thing. We can just go. Stand up and go to the door, and go. Right now.

MARITA: I'm not going anywhere.

CHARLES: (*After a pause*.) All right. I respect that. That's fine, for now. I know you don't mean it—you only think you do. You'll come 'round once we get there.

(MARITA *turns away*.)

Or we could go somewhere else, if you want. Wherever you want. Get in my car and just keep driving. Vancouver maybe. Alaska even.

MARITA: No.

CHARLES: Look: I'm trying to be nice about this. It's wrong for you here, and we both know it. You've gotta come with me. Now. You've got to.

MARITA: I said move away from me. Do I need to call Mr. Brennecke?

CHARLES: You mean that old guy out in the hallway with the mop? That fat guy?

MARITA: He's a retired city policeman.

CHARLES: I think I could take him, don't you?

(*A beat.* CHARLES *moves apart.*)

She is blessed among all women. I am not just saying that. God made her in the image of the Blessed Mother. Only she's even purer than the Blessed Mother. Know why? Because not only has nothing ever gone into her—if you know what I mean—but nothing ever came out of her either—and something did come out of the Blessed Mother: Jesus. The only thing that ever came out of Marita is pee.

And blood.

(*He and* MARITA *move into other lights and pick up telephones.*)

MARITA: I saw you too, you know. Outside my window. Across the street. Under the maiden-hair tree.

CHARLES: The gingko.

MARITA: Days and nights. All those hours. I wouldn't let you see me seeing you. I wouldn't let you know I knew.

CHARLES: But I did know.

MARITA: I know.

(*They put down their telephones and return to the table.*)

I said I was afraid before.

CHARLES: And I said I don't want that.

MARITA: I was afraid of myself. What I might do. If you said come away with me.

CHARLES: Come away with me.

MARITA: (*After a pause.*) I'm not afraid any more.

CHARLES: Just tell me what you want.

MARITA: I want you to go. Pick a place that's far from here and go. Alone.

CHARLES: I can't—

MARITA: You can. For me. Give it to me for a gift. Give me my life back.

CHARLES: That's what I'm trying to—

MARITA: Haven't I been constant for you—all these years—no matter what you did or said to me? Haven't I listened? Haven't I prayed to God for you, every morning, every night? Yes? Yes. Now you can give me something back: stop this. Stop it all. Stop . . . holding me captive in your mind.

CHARLES: I can't control what—

MARITA: You can respect me, Charles, respect what I want—because I'm a human being, a separate human being. We are not one soul. You are very wrong to think that we are.

CHARLES: I don't think—

MARITA: Don't take my word for it: check your catechism.

CHARLES: What's different now? There's something—

MARITA: I am. I am putting you away from me, Charles. That's why I asked to see you today, after all this time. So I could send you away.

CHARLES: Would you just look at me?

MARITA: I'm looking. I don't see you anymore.

CHARLES: (*Turning aside.*) But I'm right here. I'm wherever you are, always, wherever you go, no matter how far. You could go to the end of the world. There's a wall at the end of the world, you know. High as the sky—as far as you can see, in both directions. It separates the world from what is not the world.

I am the wall at the end of the world, Marita. There's nowhere beyond me for you. Beyond me there's only the sun: you'd be staring straight at the sun. Straight at the Face of God. You'd burn up. (*He turns back to* MARITA.)

MARITA: Get out of my way.

CHARLES: You're hurting me.

MARITA: You're hurting yourself.

CHARLES: And not just me: you're hurting Jesus.

MARITA: (*Turning aside.*) Don't you try to tangle me: you can't. I am as smooth as a bullet now. I will cut clean through you.

I am on my way to Jesus. You can't stop me. Nothing can. I am obeying Jesus. I am the tide obeying the moon. You are a pebble I wash over.

CHARLES: (*Moving apart.*) You are my road. I travel you. Every day another mile, another piece of you.

Even before I met you—even while I was waiting to meet you—I knew you were there, waiting for me.

My whole life is leading to you.

(*He and* MARITA *move into different lights.*)

MARITA: I'm touching you.

CHARLES: Just touching your hands.

MARITA: My hand on you. Holding you. Feeling the heat of it, the blood in it. Flowing in my hand.

CHARLES: Washing your hair. It's heavy in my hands, and sweet, like honey, running through my fingers. Shining.

MARITA: Planting you inside me, in the earth of me, in the dark. Breaking me like earth.

CHARLES: Watching you sleeping. Cool in the morning beside me. Chaste. And white.

MARITA: Taking you inside me, Charlie, painting me with light inside. Making the darkness bright, like God did. Does.

CHARLES: Breathing with you. With the Lord in you. Slipping under your eyelids as you sleep. Gliding out of you on your breath. I'm breathing your breath. I'm breathing Him.

MARITA: Wrapping all around you—tight—so tight it bruises you. Bruises me. Pulls it out of you. And into me. Swollen. And dripping with you.

CHARLES: Squeezing oranges for you. For your breakfast.

MARITA: Then burning to ash, to cinder. And blowing away on the wind.

(*She moves apart and kneels.*)

Bless me, Father, for I have sinned. It is one week since my last confession—Father, I confess the sin of impurity.

In thought, yes. Not in action. Not with him. Only with myself.

He calls me on the telephone.

Not at all. He's dead serious.

About what he's going to do to me—if I won't love him, do what he says.

Of course I do. He just keeps calling back, until I'll talk to him—until I'll listen. He'll call all night sometimes.

He can't get me out of his mind, he says. He says a lot of things. It shames me, what he says, but I listen. I go along with it.

No, nothing like that. I don't think he knows too much about that. He talks a lot about Heaven and Hell. Tells me what God tells him.

I'm the one with the impure thoughts. (*She rises and returns to the table.*)

He's only fourteen years old.

CHARLES:	(*Rejoining* MARITA.) Couldn't we just talk about it? Please?
MARITA:	We have been talking for fourteen years. I want some peace now. In the time I have left here.
CHARLES:	Where are you going? I thought you said—you're not going anywhere, not unless I—
MARITA:	I'm dying. Does that count?
CHARLES:	That's a lie! You're only saying that. To make me go away.
MARITA:	Look at me, Charles. Just look. You must know it's true.
CHARLES:	You can't!
MARITA:	I'm sorry.
CHARLES:	I won't let you.
MARITA:	Oh. Do you have a cure for cancer? Did God give you that, too?
CHARLES:	He could cure you—if you we pray—
MARITA:	Just leave me.

CHARLES: But you need me.

MARITA: I abide you. I have abided you for fourteen years. And now it's over. Now I'm dying. I can't carry you anymore. I won't. I have to get ready to go. Alone.

Separate from me.

CHARLES: I can't! Don't you hear me saying that? I won't.

I haven't been this close to you—alone with you in a room—in fourteen years. Not since St. Martin's. I'm not leaving here today without you.

MARITA: How many times in fourteen years did you move from where you were living, just to stay near me? How many times did you quit a job and have to find a new one? Was it every time I was stationed somewhere new? Ever since I left St. Martin's? Practically every year? Have you done nothing else with your entire life but follow me?

CHARLES: What I did I did for you—and I'd do it again. I'd do it the rest of my life. There's no way I'm losing you. You are all there is.

MARITA: How many girls have you let down?

(He doesn't answer.)

I'm so sorry for you.

CHARLES: Then come with me! Stay with me!

MARITA: Not that sorry.

(He moves to strike her. She does not shrink. He does not strike.)

CHARLES: That is not the way you talk.

MARITA: What do I have to say to you then, to make you understand? What do I have to do?

(*He crosses himself and clasps his hands in prayer, but does not look away from her. Pause.*)

MARITA: Should I get down on my knees and elbows? Show you how I really feel, underneath it all? How I've always felt—right from the day I first saw you?

CHARLES: Hail Mary, full of grace, the Lord is with Thee—Please don't make me—!

MARITA: You were never the perpetrator. You only thought you were.

CHARLES: Blessed art Thou amongst women—What are you trying to—!

MARITA: Why have I put up with you for all these years? All your whispering at me! Pathetic little threats! Why? Haven't you ever wondered? Can't you guess? I'll give you a hint: it was more than Christian charity. (*She moves to him.*) It's you, Charlie. (*She reaches for his penis, but does not touch him.*) It's this. It's always been this.

(*He steps back.*)

You must have known.

CHARLES: Hail Holy Queen, our life, our sweetness, and our hope. To Thee do we cry—No!

MARITA: Think you can give it to me?

CHARLES: To Thee do we send up our sighs—Stop asking me—!

MARITA: (*Advancing on him through the following.*) Think you can handle me? What if I did come with you? What would you do with me? You wouldn't be able just to hound me anymore—like you've been doing for half your life. I won't give it up for a chicken-shit loser, Charlie. You'll have to deliver the stuff.

CHARLES: (*Moving away from her.*) Stop it.

MARITA: Have to give it to me . . . all of it . . . your mouth . . . wet . . . making me wet . . . drinking me . . . making me ready . . . I'm ready right now, you know . . . I'm wet . . . Can't you smell it? . . . Can't you feel me . . . wrap around you . . .

squeeze the juice out . . . out of you and into me? . . . into the dark inside of me . . . hot and wet, and liquid wet—(*She is nearly on top of him.*) And I won't ever let you out.

CHARLES: (*Seizing her to stop her*) No!

> (*They are face to face. A pause. She kisses him, with passion, hard and long. Another pause. He draws back and backs away.*)

MARITA: What's the matter, Charlie? Just not up to it, huh? Well, that's what I was afraid of. I guess you're just a plain old pervert after all. You don't really have it. All you can do is talk. How could I ever have thought you were the one? You might as well still be fourteen. If I'm going over the wall, Charlie, I'm going with a man.

CHARLES: (*Backing toward the door.*) No . . . no . . . no . . .

MARITA: Yes.

> (CHARLES *exits.*)

(*Calling after him.*) Don't trip over Mr. Brennecke on your way out!

> (*Alone now, she falls into her chair, sobbing. Pause. She rises and moves into another light.*)

I asked if they would bury me above Camilla Hall. Up on the hill. At the end of the road. You know where.

Come there—like you said you would. Come whenever you want to. Every day— every night. They never close the gate.

Say whatever you want to me then. I'll listen.

> (*The lights fade to black.*)

END

Joe Byers

Boston-based Joe Byers is the author of Heideman Award finalist *Pee Shy* (Actors Theatre of Louisville), Arch and Bruce Brown Playwriting Foundation Competition winner *Shakerman,* and Palm Springs National Short Play Fest winner *The Woman with No Nose.* His plays have been produced from New York to Mexico. Next up: *Pocket Pool: the Life and Loves of Masturbatin' Melvin Armstrong, TV Sex Guru!* He can be reached at joe.byers@forum.com

What Are Friends For?

Gloria g. Murray skillfully handles a cast of six characters, giving each a clear and easily identifiable personality from his or her first entrance. For example, Gail is the distressed wife who has just learned her husband is gay; the overweight Edna is obsessed with food and her size; Margie is defined by her smoking and painting; Brandon is narcissistic, gay, and easily distracted; Gary is bisexual, willing and able to flirt both ways; and Harold, Gail's husband, is only heard dying—or not dying—offstage. These traits and preoccupations drive each character's actions throughout the play, identifying them clearly for the audience and underpinning the comedy, as with Edna's fixation on food, which distracts her continually from appropriate social responses to complications like Harold's possible death or revelations of sexual preference that shock others and drive them to extreme behavior.

Murray uses the staples of farce in plot as well as character, building on confusion, broad physical action, and improbable occurrences. But her play's dark comedy arises from complications and choices—death or life, straight or gay—that frequently provide the basis for serous drama. Near the end of the first scene, the farce declares itself, with a character trying to knock a door down, exits and entrances following fast on each other, and estrogen pills mistaken for Valium. Murray also makes effective comic use of incongruity—a technique based not merely on misleading the audience in order to surprise, but on confounding expectations the audience brings into the theatre, e.g. the sense of what may be socially or linguistically appropriate. An example from the dialogue is Edna's admonition that "you should always keep Valiums around the house, along with other necessities of life, like a toilet plunger or a three-way bulb."

This fine comedy uses the physical, the unexpected, and action topped by action to build its comedic force. Characters tumble from one situation to the next, stepping over bodies, crushing heart pills beneath their feet, and taking the audience on a merry ride.

Gloria g. Murray

What are Friends For?

CHARACTERS   BRANDON: a young man with dyed blonde hair.

EDNA: an overweight, middle-aged woman with short, bobbed hair.

GAIL: a thin, middle-aged woman with dark, curly hair.

GARY: Rita's boyfriend.

HAROLD: Gail's husband, who remains offstage.

MARGIE: a tall, thin, dark-haired woman. An artist.

RITA: Edna's twenty-something daughter.

SETTING   The kitchen of GAIL's house. The house's front door and the door to GAIL and HAROLD's bedroom lead off the kitchen.

(GAIL *is seated at the table, a cordless phone clutched in her hand. She is dressed in jeans and a T-shirt. Adjoining GAIL's kitchen is another kitchen, EDNA's. EDNA is seated at her table. She is dressed in a terry bathrobe and is also holding a phone. GAIL speaks into her phone.*)

GAIL: Edna, it's me, Gail. Are you busy?

EDNA: (*Sipping from a coffee mug.*) No, not really. I'm not working today—the school didn't call. I was just having my coffee.

GAIL: Oh, thank god!

EDNA: (*Startled.*) Gail, what's wrong? You never use the word GOD. You're the world's #1 atheist.

GAIL: (*Sobbing, her hands trembling.*) Oh Edna, something terrible, Oh god, something terrible . . .

EDNA: What, what has happened? Is it the dog? Are you having another one of those panic attacks? I thought you were recovering with that support group.

GAIL: (*Trying to catch her breath.*) Oh my god, oh my god!

EDNA: (*Sternly.*) Gail, stop with the OH MY GODs! You're scaring me. Now what the hell has happened? I can't make sense out of anything you're saying.

GAIL: (*Whispering.*) Something . . . something's happened to Harold.

EDNA: (*Sounding relieved, she picks up the TV remote and flicks the channels.*) Oh, is that all? Calm down.

GAIL: You don't understand. Come quickly, please.

EDNA: Gail, it's 7:30 in the morning. I'm not even dressed.

GAIL: (*Demanding.*) Then get dressed, please, come quickly!

EDNA: (*Sighing, she shuts off the TV and swallows the last sip of coffee.*) Okay. Just calm down. Should I call a doctor? Is Harold sick or is he drinking again? Is that it—he's drunk? For god's sake Gail, I told you AA doesn't work.

GAIL: No, no doctor, just come.

EDNA: Okay, Okay, I'll be there, just calm down. I'm going to call Margie. I can't handle this myself. I don't know what to do when you get all hysterical.

GAIL: (*Softly.*) Okay, please . . . just come.

> (*She hangs up the phone and gets up slowly. There is a door to another room. Cautiously, she peers inside, then shuts it quickly.*)

Oh my god, oh my god!

> (*A few moments later there is a knock at the door. GAIL opens it and EDNA is standing there. She is a stocky woman dressed in a sweat suit, sweat pants and sneakers. There is a headband around her head and exercise bands around her wrists.*)

EDNA: I'm on my way to the gym later. I thought I'd take advantage of my day off. I really have to get some of these pounds off. (*She squeezes her middle, makes a disgusted face and looks over at the stove.*) You've got coffee—good! And what about a little something—I'm starving? (*She eyes the muffins on the counter and grabs one.*) Hmmm, I love muffins. What kind is this? (*Takes a bite.*) Blueberry—my favorite! Did you make them from scratch or from a mix?

GAIL: (*Impatiently.*) Edna, shut up!

EDNA: WHAT?

GAIL: (*Starting to cry.*) Edna, I'm sorry—I didn't mean it. Thanks for coming. (*She throws her arms around EDNA's neck.*)

EDNA: Gail, please, you're choking me, besides, I can't digest.

GAIL: (*Removing her arms.*) I'm sorry.

EDNA: (*Firmly, grabbing another muffin before sitting down.*) Okay, now tell me exactly what's happened. I called Margie—she was beginning another painting when I called but she's on her way. Oh god, (*Rubbing her stomach*.) my irritable bowel is starting.

GAIL: (*Trying to talk calmly*.) Harold is not drinking again. It's not that. I almost wish it was. He's, he's . . . having an affair.

EDNA: (*Laughing*.) Are you crazy? Harold hates women!

GAIL: (*Looking straight at* EDNA.) Yes, that's true. That's why it all makes sense.

EDNA: What? Nothing you've said so far makes sense.

GAIL: Edna, Harold is having an affair with another man.

EDNA: What?

GAIL: (*Nodding*.) It's true.

EDNA: That's ridiculous.

GAIL: I know, but believe me, it's true. I saw them . . . together.

EDNA: (*Incredulous*.) You what?

GAIL: I saw them at Mickey's Bar & Grill. Sometimes I pass there on my home from the support group. No, that's not true. I was checking to see if Harold was drinking again and I passed and looked inside and that's when I saw him at the bar with this really gay looking guy, dyed blonde hair and young, of course. (*Brushes her hair back, looking indignant*.) Well, they were really talking intensely.

EDNA: So, is that all?

GAIL: (*Annoyed*.) Listen, just listen. I see Harold put his arm around this guy and then . . . he . . . kisses him—right on the mouth—right there in Mickey's bar when they're playing the song Harold and I used to dance to: "We Belong Together". I couldn't breathe, my heart was pounding so hard I just ran right out into traffic . . . I almost got hit by a car!

EDNA: (*In amazement.*) Wow, that is really wild! I never would have believed it.

GAIL: Is that all you can say?

EDNA: (*A little sheepishly.*) I'm sorry Gail. I realize how awful all this must be for you, but you know, it is sort of funny, don't you think?

GAIL: (*Glaring.*) I don't think it's funny at all!

               (*There is a knock at the door. GAIL goes to answer it. In the meantime, EDNA starts to take another muffin, shrugs, then breaks it in half. A tall thin woman enters. She is wearing black spandex pants, a long paint-stained shirt and sandals. Her hair is pulled back in a ponytail.*)

               (*Motioning for her to come in and sounding relieved.*) Oh, Margie, thanks for coming.

MARGIE: (*Sitting down.*) Hi Edna. (*To GAIL.*) When Edna called and said it was an emergency, I was just starting my new painting—seaweed, a canvas of seaweed with a coke bottle and a Dunkin' Donuts box right in the middle. Doesn't it sound intriguing, sort of like surrealist impression with a touch of Warhol? (*Turns to GAIL.*) Gail, honey, can I have some tea please?

GAIL: Sure. (*She puts some water in a teapot to boil.*)

MARGIE: (*Lighting a cigarette.*) So, what's happened?

EDNA: (*Blowing the smoke away with her hand.*) Do you have to smoke? I'm trying to get healthy.

               (*GAIL and MARGIE look at one another and smirk, but MARGIE puts the cigarette out.*)

               (*To MARGIE.*) Harold's having an affair—with another man.

MARGIE: (*Looking bored.*) Oh, is that all?

GAIL: (*Exasperated.*) I don't know why I called you two over anyway. What kind of friends are you? (*She begins to cry.*)

MARGIE:	(*Grabbing her hands.*) Calm down, please. We're here to help. So you found out Harold's having an affair—you know for sure?
	(GAIL *nods, and lets* MARGIE *hold her hands.*)
	Does he know you know?
GAIL:	(*Nods.*) After all those years, all that drinking I put up with, all those Al-Anon meetings—"Easy does it, Just for today, God grant me the courage, blah, blah, blah"—and I wasn't even religious—had to go along with all that twelve step stuff. (*She shakes her head.*)
EDNA:	I know, my mother did it with my father, only he never stopped, died of cirrhosis—we all celebrated at his funeral—so glad it was finally all over. Almost all of AA came and we had to make about ten pots of coffee and pass out all those pamphlets—tons of them, they even brought them in a carton. And everyone kept hugging us and saying if only he had found Jesus and AA—he could have been saved. And all the while under her breath my mother kept saying, "Thank god!"
GAIL:	(*Getting up.*) There's the tea. (*She pours a cup for* MARGIE *and herself.*) I saw him with that . . . that disgusting man and he just said, "What man?" and kept stuffing clothes into a suitcase. The one at the bar, I told him, "The one you were kissing." Well, he looked stunned, and then nodded and began gasping for breath. You know, he's got this heart condition, and I began crying hysterically and said "Then it's true, you bastard!" Well, he looked stunned, then nodded and began clutching his chest. I asked him how long it had been going on and he looked sad and said probably all his life, that he couldn't pretend any longer, the alcohol was just a cover-up, that it kept him from really looking at it but when he met Brandon he knew it was all over. (*She pauses, wiping tears from her eyes.*)
EDNA:	(*Touching her hand.*) Go on.
GAIL:	At that point I began beating at his chest with my fists. I called him a bastard, screaming that we had a child together, how could he? I even picked up the Al-Anon book and began pounding it on his head. He tried to get away; he grabbed the suitcase and began dragging it across the room when he clutched at his heart and fell into a chair. He started yelling about the pain—and that I should get his medication . . . and then . . . he just . . . passed out. Oh, god—it was awful.

EDNA: (*Alarmed.*) What did you do?

GAIL: (*Lowering her voice.*) I grabbed his pills and my hands were shaking so bad I dropped them and they were all over . . . there—see them on the floor near the sink. (*They all look at the pills.*) And I couldn't move. I just stood there, leaving Harold inside alone, unconscious or worse—(*She starts to cry.*)—to die!

EDNA: My god Gail, how could you?

GAIL: (*Whimpering.*) I don't know, I just hated him so much I . . .

MARGIE: And did he?

GAIL: Did he what?

MARGIE: Die? Is he still alive?

EDNA: Gail, can I have another muffin?

GAIL: (*Blowing her nose.*) Sure, help yourself. Margie, I don't know—I just don't know. I was afraid to go back in.

MARGIE: (*Jumping up.*) I can't believe you! I can't believe you would just leave him there. You've got to get rid of the body!

EDNA: (*Finishing the muffin, sounding alarmed.*) Margie, what are you saying? Gail's not a murderer! We've got to get a doctor. We've got to help Harold. After all, he is a human being.

MARGIE: I'm not so sure!

GAIL: (*Holding her head.*) Please . . . stop! I can't even think anymore. What if I call a doctor? They'll wonder why I didn't give him his medication . . . I'm so confused . . . Oh god!

EDNA: Gail. (*Trying to calm her down.*) Alright, no doctor. Let's just see if Harold is okay. That's the first step, right Margie?

(MARGIE *nods passively, and sips her tea*)

284

MARGIE:	I'm so glad my Ed left. I haven't seen him for almost ten years and that's fine with me. The kids keep calling him, but he's just too busy with his twenty-year-old hippie, smoking pot and trying to make a love baby. I hear she writes pretty bad poetry.
EDNA:	(*Wistfully.*) Well, I sort of miss Frankie. He used to say how fat turned him off, then he goes home to mama Mangani, all 365 pounds of her and her homemade canolis and sauce. I'm a good cook but I couldn't compete with that. Besides, she'd be at the stove all day and night, stirring that damn sauce. The kitchen cabinet would be full with cans of tomato purée and crushed garlic. Well, I'm going to get really thin, then you'll see—I'll walk past that house in spandex pants and wiggle my ass right under that old lady's nose.
GAIL:	(*Impatiently.*) Please Edna! Go look and see if . . . if . . . Harold's still alive.
EDNA:	(*Nervously.*) Me? I don't know . . . I don't think I can look at a dead person.
GAIL:	(*Accusingly.*) Oh, what kind of friends are you!
MARGIE:	Calm down, I'll go. I'm not afraid of dead people. I even thought I might start painting them—you know—open coffins. I don't think it's ever been done. I think it could be very interesting.
GAIL:	Please, just go and check on Harold.
	(MARGIE *gets up, goes to the door. She opens it slowly and calls out his name. There is no answer.*)
MARGIE:	HAROLD! Are you awake? (*Again calls out.*) Harold? Are you awake? (*No reply. She gets a little closer.*) HAROLD!
	(*She goes inside, closing it behind her.* GAIL *and* EDNA *sit there quietly, looking at each other. After a couple of minutes* MARGIE *comes out.*)
GAIL:	Well, is he . . . is he . . . ?
MARGIE:	(*Shrugging.*) I'm not sure . . . I tried to check his pulse, but I could barely feel it.

EDNA: Oh no!

               (*There is a knock at the door, startling them.*)

GAIL: Oh god, who is that now?

EDNA: (*Patting her arm.*) Don't worry, I'll go see. (*She opens the door.*)

               (*A thin, feminine-looking man is standing there, his hair streaked blonde. He is dressed in a floral shirt, shiny black pants and sandals. There is a touch of rouge on his cheek.*)

               (*Staring.*) Yes?

               (*He pushes past her.*)

MARGIE: (*Suddenly realizing who he is.*) I can't believe he came here!

GAIL: (*To the man.*) Who are you?

BRANDON: (*Ignoring* MARGIE.) I'm Brandon . . . Harold's . . . friend. He asked me to come. He's expecting me.

GAIL: (GAIL *stares at him.*) Expecting you?

BRANDON: (*Looking nervously around.*) Yes, well, where is he?

GAIL: I can't believe you came here. You have nerve, Brandon, you really do!

BRANDON: (*Defensively.*) I'm sorry, I really am, but I had to come—Harold needs me. I suppose you know the whole thing by now.

EDNA: (*Sarcastically.*) Of course. We all do.

               (BRANDON *glares at her.*)

BRANDON: Gail, can I see him?

               (GAIL *looks frantically at* EDNA *and* MARGIE.)

MARGIE: (*Whispering to* GAIL.) Don't worry, we'll handle this. Brandon, Harold is . . . is sleeping at the moment. He wasn't feeling too well and he decided to take a nap. Why don't you sit down and have some tea with us?

BRANDON: (*Trying to move toward the other door.*) No, I think I'll just go and check on Harold.

EDNA: (*Jumping up, she grabs his arm.*) Oh no, Brandon, Harold really needs his rest. His heart was giving him some trouble. You know—his condition—and he just needed to lie down. Here sit down, these blueberry muffins are delicious. (*She grabs one, pushes it at him.*)

BRANDON: (*Trying to push it away.*) Really! I don't want any. I watch my weight, you know. (*Eyeing her plump body with a disdainful look.*)

MARGIE: (*Sweetly.*) Brandon, I must say you have such a wonderful lean physique. I'm an artist, you know, and I would just love to paint you—that marvelous bone structure, those gaunt cheekbones—Vonderbar!

(*She walks around, examining him carefully*)

BRANDON: (*Relaxing a little.*) You really think so?

MARGIE: Absolutely! As an artist, I would never joke about a thing like that.

EDNA: (*Nodding.*) Besides being such a talented artist, you could even say—a genius, Margie is one of the most truthful people I know. She believes in revealing one's soul in art and life as well.

BRANDON: (*Intrigued, he smooths back his hair, crosses his legs*) Really! I wanted to be a Buddhist once. I studied a bit—was going to India to find my own Guru—then, I don't know . . . I just got sort of got side-tracked. But I do so admire genius and genuine talent. Oh Gail honey, do you mind if I do have a bit of tea?

GAIL: (*Trying to hide anger.*) Of course, Brandon. What would you like, milk or lemon?

BRANDON: Oh, lemon would be fine, and maybe one of those delicious-looking muffins.

(GAIL *shoves one on a plate and pushes it at him.*)

GAIL: Enjoy!

BRANDON: (*Taking a bite.*) Thank you. Hmmm . . . these are good. So, Margie, I could be available for a sitting if you like.

MARGIE: Darling, I would love it. Just give me your number and I'll call you with a definite time.

(BRANDON, *smiling, nods. He takes out a pen and scribbles his number on a napkin.*)

EDNA: So, where did you and Harold meet?

(MARGIE *motions with her hand for* EDNA *to be quiet*)

BRANDON: (*Jumping up.*) You know, I really don't know why I'm sitting here—not that I'm not enjoying your company, but I did come to see Harold. Maybe he's awake now, so if you ladies will excuse me, I'll just go and see . . . Which way?

(GAIL *points to the bedroom. He opens the door, softly calling* HAROLD's *name, and closes it behind him.*)

GAIL: Do you believe that . . . that . . . queen—that arrogant . . .

EDNA: (*Putting her arm around* GAIL.) I know honey, I know.

(BRANDON *comes running out of the room. His hands are shaking and he can hardly speak.*)

GAIL: What's wrong Brandon? You look terrible.

BRANDON: (*Waving his arms frantically.*) It's Harold, Harold . . . he's . . . he's not moving, I called his name and went to . . . well anyway, I think maybe . . . maybe something has happened to him . . . Oh my lord—my dear, sweet Harold!

MARGIE: (*Snorting, she whispers.*) This is making me ill.

BRANDON: (*Hands fluttering.*) Oh, I'm feeling a bit dizzy . . . I . . . I . . . think I might faint. I get that way when I'm very nervous.

EDNA: Here, sit down.

                   (*She helps him into a chair.*)

BRANDON: (*Weakly.*) Thanks. Oh, yes, I'm definitely going to . . .

GAIL: Are you sure Harold wasn't moving?

BRANDON: (*Nodding.*) I'm feeling really dizzy. I . . .

                   (*He passes out, his body going limp in the chair.*)

MARGIE: Oh no, now we've got two of them. Can you believe this?

EDNA: (*Shaking him.*) Brandon, Brandon, get up!

GAIL: What are we going to do now?

                   (*At that moment there is a knock at the door. GAIL jumps up and goes to answer it.*)

                   Oh, what now?

                   (*She opens it to find a girl of about twenty standing there. The girl is carrying a suitcase and her face looks as if she has been crying.*)

                   RITA!

RITA: Hello, Mom. (*She puts the suitcase down and hugs GAIL.*) I'm so glad to be home.

GAIL: (*Flustered, hugging her back.*) What are you doing here? Where's Gary?

EDNA: (*Trying to shake BRANDON into consciousness.*) Hi Rita.

MARGIE: Hi Rita.

                   (RITA *nods in acknowledgment, then throws her suitcase down and slumps into a chair.*)

RITA: Gary!—Oh, that . . . that no-good deceitful little . . .

GAIL: (*Concerned.*) What's happened? I thought everything was fine with you and Gary?

> (*By now* BRANDON *has completely fainted. He falls off the chair while* EDNA *steps over him.*)

RITA: You won't believe it, you just won't believe it, but it turns out . . . brace yourself Mom, Gary . . . handsome, virile Gary . . . is . . . (*She starts to whimper.*) bi—bisexual!

> (MARGIE *tries not to smile.*)

EDNA: (*Astonished.*) Are you kidding?

GAIL: (*Shocked.*) Gary? Rita . . . are you sure?

MARGIE: What a question! (GAIL *glares at her*)

BRANDON: (*Fully awake now.*) What happened?

MARGIE: You passed out, that's all—I think you should leave now, Brandon. We're having a family crisis.

BRANDON: (*Slowly getting up, swaying a little.*) Oh, I feel so woozy. What about Harold? I thought . . . You know, I don't think he was sleeping . . . I'm just a little confused . . .

EDNA: (*Pushing him toward the door.*) He's sleeping! Go home, don't worry, we'll call you when Harold's awake.

BRANDON: Are you sure? . . . don't forget . . . I'm still feeling a little weak . . . You have my number?

MARGIE: (*Waving the napkin.*) Right here, honey.

GAIL: (*Softly.*) Brandon, please . . .

> (*She pushes him out and closes the door after him.* MARGIE *blows her nose in the napkin and throws it into the garbage.*)

RITA: Who was that?

GAIL: (*Suddenly defeated.*) Your father's lover.

RITA: What?

GAIL: Seems like we're in the same boat.

RITA: (*Adamantly.*) I don't believe it! Mother, you're making this up, aren't you?

> (GAIL *stares at her and shakes her head.* RITA *jumps up, knocking over* BRANDON's *tea.*)

Oh god, this is the worst day of my life! I can't believe this is all happening. I can't deal with any of this—have you any Valiums?

EDNA: (*Taking one out of her pouch.*) Here, honey . . . (MARGIE *hands her two.*)

RITA: (*Swallowing them with some water.*) Thanks, I'm going upstairs. I've got to lie down. Oh, and where is he . . . ? Where is my father . . . ?

GAIL: Ah . . . he's just resting honey. He wasn't feeling too well. This has all been too much for him. Actually, for all of us. Now you go upstairs to your room and get settled. I'll be up shortly, and somehow we'll try and sort all this out.

RITA: (*Taking her suitcase and going to the door.*) Alright, I'm so tired . . . but Daddy . . . I . . . I can't believe what's happened . . . and that man . . . that . . . (*Shaking her head, she goes upstairs.*)

HAROLD: (*From the other room.*) Gail, are you out there? Gail?

GAIL: (*Stunned.*) Oh my god, it's Harold!

EDNA: Then he's not . . .

MARGIE: Answer him!

GAIL: Yes, Harold. What is it?

HAROLD: Gail, where are you?

GAIL: Oh my god, I've got to go to Harold. But, can you believe . . . that . . . that man, that arrogant . . .

EDNA: Calm down, at least Harold's alive.

MARGIE: That's right, just think what would have happened if Harold had really died.

GAIL: (*Nodding and touching her hand.*) Thanks, you're right. I know—I am relieved, but I can't help it—that man has wrecked my life.

EDNA: (*Putting her arm around her.*) I know, honey, I know.

MARGIE: Gail, do you want us to leave now?

GAIL: No, please, stay—I'm going in to talk to Harold.

           (*She goes into the other room and* MARGIE *and* EDNA *look at one another.* MARGIE *lights up a cigarette but* EDNA *says nothing.*)

EDNA: That man was absolutely revolting.

MARGIE: (*Laughing.*) Can you imagine, he believed that garbage about wanting to paint him? Poor Gail. She's really been through hell.

EDNA: I hope she comes through this . . . she's really not good in a crisis, not like us.

           (GAIL *comes out of the room. Her shoulders are slumped, and she sits down, saying nothing.*)

MARGIE: How does he feel, is he all right?

GAIL: (*Tiredly.*) He says he has a headache and feels weak, but he seems to be okay. Well . . . he is alive. Anyway, he doesn't want to come out, not until you two leave. I think he's embarrassed. And, yes, he's definitely leaving. I told him Brandon had come by and he was so happy—you should see him light up just at the mention of his name.

(*She puts her head down.* MARGIE *and* EDNA *get up.*)

MARGIE: As long as you're okay.

GAIL: For the moment, but if the panic comes back, and I know it will, can I call you guys again?

EDNA: (*Hugging her.*) Of course. But make sure you have plenty of Valiums in the house—you should always keep Valiums in the house, along with the other necessities of life, like a toilet plunger or a three-way light bulb.

MARGIE: (*To* GAIL.) Honey, call anytime. You know, it's almost a shame. Harold could have been my first corpse painting.

GAIL: I can't believe this has happened. I don't know how Rita's going to cope with all this—she's already on anti-depressants. I'm just so scared of what will be become of us. Maybe I'll go back to school—pursue journalism, I've always wanted to do that. (*Shaking her head.*) I don't know. Anyway, Harold does have to support us.

EDNA: (*Nodding.*) Of course. You'll be fine, Gail, and at least he didn't die.

GAIL: (*Whispering.*) I know.

HAROLD: (*From the other room.*) Gail! Can you get my pills? I'm having more chest pain. GAIL!

GAIL: (*Getting up quickly, she looks down on the floor, then cries out.*) Oh no!

EDNA: What is it? What's wrong?

GAIL: (*Frantically.*) What happened—What happened to the pills? They're all crushed, every single one.

EDNA: I think we all must have stepped on them.

HAROLD: Gail, my pills!

RITA'S VOICE: (*OS.*) Mom, is that Daddy yelling?

GAIL: (*To* RITA.) It's all right, honey. I'll take care of it. (*To* MARGIE *and* EDNA.) I've got
               to do something. What can I give him, until I get the prescription filled? I'll tell
               the pharmacist it's an emergency.

EDNA: What about Valium?

GAIL: (*Nodding, she reaches for a medicine bottle, squinting.*) I think this is them. (*She
               takes out some of the pills.*) Oh, where are my glasses? Yeah, they're yellow. I'll
               give him two of these. They say Valium is good for the heart and hopefully it'll
               relax him.

MARGIE: Sure. In the meantime I'll call the pharmacy. Where's the number?

               (GAIL *hands her the number and goes into the other room to* HAROLD.
               In the meantime MARGIE *starts to dial the pharmacy.* GAIL *comes
               out and goes to put one of the pills back in the bottle when she begins
               screaming.*)

GAIL: Oh no!

MARGIE: (*Still holding on.*) What is it Gail? What's wrong?

GAIL: I don't believe it!

EDNA: Believe what? What's wrong?

GAIL: I thought they were Valiums, but they're not. They are the same color . . .

MARGIE: Well, what were they? What did you give Harold?

GAIL: (*Stunned.*) My estrogen. I gave Harold my estrogen pills.

MARGIE: (*She starts to laugh*) A bit apropos, I think.

EDNA: I don't believe it!

               (*There is a knock at the door.*)

GAIL: Oh, who is that now?

BRANDON: (*From behind door.*) It's me, Brandon! I must see Harold, and I won't leave until I do. Let me in. There's something very strange going on here.

GAIL: DON'T ANYONE OPEN THAT DOOR!

(EDNA *and* MARGIE *both nod.*)

Go away, Brandon! We don't need you here—not now—or ever!

BRANDON: (*Banging on the door.*) I'm not leaving! I'm going to break this door down!

MARGIE: Hah!

(*They can hear* BRANDON *throwing his body against the door and then a thud where he has fallen. He cries out.*)

BRANDON: Oh my god, my shoulder, I think I've broken it!

GAIL: Margie, I think you'd better call nine-one-one instead of the pharmacy.

RITA: (*From upstairs.*) Mom, can you come up, please? I really need to talk about all this!

GAIL: In a minute, honey, I've got something I need to deal with first. I'll be up in a minute.

RITA: Okay, but if Gary calls you . . . you tell him . . . you (*She begins to cry.*)

GAIL: Please . . . Rita . . .

MARGIE: (*Nodding, she starts to dial nine-one-one.*) This has gone much too far. (*Into the receiver.*) Hello, nine-one-one, can you come right away? We have a very sick man here, no—make that two . . . . Yes, The address is forty-two East Fourth Street.

BRANDON: (*Yelling from behind the door.*) Help! Oh somebody, please help!

GAIL: (*She opens door, says wearily.*) Don't worry, Brandon, don't move, help is on the way.

(*She sits down on the kitchen floor and begins cleaning up the crushed pills with her hands. EDNA comes over and slumps down beside her, puts her arm around her.*)

MARGIE: They're on their way. Let's all just relax . . .

BRANDON: (*Behind door, still yelling.*) Please someone—Help!

(*There is another knock on the door.*)

GAIL: Oh no! Who is it now?

(*A voice behind the door yells out.*)

GARY: Rita! It's me, Gary. Open the door—I need to see you!

GAIL: Gary? Oh no! Please leave Gary. Rita doesn't want to see you right now.

GARY: (*Behind the door, to* BRANDON.) Oh. Who are you, and what happened?

BRANDON: I'm Brandon, and I've . . . hurt my shoulder, maybe broken it.

GARY: (*Still behind door.*) Here, let me help you, just rest on me . . . there . . . isn't that better?

MARGIE: Oh, for god's sake!

RITA: Mom! Who is that—Gary? I won't see him. Tell him to leave!

HAROLD: (*Yelling.*) Gail, are you there?

BRANDON: (*Behind door.*) Harold, is that Harold?

EDNA: I think I need another muffin. All this chaos has made me sooo hungry.

BRANDON: (*Behind door.*) Thank you, Gary, you're very kind . . . and so . . . so gentle . . .

MARGIE: Ugh! Gary, could you please leave? Rita doesn't want to see you! (*She takes out a cigarette, stares at her friends, takes a puff.*) And don't anyone say a word!

(*In the background there is the sound of ambulance sirens. The lights fade to black.*)

(*Lights up. A few hours have passed. RITA comes into the room in a terry bathrobe and looking disheveled. She looks around, shrugs, and sits down at the table when there is a knock at the door. Wearily, she gets up to answer it. GARY is standing there.*)

RITA: Gary! What are you doing here? (*She tries to push the door closed, but GARY forces it open.*)

GARY: Rita, please listen . . . I love you! I don't want it to be like this with us.

RITA: (*Trying to pull away.*) Hah! Love me! Me . . . and what is his name anyway?

GARY: (*Pleading.*) Rita, please listen—it was just a . . . a one-night stand . . . I mean, I don't know . . . a crazy mistake. Please . . . (RITA *glares, saying nothing.*) Do you want to talk about it?

RITA: (*Shaking her head.*) No, I suppose not.

GARY: (*Touching her arm.*) I love you, please believe me.

RITA: (*Softening.*) Really, do you really mean it?

(GARY, *realizing he has won her over, nods emphatically and pulls her to him.* RITA *jumps into his lap, they kiss while he begins to undo her bathrobe. There is a knock at the door.*)

GARY: (*Annoyed.*) Go away!

EDNA: (*Calling from behind the door.*) Let me in. It's me, Edna.

(*Jumping up,* RITA *straightens her robe, goes to the door, opens it.* EDNA *walks in.*)

EDNA: (*Hugging* RITA.) Oh honey, you're finally awake.

RITA: Where is everyone? Where's my mother . . . and Daddy? I thought I heard an ambulance, but I was so drugged after those Valiums.

EDNA: (*Sitting down*.) How many did you take? Oh, no more muffins? (*Looking around*.) Where did they all go?

RITA: You ate them all! So what has happened? Please tell me . . .

GARY: Yes, Edna, Rita has been frantic with worry.

EDNA: Oh hi, Gary. Well, not to worry. Your dad is going be fine. They've got him hooked up to a heart monitor and he's finally getting the right medication. They said it was a mild heart attack, but the doctors are very optimistic.

RITA: (*A little relieved, she sighs*.) But Mother, how is she?

EDNA: Shook up, of course, but Margie is with her and you know how capable she is.

RITA: (*Touching* EDNA's *hand*.) Thanks. You and Margie are such good friends.

EDNA: (*Proudly*.) Of course—after all, what are friends for? And oh yes, Brandon, well, he bruised his shoulder pretty badly but they've bandaged it up and he'll be okay.

RITA: (*Suddenly remembering*.) Oh god, then it's true—about him and Daddy?

EDNA: I'm afraid so, honey. (*She reaches out to pat* RITA's *hand*.)

GARY: I just can't believe Harold would . . . go that way. I mean . . . I admit Brandon is quite a charmer. (RITA *glares at him and he laughs apologetically*.) Just kidding honey.

RITA: Oh, what will happen to my mother, to all of us?

GARY: Don't worry, everything will be fine. You'll come back and stay with me. (*He whispers*.) I love you, Rita.

RITA: I love you too, Gary, but you must promise . . . never . . . never to do that to me again!

EDNA: Rita, you and Gary belong together. Your mother will be just fine. Margie and I will see to that.

(*There is another knock at the door.*)

(*Getting up.*) I'll go.

(*She opens the door. MARGIE is standing there with BRANDON. His arm is in a sling, the other flung around MARGIE's shoulder. He smiles nervously.*)

BRANDON: Hello, hello everyone. Don't worry, I'm just fine—nothing broken, just a bruise. They say it will take a few weeks, but I'll be as good as new.

(*They all roll their eyes as if to say who cares.*)

EDNA: (*Politely.*) That's wonderful Brandon.

RITA: (*She goes to lunge at BRANDON.*) Oh you . . . you . . . egotistical little fag!   You . . . you . . . homewrecker!

(GARY *grabs her arms, tries to hold her back.*)

BRANDON: (*Looking wounded.*) Rita, I'm sorry, but I really do love Harold. Before I met him, well, I was just floundering—picking up guys in bars—one night stands, you know . . .

RITA: (*Holding her hands over her ears.*) I really don't want to hear this!

MARGIE: (*Firmly.*) BRANDON, SHUT UP!

BRANDON: (*Looking bewildered.*) Well, really. I was just trying to comfort Rita.

MARGIE: (*Incredulous.*) You really are something else, Brandon.

(EDNA *nods in agreement.*)

BRANDON: Then here's something that will certainly cheer you up. Your father has decided not leave your mother. I suppose you're all satisfied. I guess for Harold this was just . . . a fling.

RITA: (*Surprised.*) Really?

MARGIE: (*Nodding.*) Yes, honey, Harold has finally come to his senses, the little he does have . . . (*Laughing.*) Or maybe it was the estrogen that helped clear it up.

EDNA: Oh Margie, that's wonderful. I think that's really what Gail wants. (*She turns to* BRANDON.) I'm sorry . . . I know how hard this must be for you.

BRANDON: (*Haughtily.*) Oh, don't worry about me. I'll be just fine! With my good looks and charm . . . I'm sure I'll have no trouble finding someone, ah, worthy of my affection.

GARY: (*Sarcastically.*) I'm sure you will, Brandon.

(BRANDON *smiles seductively at him then shrugs his shoulders, crying out in pain.*)

MARGIE: (*To* RITA.) Your mother will be home soon. She's just waiting to be sure Harold is stabilized.

(*The phone rings and they all look at each other.*)

RITA: Could you get it, Margie, please . . .

MARGIE: (*Nodding, she picks up the phone.*) Yes, yes, this is her friend . . . yes . . . hmm, (*Raises her voice.*) Oh, are you sure? Really! Oh far out! And how is she taking it? Oh sure, we'll all be here waiting. Thank you, doctor, for letting us know.

(*Laughing, she sits down.*)

RITA: (*Alarmed.*) Margie, what is it? Tell me!

EDNA: (*Also alarmed*.) Yes, tell us—What's happened? Is . . . is Harold . . . ?

(MARGIE *continues laughing*.)

BRANDON: Yes Margie, please tell us what's wrong?

(MARGIE *reaches for a cigarette, dangles it between her fingers. EDNA grabs it away*.)

MARGIE: Not to worry—nothing has happened, except . . . well . . . it's Gail . . . it seems she became dizzy and the doctor made her lie down. I mean after all this, who wouldn't be? And then he examined her—just to make sure she was all right and ordered some blood work.

RITA: (*Nervously*.) Yes, and?

MARGIE: Well, she was taking the estrogen because of . . . you know . . . the changes, and with her system a little mixed-up. (*They all stare at her, waiting*.) It seems Gail is . . . pregnant. She's having a change-of-life baby.

RITA: WHAT?

EDNA: (*Jumping up, she squeezes* MARGIE, *who begins gasping for air*.) Oh god, that's so wonderful . . . and . . . so strange. I mean, I thought her and Harold . . . you know . . .

BRANDON: Ugh! How positively revolting!

GARY: Oh Brandon, shut up! (*He puts his arm around* RITA.) Well, honey, you've always wanted a brother or sister.

RITA: (*Calming down a little*.) Well, I suppose . . . maybe . . . maybe this is not the worst news we've had today. It's just so weird thinking of my mother . . . at her age . . .

(*No one notices* BRANDON *slip a piece of paper into* GARY's *hand. He smiles and whispers "my number" to which* GARY *gives a slight shrug, then smiles slyly back*.)

MARGIE: (*Standing up.*) You know, I just thought of a new idea for my paintings. I think maybe corpses are a bit too morbid. What do you think: mothers and newborns, maybe on a beach, sun shining down on their naked bodies, the babies sucking on—not breasts, but coke bottles—you know, sort of Mary Cassat with a touch of Warhol?

(*The lights fade to black.*)

END

Gloria g. Murray's work has appeared in many literary journals, including *CQ Quarterly, Poet's Guild Journal, Blue Unicorn, The Pittsburgh Quarterly, Pearl,* and others. She has received several awards for poetry and has published two chapbooks, *Walking on Eggshells* and *The Tasting of Cherries.* Her new book, *In My Mother's House: New and Selected Poems,* is now available.

Gloria g. Murray

Too Much of Me

James Magruder's excellent play exemplifies the proposition that the nature of a play's characters invariably determines not only their responses to a play's complications, but gives rise to the complications themselves. Reaching beyond the stage for a universally recognizable example, we offer the beloved monkey from children's literature, Curious George. George lives up to his name, and his curiosity always leads to the major complications in each story. Similarly, the nature of the characters in *Too Much of Me* leads to the complications of this dark comedy.

A homophobic former stripper and prostitute who has been "saved" and become an ultra-traditional Christian, Georgette has created strife in her son Vergil's life for many years, and she continues as the source of dramatic conflict in the play's action. Her narrow beliefs and extreme, in-your-face ways of expressing herself make her a force to be reckoned with—which is exactly what Vergil's new lover Dennis must do. And this encounter, a real test of fire that could have destroyed them, causes Dennis and Vergil to bring forth inner strengths that cement their relationship.

Georgette, in turn, redeems herself at the very end by presenting her son with a treasured heirloom she had claimed to have sold in a yard sale. This final gesture provides the happy ending that creates a comedy from events that could have led to tragedy. The battle between Georgette, her son, and his partner is a delight to watch because the wit of the dialogue springs virtually unmediated from the nature of the characters. In the end, Georgette accepts that she no longer has the upper hand she enjoyed when Vergil was a child. As the play closes, however, Magruder slyly suggests that Georgette may have simply begun a new campaign for supremacy, one that now includes Dennis as well as Vergil.

James Magruder

Too Much of Me

CHARACTERS   VERGIL.

GEORGETTE: his mother, a woman of great cheer and hostility.

DENNIS: his boyfriend.

SETTING   The living room of Vergil's house, the present.

(DENNIS *and* GEORGETTE *are talking in the living room of* VERGIL's *house.*)

DENNIS: My boy's name is Matthew. He's thirteen.

GEORGETTE: Matthew! So that makes Nina, Tess . . .

DENNIS: —ie. Tessie. Sarah—

GEORGETTE: Sister Sarah and Matthew. Brother Matthew. Gracious, four children! Matthew is such a special name. He was the most handsome Evangelist, blond, blue eyes, good teeth, strong oh so strong, he was the Nordic one—let us just give praise to Matthew. I always say in teen reach-outs that Matt was the Paul McCartney of the first Fab Four.

DENNIS: Really.

GEORGETTE: The fabbest four of all, oh praise 'em.

DENNIS: Which one was Ringo?

GEORGETTE: Luke, stupid. (*A beat.*) I see you're a spring.

DENNIS: Excuse me.

GEORGETTE: With blue undertones. That shirt is all wrong for you, Dennis. You look like nobody loves you. Take it off.

DENNIS: What?

GEORGETTE: I said take it off.

DENNIS: Well—I can change if this one bothers—I have other shirts—

GEORGETTE: I said take it off. We're family right now. (*She laughs.*) I want to show you something, wrench it off right now, goosie boy.

(*As* DENNIS *starts to remove his sport shirt,* GEORGETTE *pulls out colored swatch samples and a mirror from a carpetbag.*)

DENNIS: Are you sure I can't get you something to—

GEORGETTE: NO, I said I was FASTING! Hold still, goosie boy! (*She begins to lay the swatches over his white t-shirt against his shoulders.*) Pastels are just the thing for a man with your skin tone. Peach. Lime. Tutti-frutti. I wear jewel tones myself and make a joyful noise unto the Lord. Without my Lord's jewel tones I'd still be whistling Dixie out my cooter. Ooh, what pretty eyelashes, don't suppose you curl 'em, I should call you Denise. Periwinkle—that looks great on a father of four. What do you think of that? In a nice crêpe-de-chine. Periwinkle is so restful.

DENNIS: I don't have much occasion to wear crêpe-de-chine.

GEORGETTE: You don't? Well just who am I talking to then? (*Continuing with the swatches.*) Melon. Banana taffy. You need to get to the gym, son. Verg won't put up with this. Let's try the lime again. Lime.

(*She jams her hand down DENNIS's back. He jumps up.*)

DENNIS: What are you doing!

GEORGETTE: You need to wax that.

DENNIS: Get out of there!

GEORGETTE: I have the technology.

DENNIS: Don't touch me!

GEORGETTE: What are you being so sensitive for? Didja recover a memory or something? (*She laughs.*)

DENNIS: I'm just sensitive there. That's all.

GEORGETTE: Well don't I know it now. None of you people were born in a manger, oh no, you people are all so special and supersensitive.

DENNIS: I suppose by that you mean gay people.

GEORGETTE: No, I suppose I mean dick-smokers and bungholers. The wax is in here somewhere—

DENNIS: Wax?

GEORGETTE: For your back. We're gonna clean it off for Verg.

DENNIS: He likes my back the way it is.

GEORGETTE: That's what he says now. I'm his mother. I listen between the lines. Maybe you don't do that with Huey, Dewey, Louie, and Matthew, but I listen to my kids, always have. The first things Vergil says to me about one of you all wind up being the first things he wants gone. That last one—name rhymed with spay—what was it? Oh hell, anyway, Verg calls up and says Mommie, I met a man. Tell me about him, Vergil, I say. Rock my world—I don't say that. He's got his own house, Mommie, and he's uncut. Uncut? I thought Lord he's an A-rab, how'm I gonna bring him to You, A-rab on top of in the lifestyle, but it turned out he wasn't A-rab, he was just a lawyer. And a first class android. Well. Found the wax, praise Jesus. Now the last thing I heard about this one—rhymes with lay, help me out here, Dennis—last thing I heard is I hate his dark, smelly house, Mommie, and I hate his dark, smelly jigger. I say what, don't he clean out his jigger? What did you call Matthew's jigger growing up?

DENNIS: Penis.

GEORGETTE: That's interesting. I called it a jigger. And I made sure Vergil knew to keep after it with soap and a rag. What did you call your girls's cooters growing up?

DENNIS: Vaginas.

GEORGETTE: I called Lucy's a jinie. This wax has to melt real slow. And that was that, no more gay spay android lawyer on my prayer list. (*A beat.*) But I know, you're different, this time it's the real thing. Why you've known each other for two whole weeks, haven't you?

DENNIS: Ten months.

GEORGETTE: Do you want to know what he said to me about you?

DENNIS: Not particularly.

GEORGETTE: He said, Mommie I met a man, like he always does. Tell me about him, Vergil. Rock my world. Well, Mommie, he's as Irish as Paddy's pig, he's got four children, and his back's a bush. (*A beat*.) I'm on your side, Dennis. The one thing you have to learn about me is I. Love. People. Can't help it, I just love 'em. I'm gonna love you as one of God's own children, and I don't want you to rhyme with anything three months from now. I'm getting too old to keep up with the stack of jacks Vergil drags home. So let's just accept that I know my little boy too, and wax your back before he makes you put those precious babies of yours up for adoption.

DENNIS: He doesn't call you Mommie.

GEORGETTE: No?

DENNIS: When he calls you, which is Christmas, your birthday, Mother's Day, and whenever you've strung Lucy out, he calls you Mother. He called you a couple of weeks ago because Lucy told him you've been taking rifle lessons.

GEORGETTE: We are in constant communication, Dennis. I have long distance. I have call waiting. I have re-dial. I have that feature that lets me know who called while I'm sitting on the pot, star sixty-nine, total recall dial.

DENNIS: Outside of that, he either calls you "That Woman" or "The Dollar-Dip of Deasley, Texas."

GEORGETTE: Sticks and stones, sticks and stones! My past is known to all; I have no shame, Jesus met the woman at the well, and I was she! I have washed His feet with my tears, my sin was burned away in the white hot flame of Jesus. Vergil has always been jealous of my conversion.

DENNIS: I'm not sure that's how he'd put it.

GEORGETTE: Well you know best now, don't you? I dance for the Lord now.

DENNIS: In pasties?

GEORGETTE: (*A challenge.*) So you wanna mix it up with Mommie? Well I think that's good, that's a very good sign. Verg usually picks 'em puny. If the good Lord told me, Georgette I want you to be Cotton Queen again, you bet I'd put on my pasties and cooch my way back to the title, cause there are those who are with Him and those who are against Him. Lucky for me, He hasn't asked me to, I'm such a fa—big girl now. My figure's just a bowlful of jelly. Look.

(GEORGETTE *performs a brief, modified bump and grind.*)

DENNIS: His therapist calls you the mother with no boundaries.

GEORGETTE: Do your babies call you manpussy?

DENNIS: (*After a beat.*) What are you doing here? Vergil will just hate this.

GEORGETTE: I believe I mentioned I was on my way to Florida to wait out the tribulation. I've got a double-wide trailer with a gas-powered generator, a food dryer, and an artesian well, I'm all set for the last days—(*Angrily.*) I have told that little shit a thousand times he doesn't need a therapist! Jesus meets every need. There was nothing wrong in the way he was raised. (*She starts rummaging in her bag again.*) Now let me ask you something Dennis, do you live here or do you just lay up in my boy's bed and keep him from Christ?

DENNIS: That's none of your business.

GEORGETTE: Lighten up Lana, I'm just wondering who cleans this house. (*She has found a can of spray polish.*)

DENNIS: Vergil has a maid in on Thursdays.

(*This information stops* GEORGETTE *in her tracks.*)

GEORGETTE: A maid? He—my—but I. I taught him to clean. To be clean. And to clean.

(*She sets the polish down. She sits. All the air has gone out of her.*)

The mother of your children, where is she?

DENNIS: Out of the picture. Never in the picture, really. I raised them myself.

GEORGETTE: Me too. Just the two though, not four. (*A beat.*) And how do they feel about your—conversion?

DENNIS: The girls are thrilled, very happy for me.

GEORGETTE: Wow. That's different.

DENNIS: Vergil's just great with them. I think they all really enjoy each other. He's always wanted children, you know. He's looking into adoption.

GEORGETTE: (*Lying.*) Oh, I know, I know. Children are the greatest gift on earth, they are, they just are.

DENNIS: Matthew's harder to read. I think he might be afraid I'm going to get hurt.

GEORGETTE: (*After a beat.*) You're going to get hurt? You're going to get hurt? Haven't you got something backwards? Now I am being as tolerant as I know how to be, but I am sorry: a thirteen-year-old boy needs a man to look up to, to be proud of, to show him the world of men—what he doesn't need is a cocksucking, cornholing pervert for a daddy! What is a grown man with four kids of his own smoking jiggers for? You're going to get hurt? Shame on you, mister! The Devil has got up between you and the covenant of parenthood and, and—fatherness, and you have got to cast him out! Cast him out right now! I've got some literature about the ex-gay movement you need to burn into your brain.

DENNIS: He told me you were insane, but never, he never said how hateful you were.

GEORGETTE: Hateful?!

DENNIS: Have you even read the *New Testament,* I mean, other than to decide which evangelist you want to sleep with? The message is love.

GEORGETTE: These are the end times, Miss Dennis the Menace! Armageddon! The power grid is going out permanently! I don't have the time—I don't have the inclination!—to turn the other cheek when the world is ending in six months. I am a sanctified Christian. I am saving and taking all who I can with me.

DENNIS: Why would you want to take Vergil along? I thought homosexuals were going to be cast into the pit of Hell.

GEORGETTE: Cocksuckers have been around since when they first ran out of goats. We are all God's children. Hell, James the Lesser took it up the ass from the rest of the apostles. That's why he was called James the Lesser.

DENNIS: He's not going with you. He'll never go with you.

GEORGETTE: Look at this. (*She means the coffee table.*)

DENNIS: You just want him all for yourself. Nobody else can have him.

             (GEORGETTE *starts spraying and waxing the tables with spray polish.*)

GEORGETTE: A boy never stops needing his mother. Just like your babies needed a father 'til the Devil come up between you. They still need you. Listen! (*She stops.*) Do you hear that? Don't you hear 'em crying out for their daddy? I know I do. (*She resumes her task.*) I don't know what kind of Hispano-Rican is cleaning this house, but she is overpaid. Sure as blazes doesn't know how to bring out a fine wood grain. There. Some bit of better.

DENNIS: Where in Florida are you relocating?

GEORGETTE: Opopka. Shooting distance from the Epcot Center. Now between you and me, Dennis, I think some of those Disney characters border on idolatry. Now you take Goofy for instance—my spirit has told me that Goofy was sent straight from the pit of Hell—I've prayed long and hard over Goofy, but Lord, I love those flume rides. Whoosh! Praise Jesus for water slides. Whoosh! Whoosh! Put me on a log and whoosh! Did you just let one?

DENNIS: What?

GEORGETTE: Did you fart? Or was that me?

             (GEORGETTE *lights a match and waves it between* DENNIS *and herself. We hear* VERGIL *from offstage. When* GEORGETTE *hears his voice, she quickly manages to freshen her lipstick, adjust her bosom and clothes, and check her hair.*)

VERGIL: (*Offstage.*) Dennis? What is all this crap doing in the hallway?

DENNIS: In here.

VERGIL: (*Offstage.*) I almost broke an ankle—

            (VERGIL *enters, carrying two industrial-sized containers of peanut butter.*)

There are ten tubs of this out there. You know I'm allergic to peanuts. Are you trying to kill me?

GEORGETTE: I told you never to receive that, Vergil. You were healed of that peanut allergy long ago.

VERGIL: Oh my god, what are you doing here? Get—Jesus, this is some warning. You let her in?

DENNIS: Did I have a choice? She walked in.

GEORGETTE: Kiss your Mommie hello.

            (GEORGETTE *stays put, forcing* VERGIL, *who is still holding the tubs of peanut butter, to cross to her for an embrace.*)

How do I look? Terrible, I know. Total big girl time. Ten more pounds and—

VERGIL: —you could apply for statehood.

GEORGETTE: You like my hair? Vergil always told me how to dress my hair. Kiss your honey hello.

            (VERGIL *doesn't move to* DENNIS.)

VERGIL: So you've met why I'm fucked up.

DENNIS: All is forgiven.

VERGIL: I see she got your shirt off already. Let me guess—you're a spring.

DENNIS: With blue undertones. Did you know James the Lesser was butt boy to the apostles?

GEORGETTE: Oh baby, I got a good feeling about this one. He's got grit. Won't put up with all your fiendish ways.

VERGIL: You know what, Mother? I am allergic to peanuts! My head swole to twice its size and my throat closed up. They nearly had to perform a tracheotomy. I'd be dead if Grandma hadn't finally wrenched the car keys out of her hands.

GEORGETTE: Sweetheart, He has held you in the palm of His hand since the day you were born.

VERGIL: What is all that peanut butter doing in my hallway?

DENNIS: She's stockpiling. That's our share for Armageddon.

GEORGETTE: Five tubs go to Lucy. I just have a box number for her, no address, so see that she gets it.

VERGIL: Lucy doesn't eat peanut butter.

GEORGETTE: I don't see why not. It's pure protein.

VERGIL: How are the shooting lessons going?

GEORGETTE: Laugh all you like, but it's gonna come in handy when people start slaying each other over bottled water and a six-pack of Slim Jims.

VERGIL: (*A new thought.*) Hey, where's dickface? He's not stinking up the powder room, is he?

(*This section—until the mention of the teapot—is spoken very rapidly.*)

GEORGETTE: No. He's closing the house.

DENNIS: Who's dickface?

GEORGETTE: He's got his own timetable, always has. (*To* DENNIS.) Dickface is Paul.

VERGIL: (*To* GEORGETTE.) So you're really going through with it.

GEORGETTE: Child of mine, it's really over, praise Jesus, it is really over.

DENNIS: Who's Paul?

VERGIL: My stepfather. The meanest of all God's creatures.

DENNIS: You have a stepfather?

VERGIL: You've shut down the house.

DENNIS: Why didn't you tell me?

VERGIL: You don't give power to the Devil by speaking his name.

GEORGETTE: Amen to that, sister. I taught you right.

DENNIS: Anything else important I don't know that I should?

VERGIL: My stepfather is not important. The house, Mother?

GEORGETTE: Sold it, sold everything, every last thing. Free of all earthly ties that bind.

VERGIL: Wow. That's some retirement plan. (*A beat.*) Did you bring me my teapot?

GEORGETTE: Teapot?

VERGIL: Grandma's Limoges teapot, where is it?

GEORGETTE: That old thing? Honey, I had a yard sale.

VERGIL: I don't believe this!

GEORGETTE: Disposing of a ten-room house on my own and I'm supposed to remember a teapot?

VERGIL:	Not a teapot. Memi's (*Pronounced 'me-my'.*) teapot.
GEORGETTE:	You don't need a teapot. You need water, a source of protein, a self-standing gas-operated generator, a means of protection, and Jesus.
VERGIL:	That teapot was coming to me! She wanted me to have it.
GEORGETTE:	You are such a faggot sometimes.
VERGIL:	And you're still a fat old whore with blue eye shadow.
DENNIS:	Vergil, take it easy—
VERGIL:	What?
DENNIS:	She's your mother.
VERGIL:	That's right, she's my mother, and she has to take it. That teapot was coming to me. She sold the rest of the service, piece by piece, to keep herself in Jim Beam.
GEORGETTE:	Really? I remember selling it off to pay for your schoolbooks and your band fees and your choir uniform—with your Memi's blessing. She said sell the teapot too, but I knew how much it meant to your candy ass.
VERGIL:	So you sell it at a garage sale?
GEORGETTE:	And got a good price for it too! The world is ending! Open your eyes!
DENNIS:	Vergil, why didn't you just take the teapot before all this happened?
VERGIL:	What did you say?
GEORGETTE:	Now that is an excellent question, Dennis.

(*A standoff.*)

You know what, I'm feeling kind of peckish.

DENNIS: You told me you were fasting. I swear she did, Vergil.

GEORGETTE: My fast is over now. Time to break it.

DENNIS: Vergil, did you tell your mother I had a hairy back?

VERGIL: No.

DENNIS: Did you tell her I was as Irish as Paddy's pig?

VERGIL: You're German.

DENNIS: No kidding. Did you tell her I had four children?

VERGIL: No.

DENNIS: What did you tell her about me?

VERGIL: Nothing.

DENNIS: Nothing. (*A beat.*) What would you like to eat, Georgette?

GEORGETTE: Oh, I do think this one's a keeper, Verg. Hang on to this Harry.

> (GEORGETTE, *who has been rummaging through her carpetbag, has retrieved a Ziploc bag filled with powder which she hands to* DENNIS.)

If you got some skim milk, blend it up with this. Two percent'll do too. Don't worry about the lumps. It's a protein shake. There's too much of me, just too much of me, and I gotta get my figure back.

VERGIL: You look fine, Mother. You're fifty-one years old, give yourself a break.

GEORGETTE: Hold on, Dennis. Here's the wax. (*She hands the wax to him.*) Now, like I said, it's gotta melt slow. Get a saucepan.

DENNIS: Is a copper bottom okay?

GEORGETTE: Ooh, fancy—put it over a gentle flame, less than simmer, or it'll burn.

DENNIS: Lid on or off?

VERGIL: Dennis.

DENNIS: What?

VERGIL: Put the wax down. You don't have a hairy back.

DENNIS: Right, I don't.

(DENNIS *starts to exit.*)

GEORGETTE: Dennis, come here—

DENNIS: Yes, ma'am.

VERGIL: Stay away from that wax!

GEORGETTE: Look at my eyes.

DENNIS: Yes, ma'am.

GEORGETTE: Am I wearing eye shadow, blue or otherwise?

DENNIS: No.

(DENNIS *exits. It is awkward for mother and son to begin.*)

GEORGETTE: Why do you think Lucy doesn't eat peanut butter? It's pure protein.

VERGIL: Maybe because it's all the protein we had growing up.

GEORGETTE: Maybe that's why you think you're allergic to it. (*A beat.*) It's a lovely lovely home, Vergil. I was hoping I'd get to see it someday. The Lord knows you didn't get this good taste from me.

VERGIL: You can't stay.

GEORGETTE: Just 'til Paul catches up?

VERGIL: You can't.

GEORGETTE: You're right—can't disappoint your therapist, it just isn't done. (*She laughs.*) Well, what am I thinking anyway? I start teaching next week. In Opopka. Tap and toe dance. And Bible classes right up to the fiery end.

VERGIL: Dance lessons by day.

GEORGETTE: Honky-tonking by night. (*She starts to move into a dance routine.*)

VERGIL: Back where you started.

GEORGETTE: Without my little boy at the piano though, making me look good.

               (GEORGETTE *performs an odd amalgamated toe dance—soft shoe, using the books of the Old Testament—"Genesis, Exodus, Leviticus, Numbers," etc., for lyrics.* VERGIL *joins in, corrects her, reminds her how the routine went. He finally breaks it off.*)

VERGIL: Buy a boom box.

GEORGETTE: Don't I know it, child of mine, do I not know it?

VERGIL: (*After a beat.*) I want you to know I've thought about this a lot. I think it all was better when you were still stripping.

GEORGETTE: And laying up with men to put food on the table? That's some romantic notion you have. Jesus changed my life forever. He had to.

VERGIL: That's when you left though. Forsook us.

GEORGETTE: I had nothing inside me, Vergil.

VERGIL: And then there was nothing for us. You stopped looking in front of you. You didn't see us anymore. Jesus was more important to you than your children.

GEORGETTE: Well of course He is, He just is, He's Jesus, that's what Jesus means.

VERGIL:	A twelve-year-old needs his mother's full attention.
GEORGETTE:	(*After a beat.*) Verg.
VERGIL:	I said no.
GEORGETTE:	I don't want you to die in the fiery pit.
VERGIL:	I can't. I won't. The world is not ending.
GEORGETTE:	Armageddon is a fact ten feet in front of us.
VERGIL:	You're all just bored. And you're pissed off that nobody'll listen to your nutbag politics.
GEORGETTE:	I have cancer.
VERGIL:	Again?
GEORGETTE:	Cancer, you hear me?
VERGIL:	Where is it this time?
GEORGETTE:	I'm riddled with it, up and down, side to side. My CAT scans look like a lace tablecloth.
VERGIL:	He has held you in the palm of His hand since the day you put on a useful brassiere.
GEORGETTE:	You think I'm kidding? Look. (*She begins to untuck the blouse from her skirt.*)
VERGIL:	Put those back right now. This is my house. I don't need to see them anymore.
GEORGETTE:	I'm dying. I need you to take care of me.
VERGIL:	How can you lie about something like that? People really get cancer, you know.
GEORGETTE:	I'll leave Paul. He can live in another trailer. I'll just set out food for him.

VERGIL:	Please go. I'm trying to be as nice as I can.
GEORGETTE:	He won't come up between us anymore. That's what you always wanted! You want him out—he's out! I've always loved you best. I've always loved my Vergil most. See—I did see you all these years! I saw what was in front of me. I see what's in front of me now——my baby boy. I want you back.
VERGIL:	Mommie, I—
GEORGETTE:	(*Almost whispering.*) Mommie knows. Mommie loves you. (*She holds out her arms to her baby.*)
VERGIL:	Mommie . . .
	(*He takes a step towards her. DENNIS enters. They fall silent. DENNIS gives GEORGETTE her protein shake.*)
GEORGETTE:	What, no doily? Dennis, I have cancer.
VERGIL:	She does not.
GEORGETTE:	I have cancer and my only begotten son won't come care for me, won't brighten my last days. Oh Dennis, my boy used to dance and sing with me, helped me match my outfits, he was my little sparkler born on the tenth of July, I don't know whether you've seen the sweet side of him. (*She has tasted the shake.*) Lumps. Goddamit.
VERGIL:	She doesn't have cancer, Dennis. She's lonely. This is her payback, this is the thanks you get, Mother. Mother, you have to go now.
GEORGETTE:	Not until you come with. (*A new idea.*) Dennis! Dennis! You come with us, Dennis. I'd just love that. I need granbabies. Bring your brats and we'll home-school 'em. Teach 'em toe dancing and scripture. I can give them a mother's love. I'll bet they've never been to the Epcot Center. Whoosh! Whoosh!
VERGIL:	Don't make me push you out the door.
GEORGETTE:	Don't you come near me! And what is this I hear about your adopting children?

VERGIL: Dennis!

GEORGETTE: Oh, Dennis told me all about it. And I think it's the sickest thing I ever heard of.

DENNIS: I thought you were exaggerating. (*Re: your mother*).

VERGIL: Surprise!

GEORGETTE: It's not enough to have a therapist and a maid, now you have to have a child? I guess this is what they call "Homos having it all!" How on earth do you expect to raise a child with your problems? What sickos would ever let you have a baby?

VERGIL: Adoption agencies in China, Vietnam, Russia—

GEORGETTE: Foreign castoffs raised by homosexuals—those aren't gonna be my granbabies.

VERGIL: That's right, they're not gonna be your granbabies, because I'm an orphan! Orphaned at twelve! Lucy's an orphan! Lucy's an orphan with a post box! She had the right idea.

GEORGETTE: Well, if some ignorant gooks are fool enough to hand you a baby, I hope it's a girl, I wouldn't want to contemplate what you'd do with a boy. (*A shift.*) I didn't mean that, just flew out of my mouth. Baby, when you come back to Christ, we can raise one together down in Florida.

VERGIL: No, that's the sickest thing I ever heard of. I don't get it, Mother. Why do you want me so bad all of a sudden? Are you so lonely that you have to fake cancer to drag me into Hell with you and Paul and a truckload of peanut butter? What is the point of my being with you? What on earth could we do together? Your nails, your hair? Color charts 'til kingdom come? I just don't see it. I can't get through dinner and a movie with you anymore. You're exhausting!

DENNIS: Wait a minute—

VERGIL: You are an instrument of torture!

DENNIS: Time out. "Come back to Christ?" Come back to Christ?

GEORGETTE: You heard it here first. Vergil is a Christian, son, backslid something fierce, but make no mistake, he is as sanctified as I am. Vergil accepted Him as his personal lord and savior in my very presence, slain in the spirit; preacher cast out the demon of man-worship in him, demon of cocksucking, demon of fudgepacking, demon of antiquing. (*She laughs.*) Vergil called out, cried out "Cure me Jesus, heal me of my homosexuality," he even talked in tongues, didn't you honey? Vergil's rebirth was a proud proud moment for me. Born again at twenty-three.

DENNIS: Twenty-three? Vergil?

VERGIL: Mother. God makes gay people.

GEORGETTE: I know you need to believe that but no, child, the Devil gets in there. The child must be rescued from his snares. You adopting a child is a misbegotten thing. (*To* DENNIS.) You having four—well, the jury's still out on that, that's all I'm gonna say.

VERGIL: (*To* DENNIS.) I was hoping you'd never have to meet her. I'm so ashamed.

GEORGETTE: (*Livid.*) Don't you be ashamed of—I'm not ashamed of you, am I?

DENNIS: What about the grandchild you do have?

GEORGETTE: What?

DENNIS: What about Carl?

GEORGETTE: What are you getting at? Lucy's little Carl is only out of wedlock. I have forgiven Lucy of her sin. Carl's my little Latin lover.

DENNIS: Carl is a Guatemalan Indian.

GEORGETTE: No, he's Spanish.

DENNIS: And he's adopted. Lucy and Gretchen—

VERGIL: Dennis, don't.

DENNIS: Lucy and Gretchen adopted Carl.

VERGIL: Don't.

GEORGETTE: Her roommate Gretchen? What does Gretchen have to do with it?

VERGIL: Dennis, stop!

DENNIS: They're lovers. Lesbian lovers.

VERGIL: This isn't for you to say.

GEORGETTE: They are NOT. They're career girls sharing expenses, ROOMMATES, and I think that's SWEET. That kind of friendship is rare and—SWEET. You just want everybody to be gay, don't you, mister? You come swirling out of the closet in high heels and suddenly the whole world's in the lifestyle. Precious baby Carl is NOT adopted.

VERGIL: Dennis, this isn't your business.

DENNIS: Why are you so afraid of her?

VERGIL: I don't know, baby. I wish I—she won't let go.

GEORGETTE: Lesbians? (*A beat.*) That is a GODDAM lie. That's nasty. I'm not going down there. I got one of my own. Gretchen, well okay, she looks like she went to dyke school, but Lucy? She hasn't the GUMPTION. This is just a PHASE. Vergil? (*He nods.*) She is doing this to DEFY me. I spared the rod and look what I got. I have hateful, spiteful children. I don't know who raised you.

VERGIL: She's completely unable to see us. She couldn't even see—wouldn't see that my head blew up to twice its size.

GEORGETTE: I don't need to see you, godammit. There's a cord that runs between mother and child, never to be broken! Never!

DENNIS: Georgette. This Paul person—

VERGIL: Dickface!

DENNIS: Is Lucy's father.

GEORGETTE: That's right.

DENNIS: And Vergil's father is—

VERGIL: He could be anybody, doesn't matter!

DENNIS: And Vergil's father is Vergil's father. Both of your children are gay, Georgette. Fathered by different men. Did you know there's a lot of research out there suggesting that homosexuality has a genetic component? Carried through the mother.

GEORGETTE: What are you getting at, son?

DENNIS: If anyone is carrying the gene, it's you. I think you should ask Jesus why he sent you two gay children.

GEORGETTE: Are you saying I'm a carrier? Vergil? Is he saying I'm a carrier?

> (*He nods.* GEORGETTE *violently starts going through her carpetbag, pulling things out and fiercely muttering Scripture and the word "carrier." At a certain point, she pulls out some bullets. Finally she finds what she is looking for: a lipstick.*)

(*To* DENNIS.) What if one of your precious baby girls turns out bulldagger?

DENNIS: All I think any parent wants for a child, wants for his children, is that they experience love.

GEORGETTE: (*Applying lipstick.*) Fuck you! I do not receive that, I do not receive you, so fuck you! (*A beat.*) Pardon my French. I don't understand this world anymore. How blessed glad I am it's going to be over soon, so very very soon. Take me now, Lord! (*A beat.*) I'll bet your babies think you're special. All this honesty parenting bushwah CRAP.

VERGIL: They do. They treat him like a human being.

GEORGETTE: Not like some monster, you mean?

VERGIL: Not like some monster.

GEORGETTE: (*After a beat.*) I never liked my mother much. She had no use for girls. I swore to God, long before I knew Him like I know Him now, I swore when I had kids I wouldn't be the kind of mother whose kids couldn't stand to be around her when they grew up. I swore it up and down and side to side. And that's what's happened. That's what's happened, isn't it?

VERGIL: (*He has to say it.*) That's what happened, Mother. You're just too much.

GEORGETTE: (*After a beat.*) I'll see you in Heaven then. Believe it.

VERGIL: I know.

GEORGETTE: Lucy too? (*He nods.*) Jesus. Tell her I said goodbye. It was sure nice meeting you, Dennis. (*To* VERGIL.) I do like this one.

DENNIS: Thank you.

GEORGETTE: Hang on to him, Verg. Hell, there's not enough time left to switch partners and dance. When the world is over, I want you two to be taking your last breath together.

(GEORGETTE *exits.*)

VERGIL: You outed my sister?

DENNIS: Jesus Christ is your personal savior?

VERGIL: It was a vulnerable time.

DENNIS: You talk in tongues.

VERGIL: Not anymore.

DENNIS: You wanted to be straight?

VERGIL: No. I wanted her to love me.

DENNIS: (*After a beat.*) When it's over, however it's over—and god knows, she may have a point . . . where do you plan on being?

VERGIL: I sort of thought, sort of . . . here.

DENNIS: Look.

VERGIL: What.

DENNIS: There.

VERGIL: What?

DENNIS: Between us.

> (*They stare at the devil between them and do not move.* GEORGETTE *re-enters quietly. She is carrying a box.*)

GEORGETTE: I'm a litle teapot, short and stout. Wrapped, wrapped, and wrapped again. Came over from France Lord knows when with your Grandmaw's first husband. Vergil taught us to call it Limoges, not Lime-o-gez. I'd say treat it right, but I don't have to tell you all that. (*A beat.*) Hey.

DENNIS & VERGIL: What?

GEORGETTE: This is a joke. Why did God make gay boys?

DENNIS: I don't know. Why?

GEORGETTE: So fa—so big girls would have someone to dance with.

> (GEORGETTE *sets down the box and exits. They look at each other. One of them starts to move. The lights fade to black.*)

END

James Magruder is a playwright and award-winning translator of the works of Marivaux, Molière, Lesage, Labiche, Dancourt, and Gozzi. He also wrote the book for the Broadway musical *Triumph of Love* and teaches translation and adaptation at the Yale School of Drama, where he received his doctorate.

All information concerning performance rights can be obtained by contacting Peter Hagan at the Gersh Agency.

The Death of Saul

Bill Teitelbaum's intense and erudite play recounts the death of Saul, anointed as first king of the ancient Hebrews by the prophet Samuel, whose voice Saul still hears in his head as his death and the armies of the Philistines approach the cave where he hides with his servant. *The Death of Saul* is a Midrash in the tradition of Midrash Halakah, interpretations of the Old Testament by ancient rabbis. In the same sense that Midrash offers commentary on or speculation about scripture, this play examines Saul's final conflict to find depth of understanding. That he will choose suicide instead of capture by his enemies is never in doubt. Instead, he struggles with his place in God's plan and contrasts it with that of the servant who accompanies him on his final journey.

The play begins with a dramatic and beautifully poetic description of the setting—a cave on Mt. Gilboa that is fit for the death of a king. The drama ends with stones rattling down from the cave's opening, signaling the enemy's approach and serving notice that the time for final action has come. As created by Teitelbaum, the cave might well be the inside of Saul's head, where the once mighty king examines his relationship with God and his fate. Although some people in theatre seem to feel that stage directions are the director's province, descriptions of setting, character, and opening action are usually the playwright's first chance to impress a reader with the power of language and the depth and scope of the play's vision. As Teitelbaum demonstrates, if a writer can create dialogue and action worthy of production onstage, any reader must pay attention to all of the play's language.

Bill Teitelbaum

The Death of Saul

CHARACTERS KING SAUL OF BENJAMIN: mid-sixties.

SERVANT: Saul's armor-bearer, a noncommissioned officer, thirty to forty.

SETTING A limestone cave near the summit of Mount Gilboah above the Jezreel Plain, Late Bronze Age Canaan, about 1,000 B.C. In the foreground a sandy apron, boulder-strewn. Erosion has left buttress-like ribs jutting from the cavern walls. To the rear at the crest of a rubbled slope, the cave's entrance is less a doorway than a low, horizontal crease in the face of the hillside. Spilling from this crease, waning daylight provides the cave's only apparent illumination, silvering the tumbled rock.

Scene 1

(*Evening. Silhouetted figures appear at the crease, then enter the cave, first the* SERVANT, *headlong, scrabbling, dragging his burdens after him, provisions, packs, goatskins, weaponry, then reaching back urgently for* SAUL, *wounded and favoring his back.*)

SERVANT: Your hand, Sire!

SAUL: Bastards!

(SERVANT *helps* SAUL *down the slope to the cave floor amid small cascades of shale, both smeared with grime as if scorched,* SAUL *in full battle kit—a kilted tunic, a leather baldric hung with a Philistine broadsword, a full coat of coarse wool, a more finely woven woolen cloak hemmed in purple, booted sandals, and a kaffiyah with a brow-band of gold cords. Now in his sixties, irascible, thin-skinned,* SAUL *is presumed generally to be insane, that is, possessed by a divine but malevolent spirit.*)

(*Freeing himself painfully from* SERVANT'*s grasp.*) Damn you, that's still attached to me! (*Pause.*) Well, they've done for us now, haven't they. A blind man could track us the way I've bled.

(*Meantime, unslinging his bags, the* SERVANT *makes a servant's assessment of their accommodations. There is a ruined firepit, a broken gourd. He pokes gingerly at the rocks with the butt of his lance.*)

What are you looking for?

SERVANT: Vipers. Adders, Sire.

SAUL: We should be so lucky. Oh be still for pity's sake!

SERVANT: Perhaps after eating, Sire—

SAUL: Enough I said. (*Pausing now, watching as* SERVANT *gathers fuel.*) And now what are you doing?

SERVANT: It grows cold, Sire. I thought a bit of fire here, sheltered by these rocks?

SAUL: A small one.

SERVANT: Yes, Sire.

SAUL: Small I said.

SERVANT: Small. Yes, Sire.

SAUL: Good lad. (*Looking about, dubious of their safety, while* SERVANT *strikes flint to wick.*) Well, here's a proper tomb for us. I think I know this hole. (*Pause.*) You'll forgive me if I seem to suspect your loyalty. I'm not accustomed to it. You didn't know your predecessor I take it.

SERVANT: I attended our Lord David at Bet'shan, Sire.

SAUL: Lord David no less.

SERVANT: By your appointment, Sire.

SAUL: You'll bear with me. I seem not myself today.

SERVANT: No, Sire.

SAUL: Still, it's not every day we lose a kingdom, is it? (*Pause.*) Your Lord David was with them you know.

SERVANT: I heard it, Sire.

SAUL: Yes, well, trust me, he was there. The first words I ever heard from him were 'What's in it for me?' If the price were right our pretty shepherd was a proper cutthroat. (*Pause*) How will our Philistine masters reward him, do you think? Hebron? Bethlehem? That's what I would give him. Someplace I could keep an eye on him. (*Pause.*) You wouldn't have any wine in that commissary of yours.

SERVANT: (*Offering a stoppered goatskin.*) Kinneret, Sire.

SAUL: Is that so? Your health then—much good it'll do you. (*Drinks—spits.*) My God that's rotten! (*Plugs goatskin with disgust, tosses it back.*) Why is it that everyone seems capable of a potable wine but us?

SERVANT: (*Sorting through provisions.*) There are curds, Sire. A barley loaf. Pressed figs?

SAUL: I couldn't eat. My God that wine is vile. Give it here. My back is seizing up. (*Retrieving wineskin, noticing* SERVANT *still eyeing the rations.*) Don't let me stop you though.

SERVANT: It is not important, Sire.

SAUL: I didn't say it was important. (*Pause.*) Well go ahead and eat for pity's sake.

SERVANT: Thank you, Sire. With your permission.

(SERVANT *blesses the bread, then searches out a small purse of salt.*)

SAUL: I didn't know you were so pious.

SERVANT: The habits of youth, Sire.

SAUL: Yes, I remember. The prime of life for the mediocre. Before the actualities seize us. I was happy then. (*Pause;* SERVANT *eating.*) I don't suppose you sing at all? Your Lord David sang to God as if he were serenading a milkmaid. He had this bit of a prayer-song. (SAUL *offers a few bluesy meters of "How Long" in a ragged bathtub baritone.*) "How long—wilt thou forget me, Oh Lord? / How long—wilt thou hide thy face from me?" Oh come, you know that verse. Everyone sang it.

SERVANT: I know it, Sire. But I have no gift.

SAUL: 'No gift.' Man, just sing for us, to comfort our hearts.

(SERVANT *shrugs; sings.* SAUL *reacts as if struck.*)

I think I may be bleeding again. That was hideous. (*Pause.*) No mistaking Saul, is there. Last post, and even that's a cockup. I couldn't even get myself killed properly. We're all heirs of Isaac, aren't we, escaping into life with a knife at our throats? Why must things be always so difficult for Saul?

SERVANT: My father would say this was our test, Sire, to endure those things we cannot change.

SAUL: Oh did he then? Well, how nice for you. And this was your father no less. All snugly dead now I take it, enduring away ta-rum-ta-tum? (*Operatic; perhaps throttling himself.*) My lad, even your dear dead dad could not have suffered the shit that slid down this royal gorge.

SERVANT: (*Stiffly.*) No, Sire. Then perhaps you could help me, Sire.

SAUL: Oh my, mustn't trifle with papá mustn't we. (*Rising with difficulty, in phases, to assume an appropriate bearing.*) All right, I know—desperate times—death will level us—but you will notice I hope that I—am—not—dead—yet!

SERVANT: No, Sire. Your pardon, my Lord.

SAUL: (*Draws sword.*) I am Saul!

SERVANT: (*Patiently.*) Yes, Sire.

SAUL: It's not that I want to live, but I don't know what else to do.

SERVANT: You should rest, Sire.

SAUL: It's true, I'm tired. By God that was a day's work we did—didn't we today? We turned our promised land into a nation of women. A pity our Samuel didn't live to milk it. That's a true incentive for your faithful, a massacre like that. (*Morose pause.*) Nothing your priest likes better than a proper massacre. (*Bitterly inspired; rising to his feet.*) Look here will you, be a good fellow. (*Hands over sword; SERVANT accepts it apprehensively.*) Splendid. Just steady on you see, and I'll run on it.

SERVANT: (*Literally terrified.*) Sh'ma Yisroel!

SAUL: No? No, perhaps you're right. You run then and I'll hold here, how would that be? Looking off perhaps? A pensive study? You see, you'll have your footing then. A simple lunge, a thrust well-placed. Only for pity's sake let's not be pokey about it. This is no cheese you're carving so let's put some Egypt in it. (SERVANT *wails in terror, falls to ground.*) No, no, no tedious good-byes. It's just us after all. Now what's all this, not the sword I hope. Poor fellow, what is it?

SERVANT: (*Embracing* SAUL's *legs.*) Oh Sire!

SAUL: Can't be left, eh? You're too tender, lad. All right. (*Coaxes* SERVANT *erect.*) All right, how's this then—daggers! Like Canaanite lovers, off in a knot. Wait, you'll like this. Where's my dagger? Well, never mind, we'll practice without. Attend me now, simplicity itself. (*Arranging a death-pact, left hands cupped at the backs of each other's neck, right hands dagger-like, fingertips rigidly extended, pressed between each other's ribs.*) There we are then, close as mice—then daggers right, left hand so, a sharp embrace, and off we go. Right? Right then, let's have those daggers. Goddamn it, man, where's my dagger? Lances then? My God, the quality of the help you get. What in the world is the matter with you! Won't you try to be reasonable? You know what they'll do if they capture us. Why do you suppose they're called Philistines?

SERVANT: But it is forbidden before Heaven, Sire! It is forbidden, my good dear Lord!

SAUL: But you mustn't be so superstitious, dear boy. Besides, I was only old Samuel's anointed. Don't you see that, my lad? It's a different thing entirely. I was never Jehovah's king of Israel—it was all a priest's canard, a shadow-play. I was never the king of Israel.

> (SAUL's *grin is terrible. To keep from falling, he seizes the man, but falls nevertheless.*)

SERVANT: My Lord, what ails thee, Sire!

SAUL: (*Clutching his side.*) I'm not quite sure. (*Now slipping to the ground.*) Perhaps I should have eaten something.

> (*The lights fade to black.*)

(*Night.* SAUL *at the fire, stripped to the waist, the* SERVANT *taking a crude suture in his side. Visible through the crease, a large moon, low in the sky.*)

SAUL: My God those bowmen were murder, weren't they? They picked us off like hares. Why couldn't we have had bowmen like theirs? (*Calling into darkness.*) Eh, old man? Some bowmen for us? Or do we simply blow our rams' horns at 'em? We do? Capital! I shall inform the cadres. (*To* SERVANT.) We have our orders.

SERVANT: Sire?

SAUL: (*In strictest confidence; wary of eavesdroppers.*) Go with the rams' horns.

SERVANT: Yes, Sire.

(SERVANT *draws a knot in the thread and bites off the trailing end, then dampens a compress. His technique is proficient, courteous but brisk, and he doesn't hesitate to enlist* SAUL's *assistance, placing the king's hand to hold the compress in place.*)

With your permission, my Lord.

SAUL: You missed your calling.

SERVANT: It is all one, Sire. While we live we must live.

SAUL: Yes, well, I'm not certain you quite grasp the situation. You're not being dull I hope.

(SERVANT *tears a length of cloth into strips and uses these to bind the compress fast, taking alternate windings around* SAUL's *waist and diagonally across his chest, at last tucking the trailing end. In all this his absorption is complete.*)

SERVANT: We have seen men die; a breath and gone, Sire.

SAUL: Yes, but it's all the difference, isn't it, that breath?

SERVANT: Perhaps, Sire, it is only that I do not think on it as deeply as you do.

SAUL: No, not yet you don't.

SERVANT: A soldier's life is forfeit, Sire. Or we cannot act. We've been dead too many too times to count. For me this is all gift.

SAUL: See, I knew it. You are being dull. You sound as if someone is going to deliver you from life with a mother's kiss.

SERVANT: (*Helping* SAUL *into his clothing.*) I only know life is fragile, Sire, that it cannot bear such examination.

SAUL: Yes, well, I don't know anything. I can't even figure out if you're an angel or an idiot. People like me are suckers for you simple fellows, you faithful servants and wise old priests. It's not you're rotten, but you're empty. You won't be questioned. Everything's a mystery or a revelation with you people.

(*Done with his ministrations,* SERVANT *places a musette and waterskin as pillows at* SAUL's *back.*)

Thank you, that's fine. (*Another morose pause.*) He was a great presence though, our Samuel, you had to give him that. Old as he was he echoed in the mind. It was all meaningless when you examined it later, but it was the kind of thing that worked in the marketplace. It seemed to take that stink of sheepshit from your nose, as if you, too, were in the presence of the living God. I always admired him that gift. I had the vocabulary but I lacked the gall for it. I always worried how I might sound to people. Better to be direct, I thought. Be yourself, a plain man playing at king. Let them think what they like of Saul, only obey the crown. (*Beat.*) It doesn't work that way of course. One hopes it does, but you need a different heart to be a king. To parade as though all the world were following behind, to throw a shadow on the wall? An ant might be an elephant in the right light. Only, I was too much of a country boy to deceive myself. (*Beat.*) Yet hocus-pocus there I was. Sort of a tailor's idea of a king. Tall you see; I had loft. Higher than a man but lower than an obelisk. Call it the height of stupidity. (*Mocking his annunciation.*) 'You, there! That's right, you, Stretch there, the big one.' I wasn't modest but even to me it was preposterous. (*Beat.*) Besides, I must tell you, life was not so bad for us in Gibeah. We were in the livestock business. Asses, goats . . . (*Beat.*) I tried to interest my father in camels at one time but he didn't trust them. Very stubborn. An ass himself in some respects. "They're ugly," he said. "They eat too much." (*Beat.*) But there I was, God's own yokel, Saul of Benjamin, son of Kish. "Rabbi Samuel," I asked, "How shall I be king?" But that was the point of it, wasn't it. My God but he was slick. I went home to Gibeah in a holy fog. (*Pause.*) Yet it turned out I had a flair for this king business. Murderers are our muses. We imagine with their impunity our brilliance will be released. I was to be his Adam. "Only follow me," he said. (*Gesturing* SERVANT *closer.*) D'you know what that beggar did? Oh this is prime. (*Aside, to darkness.*) Oh shut up! (*To* SERVANT.) Out of nowhere he arrives in Gibeah one day with marching orders. God has spoken, let Israel be avenged on the Amalekites. Men, women, infants at the breast, cattle, servants—*Kherem!* Amalek must be destroyed utterly. As though it were possible. (*Aside.*) Bitter man, there is no such thing as slaying the Amalekites utterly. All you sow is the next generation of fanatics. Use your head at least, take hostage their leaders, their sheiks and holy men. It would have taken at least two generations for them to sort that out. (*To* SERVANT.) Do you know our own scripture forbids *kherem*? They drum this into our heads from birth. Always there will be Amalek. (*Aside.*) Vile man! What was your Torah except death! Enough of blood! I was tired of it. (*Beat.*) Oh don't go. My man here was planning canapés. (*To* SERVANT.) Ah well, it was always one thing or another, wasn't it? If not the Moabites, then the Ammonites. Or the Edomites were in Carmel, profaning the altar; raiding the granaries; polluting the cisterns; someone had thrown a dead dog in the well. Twenty years I reigned in that noise! The height of my powers, and a nervous wreck. I remember when these grim hills were my refuge, a kind of Sabbath for Saul when the Philistines marched. These are the gardens God made for His fugitives—aliens to pleasure, outcast monks, reclusives and madmen, eaters of carob. Here all was clear at least. I loved these dumb stones. (*Beat.*) Then, even that went to pieces. (*Pause.*) We were on holiday at Elah. You know the place, the wadi Essant? Well-watered, good grass—another stalemate but not unpleasant. One looked forward to these martial excursions. Who knows—was I a better general then? A month or so exchanging insults, fine weather, the stars in their courses. Forty days we faced them, they on their hillside, we on ours, and twice each day they would send their champion to challenge us winner-take-all, a brute of nature with the lungs of an ox and the manner of the knacker's yard. It was restful. I would have held our position for forty years if I'd had to. But suddenly this shepherd-boy appears, a golden boy smelling after his future. Lustrous with youth, glowing with ambition—an olive-eyed wonder, a greed of place like a plague of fire in his belly. He was perfect. We would send him against their champion like a stalking horse, the meanwhile send our raiders to their rear. Not a plan of genius, I grant, but we would take their pickets, burn their tents. What would it cost us, a shepherd-boy? (*Pause, shrugging.*) Go know. (*Miming slingshot.*) Wap! Cr-a-ack! Like it had eyes for pity's sake! Down goes the freak, seven feet if he's an inch, off comes his head, and our precious rabble go mad as dogs.

SERVANT: A great victory, Sire, *barukh ha'Shem*.

SAUL: 'A great victory.' We had them! The greatest army in the world were our servants. But do we even permit them surrender? I wonder now if victory becomes us. What would we do then? How would we know ourselves? Or is this our destiny, never a nation but perhaps a stage for the odd personality? Why else are we placed here like lizards on this heap of rocks? This land is not the Land of the Patriarchs alone. It is the land of Canaan, of Ishmael, of Moab, of Edom. How shall we be a great nation? Or is it that we do not know yet what our greatness shall consist of and in the meantime we piddle along imitating the goyim? (*Shrugging now as if to admit that political philosophy might not have been his forte.*) I knew my enemy though. An exquisite mind, teeming like an anthill, and utterly unhampered by principle or qualm. Think what a gift this would be! Pure ambition and an insatiable appetite for political chicanery. Dissembling was bread and wine for our young prince. He seemed incapable of narrowing his eyes. I would witness this with amazement in the man. You have to born with such talent. God Himself reaches down. (*Intimately; a confidence.*) He knew I knew, you see, yet he would gaze on me with such melting innocence that astonishment would overwhelm even my dread of this magic boy. The angels lived in those heifer's eyes. I even cast my spear at him one night—you understand, only to see what he would do. "Majesty," he cried, "you seem . . . tense." (*Bitter, rueful.*) I should have killed him on the spot. But for a time I thought better to keep him close to me. Better in the tent pissing out? Still, I should have killed him and had done with it. It was a mistake. It would have been one less thing to worry about. (*Beat.*) It's interesting, isn't it? In my place he wouldn't have hesitated. He would have had me killed by some expendable assassin and then raised my martyrdom to his greater glory. See, now, that's a king for you, he would have worked with it. That's the stuff of legend there. He would be blameless. (*Beat.*) He'll mourn us, too, that dog. I can hear him chanting for me. (*Simpering.*) '*Yisgadal, v'yiskadahsh—*'

SERVANT: They say he spared your life, Sire.

SAUL: Yes, quite. And thunder curdles milk. (*Beat.*) Which of those wondrous tales did you hear, tell me, the cave I entered without sending ahead, or the one about the waterjar, how he passed into the bedchamber of my tent—with a servant no less, through my lines, past my guards—disguised as a windsprite I take it. That business of the torn robe was inspired. Tasty details like that lend delicious plausibility to a tale. (*Beat.*) He never spared me! It was I who spared him, more's the pity. I, Saul, did that. I should have killed him when he was near me.

SERVANT: You loved him, Sire.

SAUL: Kings must not love, we must act. Men must be nothing but mirrors for us, for our vanity, our rage, the transparency of our ambition. That may have been the one great feat of my reign, realizing what an idiot I was.

SERVANT: Surely, Sire, a man can only do his best. Even a king, my Lord.

SAUL: (*Sighing as if fatigued.*) But plain men can't allow consolation to their kings— where's your brain? (*Pause.*) They stole my life from me! Who was Saul for thirty years? This is my punishment, that I am still alive. Why else am I not dead?

SERVANT: But this is confusion, Sire. All of nature turns to life.

SAUL: But death and life are the same crime on us. Didn't you know this? It must be so. No one asks to be brought into this world. We must be summoned to this lunacy, dragged in to satisfy some poor worm's vanity—to survive himself, to bequeath his miserable property. (*Pause.*) The problem, you see, is that the father is impatient with his sons. He loves them but they challenge him. They challenge his vanity. He wants their success but fears secretly they may be better than him. Without knowing it he rivals them. It encourages their enemies. Then, bethinking himself, he indulges their passions, confusing them, and this too encourages their enemies. In their defeat the father is himself defeated. (*Beat.*) It's interesting, though, isn't it? By God, I love a good story. One wants something with a point to it.

(*The lights fade to black.*)

Scene 3

(*Midnight. Stars in profusion. SAUL restlessly awake, drinking from the wineskin, watches the SERVANT calmly occupied at the fire with a bough of wind-drift, a desiccated shrub that he patiently dismembers into finger-length twigs, feeding some to the fire two or three at a time and arranging the rest in small fastidious bundles. As in everything the SERVANT does there is presumed value and purpose in this fire-tending, and a maddening indifference to context that must eventually provoke SAUL's impatience.*)

SAUL: Busy, busy, busy. (SERVANT *shrugs politely and prepares to reply, but SAUL is preemptive.*) Please—no more homilies, I can't bear it. (*Now apologetic.*) You see? I've no one to blame, so I blame you.

SERVANT: There is no need of this, Sire.

SAUL: There is, there is. A great fraud is done. Upon you more than me. You serve in better faith. (*Pause; gesturing off.*) Perhaps I could speak to them. (SERVANT *stiffens.*) I see. Now I've offended you. Well, suit yourself. (*Pause.*) They're brutal bastards but not unreasonable altogether. Perhaps—(*Abruptly agitated,* SERVANT *holds silence but breaks twigs more vigorously.*) Good. Enough. My wives would manage me this way. (SERVANT *laughs despite himself.*) Ah, you know about that, I see. How many did you have?

SERVANT: I? Why, only the one, Sire.

SAUL: That's plenty, believe me. And children and so on?

SERVANT: Near Mount Tabor, Sire.

SAUL: Ah, then you're of Issakhar. Daberet, Khessulot?

SERVANT:	Yes, Sire, near En Hador. I see you know it.
SAUL:	(*Rhetorically*.) What—Issakhar?
SERVANT:	My wife's father was Azariah ben Rakhmiel.
SAUL:	Who? Oh, I see. Yes. Very interesting. So, tell me, how does a man make a living in Issakhar?
SERVANT:	I don't know that he does, Sire.
SAUL:	Ah. Well, still, you were happy and all that.
SERVANT:	A herdsman for wages, Sire.
SAUL:	I see. Well, no harm in that.
SERVANT:	Though I farmed a bit. One does everything then.
SAUL:	Or it goes undone.
SERVANT:	Yes, exactly, Sire.
SAUL:	A good life that. I remember it. To sleep and not to brood. One sleeps at night with loved ones near.
SERVANT:	Yes, Sire, if the loved ones sleep.
SAUL:	Yes, I daresay that's true. If the loved ones sleep. You've a head on your shoulders temporarily.
SERVANT:	Poor men have little choice in this, Sire.
SAUL:	And yet are not so easily fooled. So might a poorer man make a better king.
SERVANT:	Perhaps, Sire, if the poor man were not satisfied so easily. But life is wonderfully simple for the poor.
SAUL:	So should all of us be blessed! I would have traded all I had only to see what was before my face. That's how it is when you're a fool, the things people do

seem so deliciously surprising to you. Astounding that not everyone wants the same simple peace of mind. The relief of woe? An end of sorrow? Yet here is a man and he hates, and here is another and he yearns, and here is one who will sell his brother, and here is a liar and a thief by preference, for the pleasure and perverse satisfaction they give him. Who would have thought the world so filled? A rapist in need of compassion here? It never penetrated this yokel skull there was such absence of character in this world. Why would people do such things, I asked. I knew we were capable of error of course—stealing, lying to evade punishment—but the notion that presumably honorable men would put honor at risk? It seemed too unnatural to me. Lifelong dissimulation? Campaigns of subversion? Imagine the tenacity this requires, generations of such extravagant pretense. With less effort goals of true merit might be achieved. Well, so, there was my virtue: incredulity, dullness. I was proud of this. God would be pleased with me.

SERVANT: Perhaps He was, Sire.

SAUL: Yes, well, let's hope so. Not so much as my enemies were. (*Pause.*) You're awfully smug though, aren't you? (*Impatiently.*) Well, tell me then, what will they say of me in Issakhar do you think? Not that it troubles me, but you see, it's the time one puts in, isn't it? I mean, any man is apt to care for the things that occupied him, wouldn't you say? I mean, it scarcely matters what it might have been that he cared for past a certain point. (*Beat.*) Not that they won't survive well-enough. They always do, don't they? Bloody idiots. You see, that's all the trouble with us. One doesn't need any more in the end than any other dumb creature. The rest is all appetite. It's willfulness. We have a taste for the corrupt. We like our agéd meats and over-ripe cheese. (*Beat.*) Well, what will they say of me, for pity's sake? (*Beat.*) Yes, yes, I know all that. People reduce things to matters they can understand. He was mad that Saul, he was frivolous. He was cruel, jealous, vain—

SERVANT: Moody.

SAUL: I beg your pardon?

SERVANT: A rumor, Sire.

SAUL: Moody! (*Suddenly plaintive.*) I mean, would I be a cautionary tale for the young for example? My God, how am I different than any of these other jumped-up kings of Canaan? Every pisspot and sheepstall here has a king. They never even wanted a king, come to that, all they wanted was a judge who could keep his hands out of their pockets.

SERVANT: Still you are their king. What would you have of them, Sire?

SAUL: Shall I tell you? All right. I want an apology! It seems not too much to ask. They wasted me. Look how my foolish life is spent. What do we have except this?

SERVANT: My poor king.

SAUL: Poor enough. I tried to limit my life to what I knew. Now I'd only like someone to tell me what all the excitement was about. I have these questions, you see. (*Pause.*) Goddamnit, there were a thousand things I might have done. I thought about camels at one time. Have I spoken of this? Asses were our business of course—camels aren't practical in these broken hills. But we could have expanded. We had Amalekite breeding stock. (*Beat.*) Not that my life has been meaningless entirely I suppose. Only that it's had so little to do with me. Although perhaps it's easier to see that way, having not been my own. (*Beat.*) But I miss the dream my life began. I feel it might have been precious to me. One feels a regret for having done so little after all, of not leaving a proper seal on things. I might have let our enemies make a nation of us. But there was no map, lad. The priests owned our history. I wasn't bad for someone who never knew what he was doing, but we ran out of time too soon, we faltered too much. (*Beat.*) I look now at our bickering tribes and wonder if this was not our purpose in the world, to show merely that people might quarrel yet live and not slaughter one another? It seems modest enough spoken out, yet having done my share of slaughter, I must say this seems no small thing. It would appear we have the brains to advance but not the humility. (*Beat.*) We're like children this way, aren't we? Another's wisdom isn't good enough for us. Each has to do everything himself, so learn everything from the beginning. It dooms us. It dooms all of us. (*Beat.*) Or is it only that I would take everyone with me? (*Beat.*) I only wish now that I will not be afraid at the end, that I will remember myself well. I don't want to be bitter, you see, to be found with a sour expression on my face.

SERVANT: But God is merciful, Sire.

SAUL: You wish. (*Relenting.*) Well, perhaps so. It's only that I never hated my life so much that I felt faith like yours so necessary to me. I believed there was honor among men—some men. I had memories that were precious to me. I was not ashamed of myself yet. (*Not unkindly.*) You truly believe all that twaddle though, don't you?

SERVANT: Sire, I cannot account for the world otherwise.

SAUL: That's not faith, lad. You're just building an altar of your ignorance.

SERVANT: All faith must rest on doubt, Sire. Faith would not be real unless it were challenged.

SAUL: So you doubt, yet in your doubt you believe.

SERVANT: I must, Sire. My heart will not permit me not to believe in God.

SAUL: Fool, then what difference does it make?

SERVANT: I suppose it makes a difference to me, Sire.

SAUL: Ach! Listen to me. If one must believe in spite of one's doubts, then wouldn't it take more courage still not to believe?

SERVANT: I don't know if courage is the question, Sire.

SAUL: No, of course not. Nor do I.

SERVANT: Perhaps, Sire, as you say, humility is the question.

SAUL: You think that? Well, who knows? I know we must believe in something. My God, it would be impossible to live at all if death were inconsolable. But why in this Almighty of ours if He divides us so? If not for this Almighty God perhaps we might believe in each other. Now there we might have something. (*Weeping, gradually overtaken by grief.*) Tell me, lad, do you forgive your king?

SERVANT: I, Sire?

SAUL: I think I liked Him better in His infancy, when He had the modesty still to admit

His mistakes. There was greatness in that, He started beautifully. But since then (*gesturing*) all downhill, like an oxcart salvaged from the rubble of an avalanche. Mended axles, wheels of differing size. He's a patchwork, a bumbler. Who tells us to imitate our enemies? Is it God who gives us these hideous marching orders? Our childish smears are all over this wretched, broken-hearted God. Often I wonder how He can bear us. He must look on us with the helplessness only a father could know. What can He spare us? Can we teach one another? Or are we doomed to repeat ourselves without end by our nature? I tell you it fills me with pity that God should be so weak.

(*The lights fade to black.*)

Scene 4

(*Imperceptibly later, during the starless hours before light. The fire gutters like an oil lamp.*)

SAUL: (*At length, wiping his eyes.*) Well, what is a land except a cemetery? (*Pause.*) I must not grieve. It does not become a king to grieve. (*Beat.*) Nor does death seem so bad to me. I know it's absurd, but I've missed that rest plain men enjoy. Waking without having slept, weeping but not from grief, a kind of confusion would seize me in life. My heart ached. Like a dog seeking his center I circled myself. I missed that hope people placed in me. That hollowness of soul—I knew what that meant. No one dreamed of me now. I could not hold to things. Visions, ideas I once held in my mind, these slipped from my grasp as if a wind were bearing them away.

SERVANT: (*Peering deeply into Saul's face.*) Sire?

SAUL: (*Seeming to gaze beyond him.*) Yet it gives me peace to say these things, as if I could recall happiness in my foolish life. I wonder now if perhaps we fail to value peace dearly enough. Mere relief is the happiness of the rabble—we hold it in contempt. Yet isn't this what ecstasy is, this letting go? To feel one's fatigue with pleasure, to feel safe?

SERVANT: (*Fervently.*) Oh merciful God!

SAUL: (*Dryly.*) Yes, I'm sure. (*Beat.*) I must say though, I seem to have few regrets. I only wish that I might have held my illusions longer. Apparently life must be a dream to live it, to need that luster we give it. But I feel quiet. A strange calm empties me. There's contentment in the end of hope. (*Beat.*) It's odd, isn't it? I pursued power in my life, but even with its achievement I felt terrified. I choked with it, like a beating of wings in my chest. Dreams of unending darkness would take me—of falling, of nakedness. Now all these seem so far from me.

SERVANT: (*Abandoned.*) Sire?

SAUL: (*Feeling at his face.*) Only, I seem to know not who this is. (*Beat.*) One watches a fire consume a crop—how shall one not grieve? Yet all our years burn in fire—all that was done, all that was not done—and only a great boredom consumes me. For if I could resume my life what would matter to me, knowing I must die? Would I mend it? How would I mend it? The world does not begin or end with us. (*Beat.*) I see now how always I was outside this world. It makes the leaving almost redundant, doesn't it? As if the only world I loved was a vision I take away with me—moments of relief for Saul. With my sons. A woman whose name I no longer know. All that seems left for dead is the world of other men's delusions, invasions of our privacy.

SERVANT: (*Abruptly, seeking occupation.*) Perhaps I should look to your dressings now, Sire.

SAUL: (*Distracted.*) Excuse me? (*Pause, then gesturing.*) Ah, of course, my recent mummification. You see for a moment I didn't grasp your meaning. (*Beat.*) Man, what in the world are you talking about?

SERVANT: (*Seeking to draw* SAUL *to the fire.*) With your permission, Sire.

SAUL: But what are you doing? Are you mad?

SERVANT: But your wounds, Sire!

SAUL: (*Gently freeing himself. Calm, even sympathetic.*) Lad, believe me, I understand earlier why you wouldn't lift a hand, truly I do, but this interference now, isn't this only selfishness?

(*The lights fade to black.*)

Scene 5

(Morning. A graying dawn, shot with pink. Birds are heard—daws, crows. Huddled trembling against a far wall of the cave the SERVANT stands in prayer, his cape draped like a mourning cloak over his head, while SAUL, suffering him, crouches at the fire.)

SAUL: And so, life goes on. Who'd have thought it?

SERVANT: *(Hammering at his breast.)* For the sin of pride, Oh merciful God! For polluting the Sabbath! For the sin of greed! The pursuit of comfort!

SAUL: Still, it's a bit of relief, isn't it, this knowledge of nothing left to do.

SERVANT: For witnessing falsely! For the spilling of innocent blood!

SAUL: *(Pointedly.)* The living seem only to get in the way.

SERVANT: *(Louder.)* For the sin of mockery, of lewdness!

SAUL: *(Bellowing.)* Oh what does it take to get some peace around here! Who are you praying to, why do you keep bothering Him?

SERVANT: It comforts me, Sire.

SAUL: Comfort! And what of God's comfort? You're shitting yourself with your filthy remorse? Offer Him courtesy for pity's sake. If you entered a great man's house would you first not wash your feet? Be gracious to your precious God.

SERVANT: I haven't gotten to that, Sire.

SAUL: Well what are you waiting for! We'll be pegged like two sheepskins before you're done.

SERVANT: Yes, Sire.

SAUL: Yes, Sire—no, Sire. You're not listening to me!

SERVANT: I am afraid, Majesty.

SAUL: Look, I know that, but what shall we do with it? One grows as tired of fear as of anything else. Enough of fear. We do what we must. When we know the task, fear is only a burden to us. (SERVANT *remains distraught.*) Oh for pity's sake. You act as if God were done with you. What if it's God Who weeps and needs courage? What if it's God Who needs consolation? Can't we show a bit of mercy to Him? Surely God, too, must need kindness. God knows He must need us for something. Why else would He bother Himself?

SERVANT: But I am not worthy, my Lord.

SAUL: But you must be worthy if there is a God. Would you have Him lose His hope in us? Whose fault is it that we make a cesspool of this world? Take Him in your arms, lad. It would be blasphemy to hold your God to account.

SERVANT: (*Mechanically.*) Yes, Sire.

SAUL: Yes, well, thank God for that then. (*Pausing; suspicious now.*) And no questions? No more of this pathetic mewling?

SERVANT: No, Sire. (*Pause.*) We should go now though. (*Bolting.*) There's just time, Sire. Permit me.

SAUL: (*Open-mouthed as the SERVANT frantically stuffs their musettes.*) Go—? You poor jackass, go where? (*Heedless, SERVANT continues to pack.*) Man, why haven't we heard a jackal all night? Just stick your silly head out of that hole—you'll be yoked like an ox in half a breath. (*Abruptly.*) Damn you, stand to—I'll gut you myself! Can't you hear me? It's over. The Jezreel Plain is a Philistine parade-ground. Your own bloody David went over. Your little bride in Issakhar is probably on her honeymoon by now. (*SERVANT weeping.*) Yes, well, I'm sorry for that. But we're done here. (*SERVANT resumes his station.*) Now, are there any questions?

SERVANT: No, Sire.

             (*Abruptly a scuffing overhead of leather on stone, a chink of metal.*)

SAUL: (*Gesturing hand to mouth, whispering as he takes up lance and buckler.*) Sharply now, attend me. (*Scuffing continues. Now a rattle of falling gravel.*) Listen to those dogs. (*Spitting to moisten his mouth, then aloud, pounding the shield with his spear.*) Goyim! Bastards! Hear me, Goyim! I am Saul of Benjamin, son of Kish! I knew my father! (*Trickles of sunlit dust drift into view. Abruptly SAUL throws spear and shield aside, then, drawing his sword, examines it at arm's length as if considering its purchase.*) Well, soon we'll know everything, won't we?

SERVANT: (*In turn, hesitantly drawing his sword, then looking to SAUL.*) Sire?

SAUL: Now what?

SERVANT: Thank you, Sire.

> (*Pause. From SAUL a nod of acknowledgment, followed by an exchange of modest salutes. BOTH withdraw inward now, gathering themselves, turning their swords, going to their knees. Extended pause, light dimming, then black.*)

END

Bill Teitelbaum's work has appeared in U.S. journals such as *Bayou, Crab Creek, The Oregon Literary Review,* and *Riversedge,* as well as abroad in *Arabesques Review* and *Carillon.* His play *The Death of Saul* is the first in a cycle of one-acts called *Kings* about the early monarchs of Palestine. Bill lives in Lincolnwood, Illinois, a small Midwestern village adjacent to the larger Midwestern village of Chicago.

Bill Teitelbaum

Women in Heat

The title of Rich Orloff's play does double duty, being appropriate both to the setting—Key West in July—and to the sexual fervor experienced by at least two of the three main characters, Kim, Marge, and Charlene. Vacationing at a condominium owned by Marge's uncle, the three twenty-something Midwesterners find themselves in a setting where "nothing looks like Ohio," and where they may, as Kim says, "discover taste buds you never knew about."

Women in Heat explores the motif of "the stranger in a strange land" that has served the comic visions of writers from Shakespeare to Oscar Wilde to L. Frank Baum. Key West becomes a place where the previously unthinkable is not only speakable, but doable. Orloff's clever dialogue and inventive plotting enliven every page; and his major comic revelation—by Kim, who has initially appeared to join Marge in counseling good sense in response to Charlene's cheerful promiscuity—spins the play toward an unexpected celebration of kicking over the traces, acknowledging the disorderly impulse that animates the comic spirit.

Rich Orloff

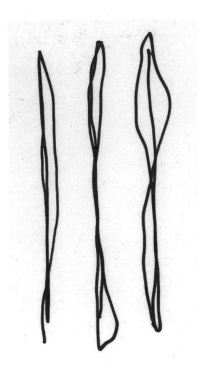

Women in Heat

CHARACTERS KIM: a woman in her twenties.

MARGE: a woman in her twenties, more shy than Kim.

CHARLENE: a woman in her twenties, less shy than Kim.

MATTHEW: a man in his twenties.

SETTING The backyard patio of a beachfront condominium in Key West, Florida.

TIME Morning.

(*The backyard patio of a beachfront condominium in Key West, Florida. A few lounge chairs, tables and such. The sounds of a beach.*)

(*KIM enters from inside the apartment. She wears a light robe and carries a cup of coffee. Not fully awake, she looks like she's sorting something out, something which makes her confused, happy, concerned, a bit nervous, and in a word, overwhelmed.*)

(*MARGE enters. She's in a jogging outfit and is completely exhausted. No person has ever been covered with more sweat than MARGE is.*)

MARGE: It's so hot.

KIM: Your uncle told you Key West was hot in July.

MARGE: He didn't tell me it'd be this hot. And humid. It's so humid.

KIM: How was your jog, Marge?

MARGE: Three miles. Three sweaty miles.

KIM: Congratulations.

MARGE: I think I've gone down a dress size from water loss.

KIM: I made some coffee.

MARGE: I just want to rest a bit, grab a book, and go into the refrigerator.

(*CHARLENE enters. She wears sunglasses and the kind of short, sexy outfit a woman would wear for a hot night of dancing.*)

CHARLENE: It's so hot; I love it!

KIM: Good morning.

MARGE: Are you just getting in?

CHARLENE: Mm-hmmmm.

KIM: Fun night?

CHARLENE: Mm-hmmmm.

KIM: Congratulations.

CHARLENE: Isn't this place great? I think Key West is God's way of balancing Dayton, Ohio.

MARGE: I don't think the Lord works like that.

CHARLENE: Too bad. He'd be more popular if he did.

MARGE: The Lord doesn't do things so we'll be happy.

CHARLENE: I know. He created parents.

KIM: Where were you all night?

CHARLENE: You remember that guy I was dancing with?

KIM: Uh-huh.

CHARLENE: Well, we both got so sweaty dancing that we decided the only way to cool off was with a moonlight swim.

MARGE: There was no moon out last night.

CHARLENE: There was when he took his shorts off.

KIM: You two went skinny-dipping?

CHARLENE: Uh-huh. And I tell you, between the surf and the waves and the stars and the breeze and the rum and his body—

KIM: Did you—

CHARLENE: Mm-hmmmm.

MARGE: In the water?

CHARLENE: Mm-hmmmm.

MARGE: Wasn't it salty?

CHARLENE: So's a margarita, and I never turn those down, either.

KIM: Couldn't wait till you got back on land, huh?

CHARLENE: I could, but apparently time and tide wait for no man.

MARGE: Charlene, do you ever think about what you do?

CHARLENE: Of course. That's why I drink.

MARGE: Do you ever wonder if you can afford to lose more brain cells?

CHARLENE: No, I've already lost the brain cells that worry about such things.

MARGE: I thought so.

KIM: Now girls—

CHARLENE: And how was your evening, Marge?

MARGE: I finished *Wuthering Heights*.

KIM: How was it?

MARGE: It was very insightful and moving.

CHARLENE: And how you plan to use this moving insight?

KIM: Charlene.

CHARLENE: Well, she's the first person who's ever come to Key West so she can catch up on her reading.

MARGE: I'm improving my mind. What are you improving?

CHARLENE: My stamina.

MARGE: Have you ever considered jogging?

CHARLENE: Have you ever considered loosening up?

KIM: Girls—

MARGE: You know, when Kim asked if you could come, I said fine, as long as she doesn't start getting on my case—

CHARLENE: I think you started getting on my case first—

KIM: Ladies—

MARGE: I'm just asking questions—

CHARLENE: No, you're judging—

MARGE: Well so are you—

KIM: Will you keep it down? I, I, I . . . I have company that's still asleep.

CHARLENE: There's someone in your bedroom?

KIM: Mmmmore or less.

CHARLENE: Is he cute?

KIM: More or less.

CHARLENE: Is he decent looking?

KIM: More or less.

MARGE: Is he human?

KIM: More or less.

CHARLENE: An anatomically correct blow-up doll?

KIM: No.

MARGE: A woman?

KIM: No.

CHARLENE: Soooooo?

KIM: "He" has four legs.

CHARLENE: Don't tell me you had a goat; it's been done.

KIM: I . . . I had a threesome last night.

                        (*The next two lines are spoken simultaneously.*)

MARGE: You what?!

CHARLENE: Right on!

MARGE: And they're still here?!

KIM: Yep.

MARGE: You brought two strangers into my uncle's condo?

KIM: Sorry.

CHARLENE: You agreed we could entertain men.

MARGE:	I meant one at a time.
CHARLENE:	I give Kim my proxy.
MARGE:	You know, I'm responsi—
KIM:	I'm sorry, Marge, I just—it just made the most sense at the time.
MARGE:	But—
KIM:	I knew I'd feel safer here.
MARGE:	You really had sex with two guys?
KIM:	Uh-huh.
MARGE:	But that's not like you.
KIM:	I know.
MARGE:	You had two guys at the same time?
KIM:	Well, some of it was at the same time, some of it was taking turns.
MARGE:	I can't imagine doing such a thing.
CHARLENE:	That's what's great about drugs. They stretch the imagination.
KIM:	I wasn't drunk. Or stoned.
MARGE:	What were you?
KIM:	Curious, I guess.
MARGE:	You know what they said about curiosity.
CHARLENE:	It's good for the pussy?

MARGE: Look, just because you don't care about safety—

CHARLENE: I care.

MARGE: Oh, yeah? With your sex life, you could give a yeast infection to the Pillsbury Doughboy.

CHARLENE: Look, you little b—

KIM: Will you two cool it?! Do you want to wake one or more of them up?

CHARLENE: Okay, details, I want details. What happened? Tell me everything. Spare nothing. Feel free to use drawings if necessary.

KIM: Well, I was dancing with these two guys, this totally cute white guy and this totally awesome black guy, and at one point I said, "I can't choose between you," and the white guy said, "You don't have to." And I laughed—and they didn't. They were smiling. Biiiiig smiles. And I thought, this will make a good vacation story.

CHARLENE: And then?

MARGE: Charlene, don't you have enough lurid stories from your own sex life?

CHARLENE: I have a vacancy in this category. So how was it?

KIM: Well, they liked it.

MARGE: Of course they'd—

KIM: Before they fell asleep, they suggested an encore—tonight.

(*The next two lines are spoken simultaneously*)

MARGE: They what?!

CHARLENE: You rock!

MARGE: You're not going to, are you?

KIM:	I, I don't know. It's not like last night was a romantic evening. I didn't think, "Gee, I hope I get both their phone numbers." But it was a, a—
CHARLENE:	Turn on.
KIM:	(*Correcting.*) An adventure. There was something about being massaged by four hands, being kissed by four lips, grabbing both their—
MARGE:	I think I've heard enough.
CHARLENE:	I haven't.
KIM:	Just once, I wanted to go too far. All my life I've been so—Ohio. I think Ohio. I dress Ohio. Just once I wanted—
CHARLENE:	An out-of-state experience.
KIM:	Yeah. That's what I wanted. Yeah. I think.
MARGE:	Are you okay?
KIM:	I think so.
CHARLENE:	You don't regret it?
KIM:	No.
MARGE:	And you're really thinking of doing it again?
KIM:	I have no idea. No, no let me correct that. I have too many ideas. And they're shouting at me all at once: "It was a mistake" "It was fun" "It's bad" "It's good." Ever since I woke up, it's like there's a debate squad in my brain.
CHARLENE:	Hey, if you had a good time, why not go for it?
KIM:	Because, well, lots of people do things once. Once is experimentation. Twice is—lifestyle.

CHARLENE: Your problem is that you think too much.

KIM: Maybe you're right.

MARGE: No, no, keep thinking, keep thinking.

KIM: You think I did the wrong thing, don't you, Marge?

MARGE: It's—I just, I just think we live in a time when everybody's looking in the wrong direction for happiness. If you're not happy, pierce your navel and tattoo your back. And when the happiness fades, pierce your eyebrow and tattoo your butt. And when that happiness fades, pierce your tongue and tattoo your arm. Pierce this, tattoo that; pierce this, tattoo that. And one morning you wake up and you're still not happy, but your body looks like Swiss cheese with decals.

KIM: I don't know. I just don't know.

CHARLENE: I say, stop thinking and go for it.

KIM: I can't stop thinking.

MARGE: You sound scared.

KIM: I am scared.

CHARLENE: What's there to be scared of?

KIM: I . . . I liked it.

CHARLENE: So?

KIM: I was just planning to do it, I wasn't planning to like it.

CHARLENE: So what's wrong with liking it?

MARGE: I like ice cream, but I think one scoop at a time is plenty.

CHARLENE: Tell me, when you're offered M & M's, do you eat one "M"?

MARGE: I allow myself one of each color.

CHARLENE: That's exactly what Kim did last night.

MARGE: Well, in my experience—

CHARLENE: What experience?

MARGE: I'll have you know more than one guy has told me I'm great in the sack!

CHARLENE: Which one of you was wearing the sack?

KIM: Hey.

MARGE: (*To* CHARLENE.) You know, you used to be a nice person.

CHARLENE: And I used to wear braids, big deal.

MARGE: Really, Charlene—

CHARLENE: I got sick of being limited by my own fears.

MARGE: I didn't know you had fears.

CHARLENE: Of course I do. Big ones. But I hate it when the fear wins. Fear is bossy; fear's obnoxious. Fear is like the worst older brother you can imagine. So I refuse to be stopped by it.

MARGE: What about the night you ended up in the E.R. with alcohol poisoning?

CHARLENE: The EMT guy was really cute.

MARGE: They had to pump your stomach.

CHARLENE: And it cured me of any desire to become a bulimic.

MARGE: You know, Charlene, sometimes I wonder if you even like sex, or if you just like rebelling.

CHARLENE: At least I have adventures.

MARGE: I've had adventures. But unlike some people, I don't send out group e-mails about them afterwards.

CHARLENE: When did you have adventures?

MARGE: It's not important.

CHARLENE: When?

MARGE: When I was with Barry.

KIM: Really?

CHARLENE: Details, I want details.

MARGE: I'd rather not reduce it to the level of gossip.

CHARLENE: Gossip is not a level reduced. It's a level achieved.

MARGE: It's none of your business.

CHARLENE: I can't believe you and Barry did anything worth gossiping about.

MARGE: Okay. I don't want to go into all the gory details, but at least once it involved ice cream. And one scoop was enough.

CHARLENE: Did you add nuts and a cherry?

MARGE: My point is, I've tried things. Lots of things. But when we broke up, I didn't think, well, "At least I've had adventures." I thought, "I'm no closer to happiness than I've ever been." (*Moving towards tears*.) And, and then I looked at the chocolate sauce on my linens, and the scratch marks on the bed post, and I thought about all the money we spent on rope, and waffles, and, and I wondered, what's the point? And then I watched the videotapes and . . .

KIM: Marge . . .

MARGE:	(*Breaking down.*) I hate this generation. I hate the pressures, the expectations. I'm so sick of having to be part of "The Young and the Horny."
CHARLENE:	(*Warmly.*) Hey . . . You want me to fix you a drink?
MARGE:	A good Christian never drinks this early.
CHARLENE:	How about if I turn some water into a piña colada?
KIM:	We should've gone to the Poconos like last year. I never question anything in the Poconos.
CHARLENE:	I never get horny in the Poconos.
MARGE:	Charlene, does the sacredness of sex mean nothing to you?
CHARLENE:	Au contraire. I think sex is God's way of saying, "You can only tan during daylight, so here's something to do at night."
MARGE:	You're shameless, aren't you?
CHARLENE:	No, but I'm willing to fake it till I get there.
MARGE:	Well, regardless of what we pretend, I think sex without love is—
CHARLENE:	Quicker.
MARGE:	Kim, honestly, what if you're in a serious relationship someday and the guy finds out what you did?
KIM:	I've asked myself that.
MARGE:	And?
KIM:	It's on my very, very long list of "I don't know."
CHARLENE:	Well, I think he'd be turned on.
MARGE:	I think he'd be pissed off.

CHARLENE: He'd get excited.

MARGE: He might get excited, but he won't stick around long enough to help you remove the maple syrup off the bathmat.

CHARLENE: Look, she's not hurting anyone, and she's not being hurt.

MARGE: (*Pointing to her heart*.) And how do you know how this is affecting her in here?

CHARLENE: She can handle it. She's strong.

MARGE: She's sensitive.

CHARLENE: She's adventurous.

KIM: (*Overlapping with the others*.)—Hey come on—

MARGE: She's mature.

CHARLENE: She's young.

KIM: —I'm right here—

MARGE: She's got a good head.

CHARLENE: And a great body.

KIM: Will you two stop it?! You two act like you know exactly who I am. Well, I don't. I thought I did, and, and . . . Damn it, why is it that every time my body has fun, my brain sets off an alarm?

(MATTHEW *enters*.)

MATTHEW: Am I interrupting something?

KIM: Yes, please do.

MATTHEW: Good morning.

KIM: Good morning.

(MATTHEW *kisses* KIM *lightly. Then an awkward silence.*)

CHARLENE: I'm Kim's friend Char—

KIM: Oh, right. Seth—

MATTHEW: I'm Matthew. Seth's still sleeping.

KIM: Right. Matthew, I'd like you to meet my friends Charlene and Marge.

MATTHEW: Pleased to meet you.

CHARLENE: Pleased to meet you.

MARGE: Pleased to meet you.

(*A bit of silence.*)

MATTHEW: Everyone seems very pleased this morning.

CHARLENE: I bet you are.

KIM: Um, there's coffee in the kitchen if you'd like some.

MATTHEW: Sounds good to me . . . Ladies.

(MATTHEW *exits.* CHARLENE *gives KIM a "thumbs up."*)

MARGE: He seems nice.

CHARLENE: You were expecting horns and a tail?

MARGE: No.

CHARLENE: Just complete horn?

MARGE: Kim, do you want us to leave you and Matthew al—

KIM: No, no, that's okay.

CHARLENE: We'll be glad to—

KIM: No, no, you don't have to—

MARGE: What a world in which just being alone with someone is scarier than sex.

(MATTHEW *returns, with coffee*.)

MATTHEW: Good coffee.

KIM: Thank you.

(*Another awkward silence*.)

MATTHEW: So is this your first time in Key West?

CHARLENE: Yep.

MARGE: Yes.

MATTHEW: Having a good time?

MARGE: Yes.

CHARLENE: Yep.

MATTHEW: Okay, and now on to the short essay questions.

KIM: I told them about last night.

MATTHEW: Ah, that does tend to turn some women monosyllabic.

MARGE: Oh, you've done this a lot?

MATTHEW: Not that often.

CHARLENE: Not that adventurous?

MATTHEW:	Not that lucky.
MARGE:	That must be so disappointing.
MATTHEW:	Ah, you're one of those types.
MARGE:	What type?
MATTHEW:	The "If I don't do it, it must be wrong" type.
MARGE:	I've done things that are wrong.
CHARLENE:	She's been banned from Haagen-Dazs.
MATTHEW:	I'm not sure I—
KIM:	You had to be there.
MATTHEW:	Well, if it was during the last twelve hours, I like where I was.
KIM:	Thank you.

(*A long silence. Nobody knows what to say next.*)

MATTHEW:	(*Whispering to* KIM.) If you'd like me to say something innocuous just to fill space, just let me know.
KIM:	Thank you.
MATTHEW:	You say "Thank you" way too often.
KIM:	My parents believed politeness was one of the greatest of virtues.
MATTHEW:	What else did they believe in?
KIM:	They were too polite to tell me.
MATTHEW:	You weren't polite last night.
KIM:	I know.

MATTHEW:	You were courteous, but not polite.
KIM:	Thank you. (*Off his look.*) I'm sorry. It's my inner "Ohio."
MATTHEW:	Did you think about our offer for tonight?
KIM:	Oh, yeah. Think, think, think.
MATTHEW:	So how'd you like to go dancing with us?
KIM:	I . . . I don't know. (*To MARGE and CHARLENE.*) You two want to join us?
	(*A long beat.*)
CHARLENE:	Define "join us."
KIM:	Good question.
CHARLENE:	(*To MATTHEW.*) Shouldn't you check with your friend to—
MATTHEW:	I'm sure Seth would love for you to both join us.
MARGE:	Define "join us."
MATTHEW:	(*Thinks, then.*) Many possibilities, no pressure.
KIM:	So?
CHARLENE:	Well um uh well um um uh, I will if Marge will.
MARGE:	Charlene, I know you don't accept that I was born again—
MATTHEW:	I don't think I'm breaking any Commandments.
MARGE:	You don't?
MATTHEW:	I figure what I'm doing is the opposite of coveting thy neighbor's wife.
CHARLENE:	How so?

MATTHEW:	One, you're not married, and two, I'm sharing.
KIM:	I didn't realize I ended up with a Biblical scholar.
MATTHEW:	That's me.
MARGE:	Have you ever read the Bible?
MATTHEW:	Not cover-to-cover, but most of the "thou shalts."
MARGE:	And you still feel it's okay to engage in, in, in—
MATTHEW:	Pleasure?
MARGE:	Pleasure without commitment. Pleasure without intimacy. Pleasure without love.
MATTHEW:	She came just as much as we did.
CHARLENE:	He's a saint.
MATTHEW:	I don't think I'm a saint, but I do think the Bible completely supports what I do.
MARGE:	Which verse?
MATTHEW:	"Do unto others as you'd have them do unto you."
KIM:	You have an unusual interpretation of the Golden Rule.
MATTHEW:	Works for me.
KIM:	I can tell.
MATTHEW:	When I went to Bible camp—
MARGE:	You went to Bible camp?
MATTHEW:	Of course. That's where I learned to make out.
CHARLENE:	Sounds like a fun camp.

MATTHEW: What can I say? Some girls were waiting for deliverance; others delivered.

MARGE: Well, none of the girls I knew made out in Bible camp.

CHARLENE: I did.

KIM: So did I.

MARGE: You did?

KIM: Once.

MARGE: Was that the night you came in late and said you had been star gazing?

KIM: Uh-huh.

MARGE: You lied to me.

CHARLENE: That was a long time a—

KIM: I didn't lie, I just . . . Marshall Mays asked me to look at the stars with him. And I sorta liked him, and I knew I could beat him up if he tried anything funny, so I said yes. And we snuck out and looked at the stars, and he put his arm around me, and he just laid it there. Thump. And then he kissed me, timidly. And we kept kissing, like two eager but inept idiots.

CHARLENE: Good ol' Bible camp.

KIM: And when I got back to my cabin, what I remember most was, was not how kissing felt, but how afraid I was.

CHARLENE: Afraid of getting caught?

KIM: No, much bigger than that.

MARGE: Afraid of going to Hell?

KIM: No.

MATTHEW:	Afraid you enjoyed it?
KIM:	No, it was more like, like, I don't know, like like one of those nameless fears, you know, the kind you feel when you're someplace that's totally unfamiliar, and all you've experienced and all you've been taught still isn't enough to guide you.
CHARLENE:	Did you and Marshall ever make ou—
KIM:	I never looked him in the face again.
MARGE:	Well, he was much taller than you.
MATTHEW:	If you want, Kim, tonight we can—
KIM:	Look out there. The palm trees. The colors. The ocean. You can look for miles and miles and miles, and nothing looks like Ohio.
MARGE:	I think last night was a lot more stressful than you've admitted.
KIM:	All I wanted was a taste of Key West, one taste, and then I'd return home to a healthy diet of Ohio. But what do you do when you discover you have taste buds you never knew about? . . . (*To her friends.*) What do you do? (*Looking out.*) What do you do?
	(KIM *looks at* CHARLENE *and* MARGE. *Neither says anything, but both reply warmly. For a moment, quiet.*)
MATTHEW:	(*Whispering to* KIM.) If you'd like me to say something innocuous to fill space—
KIM:	That's okay. I kind of like the stillness.
	(*The lights fade to black.*)

END

Rich Orloff has written ten full-length plays, mostly comedies, and oodles of one-acts. His plays have won the 1994 Playwrights First Award, 1995 Festival of Emerging American Theatre, 1997 InterPlay International Play Festival, 1998 Tennessee Williams Playwriting Competition, 1999 Theatre Conspiracy New Play Contest, 2000 Abeles Foundation Playwrights Award, 2002 Pickering Award for Playwriting Excellence, 2004 New Voice Play Festival, and a few others. Four of his one-act comedies have been published in the annual *Best American Short Plays* anthology and Playscripts (www.playscripts.com) has published seven collections of his work. For more on Rich's plays, visit www.richorloff.com.

Women In Heat is part of *Incredible Sex*, a trio of one-act comedies published by Playscripts, Inc. All information concerning performance rights can be found at www.playscripts.com

Milk

Michael Hemmingson's play offers three scenes—each with its own title—that can stand alone or function as a one-act of cumulative satirical power.

The first scene, "Biology," depicts a brief encounter on a subway train between Desmond Rosenthal, who appears in all three scenes, and Whit, whom Des may have met before as a fellow passenger. In a very short time, the two men discuss women, war, and biological imperatives, revealing a good deal about their lives and relationships. Des declares that he has killed men in "the war," that he is conducting an affair with his supervisor's wife, and that he is separated from his own wife. Whit notes ruefully that "we have to sleep with women" and admits that he has never killed; but he also volunteers that he has bought a gun and fantasizes about killing his wife. Hemmingson creates in the scene a disturbing undercurrent of suppressed violence, but as the men part we sense that they are as likely to remain paralyzed as to act.

385

"Milk," the play's title scene, brings Des together with Sheila, from whom—as we learned in "Biology"—he is separated but who "gets his mail." Des is Sheila's third husband, and appears to be the one with the power to hurt her and for whom she cares enough to feel and express consuming anger. This encounter, like the one between Des and Whit, vibrates with potential violence, and prepares the way for "Teat," in which—as the title suggests—Des finds his way back to the source, his mother Dr. Laura Rosenthal, celebrated talk show host and novelist (with obvious reference to "Dr. Laura" Schlesinger). Though Laura is the quintessential contemporary version thereof, the scene decisively reveals her nonetheless to be a typical Jewish mother, concerned with her son's every action, vindicated by the failure of his marriage to a *shiksa*, and eager for a nice Jewish grandchild. The play ends with Laura exhorting Des to drink his milk.

The fierce intensity of this play's satirical vision reaches beyond its ethnic roots to the implication that men and women may well be caught in a biologically determined Oedipal trap.

Michael Hemmingson

Milk

CHARACTERS	DES ROSENTHAL.
	WHIT.
	SHEILA.
	LAURA ROSENTHAL.
SETTING	Over there.
TIME	A few days ago.
SCENES	"Biology." A subway. DES and WHIT.
	"Milk." An apartment. DES and SHEILA.
	"Teat." A restaurant. DES and LAURA.

"Biology"

(*A subway train.*)

WHIT: So: how are things?

DES: Things aren't good. There are problems.

WHIT: At home? At work?

DES: At work. There are problems at work. I've been sleeping with my supervisor's wife.

WHIT: And your supervisor has discovered this?

DES: I don't know. If he has, he doesn't seem to mind. He's always smiling at me now, and touching me on the shoulder—this one—with his hand, like he wants us to be friends. And he keeps promoting me. Three promotions in three months.

WHIT: He must like you.

DES: I distrust him.

WHIT: Yes. Of course. I understand.

DES: My supervisor is a very attractive man. Did I mention this?

(*Pause.*)

WHIT: No.

DES: Well, he is. (*Pause.*) And I'm sleeping with his wife.

WHIT: Is the wife attractive?

DES: There's nothing terribly wrong with her. She's not disfigured in any way.

WHIT:	But you, yourself, don't find her particularly attractive?
DES:	Me? Myself? No. Not particularly.
WHIT:	But you're sleeping with her?
DES:	Yes.
WHIT:	We have to do it, don't we?
DES:	What?
WHIT:	Men. We have to sleep with women. We have no choice. It's strictly biological.
DES:	Only if you believe the biologists.
WHIT:	Are you married?
DES:	Well, yes. I'm the age for it. Yes.
WHIT:	Me, too.
DES:	Married?
WHIT:	Well, yes. I'm that age.

(They look at each other. WHIT smiles. DES smiles back. The train stops, then goes.)

DES:	I'm separated.

(Pause.)

WHIT:	You ever kill a man?

(Pause.)

DES:	Well, yes. Of course, yes. Yes. I killed men in the war. Didn't you kill men in the war?

(WHIT *shakes his head. He looks down*.)

WHIT: It's because of my feet.

DES: That's too bad.

WHIT: I never had a great desire.

DES: Desire?

WHIT: What? Oh. To kill men.

DES: It was never a matter of desire. It was war. We were given guns. The enemy was described to us. It was made clear they had committed atrocities.

WHIT: So you had no choice.

DES: It's not choice that matters. It's whatever it takes to get from day to day. That matters.

WHIT: Day to day. That makes sense to me.

(*Pause.*)

DES: So, how are things with you?

WHIT: Things aren't good.

DES: I see.

WHIT: I have purchased a weapon.

DES: Oh?

WHIT: I have it right here, in my briefcase.

DES: For protection.

Milk

WHIT: For all the thoughts I've been having. Lately.

DES: All the crime . . .

WHIT: I've been having these thoughts about my wife.

             (*Pause.*)

DES: You mean you've been thinking about killing your wife?

             (*Pause.*)

WHIT: You think I'm insane.

             (*Pause.*)

DES: I know what it means to have a wife.

WHIT: She just seemed. Always different to me.

DES: Women are.

WHIT: But we marry them.

DES: We have no choice.

WHIT: It's biological.

DES: Yeah.

             (*Pause.*)

WHIT: Why don't you tell me something about your wife. Is she attractive?

DES: Her eyes are not blue.

WHIT: My eyes are blue.

DES: There's nothing terribly wrong with her.

WHIT: No.

DES: And your wife? Is she attractive?

WHIT: She's not disfigured in any way.

(*They smile at each other. Pause.*)

WHIT: Well. Well, this is as far as I go.

DES: You live around here?

WHIT: Very near.

DES: I live further along. In a different part of the city. Nowhere near here.

WHIT: We're all getting more spread out these days.

DES: Yes.

WHIT: You know how it is.

DES: Yeah.

WHIT: Well.

(*Pause.*)

DES: Say hello to your wife for me. If you see her.

WHIT: I will. You do the same.

DES: I will. She gets my mail.

(*Pause.*)

WHIT:	Good. Well, good-bye.
DES:	Good-bye.

(*They shake hands.* WHIT *leaves. The lights fade to black.*)

"Milk"

(SHEILA's *living room. There are piles of books everywhere.* DES *appears at the door.*)

SHEILA:	I have no soul.
DES:	What?
SHEILA:	(*Stops.*) I mean—I don't mean I was born without a soul. Of course. But. I lost my soul. What are you doing here?
DES:	I said I was coming over.
SHEILA:	You did? You did?
DES:	I called.
SHEILA:	You called? Oh yes you called yes. The phone went, "riiiiing." I didn't turn the ringer off. I should've turned the fucking ringer off. It went "rrrriiiiing."
DES:	My mail.
SHEILA:	RRRRRRRRIIIIIIIIINNNNNNNG. Isn't that funny?
DES:	My mail.
SHEILA:	Your mail?

DES: I came for my mail.

SHEILA: Your mail your mail your fucking mail oh yes here.

                (She finds some envelopes and tosses the mail at him, rather violently.)

DES: Thanks.

                (They stand there.)

SHEILA: You're welcome.

                (Pause.)

DES: Um. Looks like you got more books.

SHEILA: Books yes books yes I love books. Can't get enough of them. Books are my
                new vice. I go into a bookstore—I charge a hundred dollars in books. I see
                books, I want them. I have to be reading ten books at a time. Isn't it funny?
                I'm thirty-eight years old and I've only now discovered books. Think of all the
                things I've been missing! All these years! I don't have enough time—time you
                understand?—I don't have enough time to read all the books, all the books
                in the world—well, the ones that count, anyway. The ones that can teach me.
                Enlighten me. Maybe even the books that can help me find my soul! I have to
                learn, you understand? I have to fill my head with all the great minds! Einstein,
                Meister Eckhart, Mark Twain, Carlos Castaneda, Edward Said. Do you know what
                I'm saying?

DES: Sure.

SHEILA: Sure you don't. You don't understand. Oh, I know—you've read all these books,
                right? You've read all of them.

DES: I've read some of them.

SHEILA: I bet you have.

DES: I could tell you about some of them.

SHEILA: Tell me yes tell me. "Why read these books Sheila, when I can tell you all about them?" You and your goddamn ego. YOU NEED AN EGO BLASTER! That's what you need. (Shotgun motion.) BOOM! BLAST THAT EGO! BOOM BOOM BOOM! Shoot that ego into a lot of small pieces! BOOM!

DES: Are you okay?

SHEILA: Okay? Of course I'm OHHH-KAY. AYYY-OH-KAY. Why wouldn't I be okay? What do you mean by that? Just what the hell do you mean by that remark?

DES: I didn't mean anything, I just—

SHEILA: You just you just yes you just. You always mean something by something. The words you say, that come forth from your mouth, your lips—OH YOUR LIPS!—the movements you make with your body. Going from Point A to Point B. Coming and going, yes. Coming and going.

> (*She grabs a book, opens it, starts to read, pacing around. DES sits, looks at his mail. She stops, and looks at him.*)

I'll just pretend you're not here. I'll pretend you don't exist. Wouldn't that be nice? Wouldn't that be nice? If you were just not a part of this world.

> (*She paces, he watches. She tosses the book aside, and squats up and down, and takes in several deep breaths, and makes strange body movements.*)

I'm not a part of this world, either. You understand. I'm beyond this world. Well, okay, I'm trying to get there. I've been reading about body and breath exercises, to shift the focal point of your body in this dimension, so you can enter other dimensions, other worlds.

> (*She grabs a different book, runs off to a corner, sits down, and frantically reads. He opens some of his mail.*)

I think I'll change religions. Yes, that's what I need to do. I mean, join a religion. Because I've never had religion. I don't mean join a cult. I've looked into Scientology and that's just not me. Did I tell you my parents were atheists? You know, I could go for being Jewish.

DES:	What?
SHEILA:	Judaism. That's what I'll convert to. I've been reading about The Kabbala. All that mysticism. It's fascinating. Jewish women have a special place in the world, you know. Like your mother the famous novelist and talk show host.
DES:	My mother is hardly famous.
SHEILA:	She thinks she is. Other people think she is.
DES:	She's a local celebrity.
SHEILA:	What does it matter, what does it matter? What I'm saying is that I think I'd make a very good Jewish woman.
DES:	You do?
SHEILA:	How come you never wanted me to convert?
DES:	Convert?
SHEILA:	Denial, Des. Denial. That's all you are: one big denial. It's all you've ever been. You've denied your religious and cultural heritage!
DES:	I have not.
SHEILA:	Of course you have! All the time we've been married, I have never once seen you do a Jewish thing. Okay, wait. So you did take me to your nephew's bar mitzvah. What? Five years ago? But did you wear a yarmulke? NO! Did you ever take me to your family's big Hanukah get-togethers? No!
DES:	My family has never had—
SHEILA:	EXACTLY! Your whole family is in denial. But who isn't? We live in a world of denial within denial within denial, wheel within wheel, fish within fish, galaxy within galaxy, time within time, space within space. If I don't turn Jewish, I'll be a Buddhist.
	(Pause.)

Milk

DES: You'd make a good Buddhist.

SHEILA: Or a Zen Monk! I believe I was a Zen Master in the past, and I was persecuted.
            One day I shall return to my Zen Master Form. I'm living the life I'm living right
            now to learn a lesson or two. To work out some bad karma. To be punished.

DES: Bad karma.

SHEILA: And what do you mean by that? Just what in the hell do you mean by that?

DES: I don't mean anything, Sheila.

SHEILA: (*Stands.*) Oh yes you do oh yes you do. You can't fool me. You're always full of
            little snide, off-color remarks full of hidden meanings and messages. I know
            these things now. I have yanked away the dark façade that is the awful you,
            Desmond Rosenthal! You may sit there with that smirk on your face, your
            comments and retorts minimal and slick, and this light flashes before me, PING!
            This bell sounds in my ears, RING! PING RING! PING RING! I know you're full
            of Number Two! PING! RING! I know you have ulterior motives! PING RING! I
            know you're having bad thoughts about me! PING RING! (*Pause.*) Ping. (*Pause.*) I
            sense the bad thoughts you have about me. You could be a hundred miles away,
            a thousand, and I sense them. You think bad things my way, Des, and I don't like
            it anymore. Stop doing that! You hear me? You jerk! STOP IT! STOP IT! STOP IT!
            Oh, I need to meditate. Stand back! I need to breathe! I need room! I need space!
            You're invading my white light territory, yes you are you—you—you—you Jew
            you! You evil demon! You foul omen of ill intent! Ghoul! Gargoyle! Golem!

DES: I better go.

SHEILA: "WELCOME! YOU GOT MAIL!" Go, go, and let me become one with peace, light,
            and God. Did you get anything good in the mail?

DES: Not really.

SHEILA: Nothing?

DES: Nothing.

SHEILA: I got an interesting letter in the mail today. It was from Beverly. Where is that letter? Here. "Dear Sheila," it says, "Dear Sheila, I hope you're still not angry with me and we can be friends." Can you believe that?

DES: Beverly Bonner?

SHEILA: What other Beverly is there?

DES: Oh.

SHEILA: OH! It's your bleeping fault we're not friends anymore. You know why? No you don't. I'll tell you why. She happened to mention you to me once, twice, she mentioned you, in passing, in subject, and I said, "Look, Bev," I said, "Bev, if you ever bring that man up in conversation again," I said, "I don't want to be your friend." I said. Then I find out she had lunch with you—

DES: We crossed paths, and—

SHEILA: You did it just to spite me! To hurt me! To make me crazy and mad! What did she do, BLOW YOU?

DES: Sheila.

SHEILA: So she's no friend of mine anymore. No way. The both of you—you're in cahoots. You're out to get me. Oh, my stomach! My stomach is turning inside itself! I'm going to die of stomach cancer, I know I am! Stomach, heart, brain, all full of cancerous growth! Just like my mother! I'm going to wither up in pain and despair on some fucking ratty hospital bed and die like my mother did! (*Pause.*) Well, at least I can rest assured that the universe has symmetry. I HATE YOU! (*Pause.*) You know how jealous I get sometimes. Why are you using my friends to get at me, Desmond?

DES: I'm not.

SHEILA: You're a liar.

DES: Believe what you want.

Milk

SHEILA: You're too complex, that's your problem. Maybe I should've stayed with my first husband. He was simple. He was dumb, but . . . Well, it wasn't his fault he was a hick redneck who lived in a trailer and drove a truck with big wheels. I was a hick too. Until I de-hicked myself. Is this payback? For leaving him? I didn't think he'd really care. He didn't have a single emotion, except when he got excited about hunting deer. What am I talking about? I could've never stayed with him. I was a kid, I had no business being married. I could've stayed with my second husband, I should've. He's rich now. He was always supportive, he understood me, he was a scientist. But he never wanted to have sex. So I bleeped all his friends. And now here you are, my third husband, out to destroy me, out to make my head explode and my body sprout out with a dozen cancerous tumors.

DES: I better go. I have to meet my mother.

SHEILA: I bet.

DES: For dinner.

                     (Pause.)

SHEILA: Des?

DES: Yeah?

SHEILA: Do you remember when we went to the Grand Canyon? Two years ago?

DES: Of course.

SHEILA: It was so beautiful when we got there. So clear. And cold. At night it was so cold. And we got into that horrible fight in the car. You remember?

DES: I remember you hitting me, screaming at me, scratching me with your nails.

SHEILA: I was drunk, it wasn't my fault. But we made up. And we slept in that little bed. It was so nice to sleep so close to you. In the morning, it was snowing, and we were in each other's arms. (Pause.) We drove in the snow. I was behind the wheel, because I've driven in the snow before. I knew how to deal with hydroplaning. I drove slowly. Other cars passed us by, going fast, honking their horns, angry people in angry cars.

DES: It was funny.

SHEILA: When we did hydroplane, I knew how to control the car. You said to me, you said, "It's a good thing you're driving, or we might be dead." Do you remember that?

DES: Yes.

SHEILA: Good.

(*The lights fade to black.*)

"Teat"

(DES *having dinner with his mother,* LAURA ROSENTHAL.)

LAURA: . . . so I said to Karl, "Look, you think your son getting a divorce is bad? My son is separated from a crazy *shiksa* who was married twice before and up and left both husbands and now she's up and left him. The woman will probably be on her fifth husband by the time she's my age." Why aren't you eating your baked potato?

DES: I'm full.

LAURA: Nonsense.

DES: Mom, I'm full.

LAURA: You've been losing weight.

DES: A few pounds.

LAURA: It's that New Age ninny's fault, I know it.

DES: I needed to lose a few pounds.

LAURA: You need to gain a few pounds. You'll be cold when it gets cold. Your blood will thin, your immune system will go kaput. Eat that baked potato.

DES: I'll have another bite.

LAURA: Good. Anyway, Karl's all bent out of shape about his son. I said to him, "Look, things will be okay. He'll meet a better woman soon." I worry about Karl. Not just because he's my publisher, and my new book's due out soon; because he's my friend.

DES: You're still dating him then?

LAURA: He's my friend.

              (*Pause.*)

DES: I like Karl.

LAURA: I said to him, "Kids today are getting married and divorced every ten minutes." There's a loss of connection. It's become a common theme on my show. You listen to the show, right?

DES: Sometimes.

LAURA: You need to listen to my show more often.

DES: I do. Sometimes.

LAURA: Stop watching the TV, and turn the radio on.

DES: I listened to you last night.

LAURA: That was a repeat, hon.

DES: It was good.

              (*Pause.*)

LAURA:	More and more, I get these lost souls calling up and saying, "I'm going to leave my husband." "I'm going to leave my wife." "I'm having an affair with my best friend's husband." "I'm sleeping with my boss." "I'm sleeping with my sister." All sorts of madness.
DES:	Maybe it's all made up. People call in—
LAURA:	I wish it were so. But it's not. It's all true. It's ugly out there. Drink your milk.
DES:	I—
LAURA:	Or it's these babies calling up, girls who are fourteen saying, "I'm fourteen and I'm pregnant and I don't know what to do!" They say, "Should I get married? Have an abortion?" I say, "Look, you nitwit, you moral-less character of a post-postmodern condition, you're too darn young to get married, and you're too human to kill a baby. Give it up for adoption," I say. "There are plenty of childrenless, nice couples who'd like a baby to raise." I say to them, "And you're fourteen, for Pete's sake, you have no business messing around and getting knocked up!" But it still happens.
DES:	It happens.
LAURA:	Or it's this—get this: "I think I was molested when I was a child." It's: "I hate my father because he molested me." Or: "I hate my mother because I think she molested me . . . " "You THINK?" I go. "You're not SURE?" "I'm only now starting to remember," they say. Now. Right. It's because they go to these bad bad hypnotherapists who start inserting memories. For convenience. Because prior, these poor schmucks had no lives, so they invent soap operaesque scenarios to make them feel important. It's because they watch too much TV. If it isn't molestation or Satanic rituals, it's alien abduction. You're starting to see more and more of these false memory syndrome support groups popping up in every city. It's frightening, Desmond. It scares me. But I go on. I fight my fight the best way I know how.
DES:	You've always been a fighter, Mom.
LAURA:	Of course I'm the best, I'm Dr. Laura Rosenthal. (*Pause.*) Two nights ago, I get this call-in, from a man. He says he bought a gun, and he may use it on his wife.

"Why?" I ask. "Why not," he says. "Do you hate your wife?" I ask. "She's okay as far as wives go," he says, "I just think I have to shoot her." "Take that gun," I tell him, "and do society a favor and go shoot yourself!"

DES: That's extreme.

LAURA: He was extreme. I can understand a man having a solid reason for wanting to shoot his wife—she's cheating on him, she's taken the kids, she's charged the credit cards to the hilt. I don't say I condone such an action, but I can understand it. But to shoot her for no reason? "I just think I have to shoot her." Insanity. But that is what is happening to people now. Apathy. Movements of violence for no reason at all. "Why did you shoot the kids on the playground?" "Because I hate Mondays." More and more shooting sprees, from children! "I was bored." "I don't know why." "I wanted to see the look on people's faces." It's the lack of human connection. Drink your milk. (*Pause*) Your problem, you should've married a Jewish woman.

DES: Mom.

LAURA: I mean it. I know I've never said it before. You know I'm not that religious myself, although I've been giving it a lot of thought lately—I went to Temple last week, did I tell you that? With Karl. You should've married a Jewish girl, like Helen. And you still can. I don't mean Helen. But after all the stuff with Screaming Sheila is legal and done with, find yourself a Jewish woman. Preferably ten years younger than you and not much of a bad track record. Maybe even a virgin. Marry an eighteen-year-old, that won't be so bad. You should come to Temple with me.

DES: I won't remarry.

LAURA: That's what you say now.

DES: I won't.

LAURA: You're not telling me you're going back to her?

DES: No.

LAURA: My heart jumped for a second.

DES:	I have no desire to be married. I never did. It was her idea. "Hey, let's get married," she said.
LAURA:	And you said:
DES:	"Yes."
LAURA:	Just like everyone else! "Want to have a baby?" "Sure, why not!" Without ever giving any thought to the consequences. "Let's have sex without a condom." "Okay!" Ugh.

(Pause.)

DES:	Have you talked to Dad lately?
LAURA:	Desmond.
DES:	What?
LAURA:	Are you trying to ruin a perfectly nice evening?
DES:	No.
LAURA:	By bringing up that subject?
DES:	No. Mom, I was just—
LAURA:	I have not talked to him, and I have no desire to talk to him. You may talk to him if you wish, and you do talk to him, knowing very well how much it pains my brittle heart, but he is your father, after all.
DES:	He's—
LAURA:	I don't want to hear it. I don't. You can leave, you can get up and leave right now.
DES:	I'm sorry.
LAURA:	It's not your fault. Eat your corn. Des, eat.

Milk

DES: I'm not hungry.

LAURA: I want grandchildren.

DES: Mom.

LAURA: I mean it. Look how old I am. And no grandchildren! All my friends have them.
            They tell me about them. I feel left out. I need to spoil some little crawling, crying
            thing! A tiny, precious, pretty life! I look at people holding babies and I say, "I
            wish I had one of those." Not my own, of course, not that I could. But a child
            from my child. Look, Desmond, honey, I don't care if you're married or not. I
            don't even care if it's with *Star Trek* Sheila. Or with some young girl. I want a
            grandchild. Go out there and knock someone up. I'll be financially responsible.
            I'll take care of the girl and the baby.

DES: Mother. Stop.

                    (*Pause.*)

LAURA: A moment of weakness. Sorry.

DES: Let's just . . . sit here and be quiet.

LAURA: I can't be quiet, Dessy. I just can't. Drink your milk.

DES: Mom, I wanted to—

LAURA: You have a full glass of milk, now drink it. You love milk. You always loved milk.

DES: I still love milk.

                    (DES *drinks the milk.* LAURA *smiles.*)

LAURA: You love it because I breast fed you. That's another problem with young women
            these days, they don't want to breast feed. Everything is from a bottle, artificial
            liquids going inside the babies, making them turn into artificial grown-ups. "I
            don't want my tits to sag all full of milk!" They don't understand. And I tell them,
            about you, when you were a baby, and how I'd place you at my teat for suck.

DES: Oh, Mom.

Michael Hemmingson

| LAURA: | Suckle, yum-yum. You looked so happy at my breast, cuddled next to me. So happy, with no worries. I breast-fed you everywhere. Even in public. I wasn't shy. I just whipped my tit out and you went for it, like a hungry little wild cat. People would stop and watch. There's nothing more beautiful than a woman feeding her child from her own body. |

(Pause.)

| DES: | I feel horrible. |
| LAURA: | I know. |

(Pause.)

| DES: | I'm not happy. |
| LAURA: | I know. |

(Pause.)

DES:	Dad's getting re-married.
LAURA:	I know, Desmond. I know.
DES:	She's—
LAURA:	A lot younger than him. Des, you should've married Helen.
DES:	Why do you keep talking about Helen?
LAURA:	She was a nice Jewish girl! You two looked wonderful together!
DES:	We were seventeen, Mom.
LAURA:	She was such a nice girl. She would've given me beautiful grandchildren.
DES:	Mom, Helen was not nice.

LAURA: Of course she was.

DES: She slept around with everyone. She was a slut. I didn't know this at first. But
            when I found out . . . I didn't want to have anything to do with her. And she
            didn't care. We just dated. There was nothing between us, Mom.

LAURA: Oh. Oh. Did this damage you?

DES: No.

LAURA: I'm sure she had her reasons. It wasn't her fault. Did you finish your milk?

DES: Yes.

LAURA: Do you want another glass?

DES: Yes.

LAURA: Good. Good.

            (*The lights fade to black.*)

                              END

Michael Hemmingson's plays have been
produced by the Fritz Theater and the Alien
Stage Project in San Diego, Moving Arts
and Tyburn Theater in Los Angeles, Ventana
Productions in San Francisco, Theater Babylon
and Mae West Fest in Seattle, Love Creek and
Nada in New York, and others. *Iraq* was in
the 2000 Samuel French One-Act Fest. In fall
2007, his first feature film, *The Watermelon*, will
be released by LightStorm Films and his movie
of the week *The Date*, will air on Lifetime.

Teachers Who Smoke Cigarettes

The dialogue in Danny Sklar's play fires as rapidly as the patter in a Marx Brothers' movie. And these teachers are smoking more than cigarettes. They also smoke with discontent, defiance of the system, and sexual tension. They disagree on a common target for their discontent until they are faced with the possible loss of their faculty smoking lounge. The play ends with their ironic unification against this threat.

Sklar provides each character with a clear goal or need, a dramatic technique that makes the play snap and crackle. Nancy wants the right to teach as she believes best. Carol wants the freedom to be a bad teacher. Ricky wants to attract the new teacher, Nick. Betty wants to avoid getting caught drinking, smoking, and gambling in the faculty lounge. Donna wants peace and to join the other teachers in their camaraderie in the lounge. And Jane wants to exercise administrative authority and power to control the other characters, even to thwart their desires. Nick, who initially seems attracted to Nancy, precipitates the play's major reversal when the audience and other characters discover he really wants to organize a union.

All of the characters except Jane (who perhaps simply won't admit it) want to smoke. In many plays, characters smoke and drink merely as stage business, as if to provide them with something to do. Onstage action works best, however, if it functions significantly in creating conflict and in advancing the play toward its resolution. In this play, Sklar uses the growing cultural condemnation of smoking to provide the characters with a common focus for conflict and self-revelation, and to suggest the ways in which the distraction of everyday squabbles can divert us from fulfilling our individual needs and goals.

Danny Sklar

Teachers Who Smoke Cigarettes

CHARACTERS   NANCY: mid-twenties.

CAROL: mid-twenties.

RICKY: mid-twenties.

BETTY: mid-twenties.

NICK: early thirties.

JANE: early forties.

DONNA: late thirties.

SETTING   The faculty smoking lounge of Cape Ann College, the present.

(NANCY *and* CAROL *come into the smoking lounge.*)

NANCY: I need a cigarette.

CAROL: Me too.

NANCY: Can you believe this!

CAROL: I can't believe it.

NANCY: You know what I say?

CAROL: Yeah. I know what you say.

NANCY: To hell with them.

CAROL: Yeah. To hell with them. It's like . . . It's like . . .

NANCY: Like you never taught a goddamn day in your life. I only been teaching eight years, for Christ sakes. I know what I'm talking about.

CAROL: You said it! They hire you and then do this.

NANCY: Imagine them pulling that crap again.

CAROL: The nerve.

NANCY: They change the rules of the game just like that.

CAROL: Just like that in the middle of the goddamn game.

NANCY: You read what they sent us? I oughta cut my hair. What do you think?

CAROL: Your hair looks good. I read it. Damn memos. Burns me up!

NANCY: Me too. Where's that cigarette?

CAROL: Here you are, Nancy.

NANCY: Thanks, Carol.

CAROL: Say, have you seen the new history teacher?

NANCY: They hire you and then a new administration comes in and they change the rules. They pull the rug out from right under your feet. And they expect you to keep your mind on teaching. Sure, I've seen him.

CAROL: You think they really care about teaching? When was the last time they were in a classroom? What do you think about that new history teacher?

NANCY: Jane called me into her office. Left a message on the thing saying a student complained about me.

CAROL: Now what?

RICKY: (*Enters.*) Let me have a cigarette, Nancy. I think I'm in love.

CAROL: You're supposed to smoke after.

NANCY: Shut up and give Ricky a cigarette.

CAROL: What have you done now?

NANCY: Nothing. I don't know. Yes, I do. I know what I did.

RICKY: That guy is definitely cute. You're in trouble again?

NANCY: If you're alive, you're in trouble. When I'm not in trouble, I'll be dead.

CAROL: It'll be too late.

RICKY: Too late for what?

NANCY: Shut up. (*Looking out the window.*) I see Jane coming this way. My god, you know who she looks like?

RICKY: Who? I could marry that guy. I mean, if he walked in here right now and said would you marry me, I would say yes.

CAROL: Are you crazy?

RICKY: No. Don't you believe in love at first sight?

NANCY: She looks like a psychotic Mary Poppins.

CAROL: Don't believe in nothin', kid, you'll be much happier.

RICKY: Oh, but I believe in love at first sight. Don't you Nancy?

NANCY: Are you kiddin'? I don't even believe in love. Love is for saps. Sex is much better when there's no love to it.

RICKY: Oh, you don't mean that.

CAROL: (*Looking out the window*.) This is serious. Donna just met up with Jane. I mean, Jane may be a pain in the ass, but Donna believes all that education crap.

RICKY: They wouldn't come into the smoking room.

CAROL: Don't bet on it.

RICKY: What should we do? Quick, ditch the cigarettes!

CAROL: Ricky, this is the smoking room.

NANCY: You're a teacher and they make you feel like a kid. Oh, my god, they are coming this way. They're talking.

CAROL: What are they saying? Can you make it out?

NANCY: They want to control you. That's what it's all about. The minute the job gets good and you feel you can focus on teaching and learning, they hand you all this probation crap!

CAROL: And you know what it means, all that teacher effectiveness garbage?

RICKY: Sure, it's just a matter of whether they like you or not?

CAROL: You said it!

NANCY: I mean, some of my best teachers were the worst teachers.

CAROL: I say we should be free to be bad.

NANCY: I had this professor in college—used to come to class drunk.

CAROL: Speaking of that, break out the booze you two.

NANCY: Here you go. (*Hands her a pint of whiskey.* RICKY *takes out a few bottles of beer*.)
            Who's got the cards? Anyway by the standards here, he would have been a lousy
            prof. But I'm here to tell you he was the best. Came into the class drunk, lit a
            cigarette, rubbed his face.

CAROL: I got the cards and the poker chips. All right, sit down girls. This game is straight
            five card draw.

RICKY: Don't you think we should wait?

NANCY: Wait for what? Those tight-assed broads? Call Joe's for the pizza. I'm not giving
            up our pleasure for the sake of impressing them.

RICKY: But they just came into the building.

NANCY: So what? This is Friday night. Wait a minute. (*She unrolls a poster of a painting and
            holds it up*.) Look at this. This is a goddamn Gauguin.

CAROL: What kind of pizza should we get? What do you want?

RICKY: Are you going to deal or what?

CAROL: I'm dealing, I'm dealing.

NANCY: Look at that Gauguin, would you. (*She tapes the poster of Paul Gauguin's* Hail
            Mary *on the wall*.)

CAROL: We see it. What about it?

NANCY:	This professor, Professor Myles D. Cooper, would kind of fall into the classroom, turn off the lights, light a cigarette, look around and say something like: "What the hell are you staring at? I hate those goddamn fluorescent lights. How can anyone think? What do you want to do here? You signed up for this class. What do you want to do?" He'd say just like that.
CAROL:	You gonna order that pizza? Pepperoni, that's what I want.
RICKY:	I had a teacher like that, but it wasn't until ten years later that I figured out how much I learned. He used to say, nobody gives a damn about poetry; and what the hell is a sonnet anyway? Then we'd run and find out.
NANCY:	Kipling's motto of the mongoose, "Run and find out." Myles D. Cooper used to say.
CAROL:	Do I have to do everything? Order the damn pizza. Shut up and deal the cards. I feel lucky.
RICKY:	Do you think it's a good idea to be drinking and playing cards with Jane, the dean of the college in the building and the vice president of whatever Donna's the vice president of, probably on their way up here?
CAROL:	What's with the Gauguin?
NANCY:	I'll tell you what's with that Gauguin in a second. Say, where's Betty? She's late.
RICKY:	Betty will be here. I saw her after class. She was talking to Jane and Donna. Ante up. Look at your cards and quit looking at that poster. We have to get some men to these parties.
NANCY:	What, and ruin it? Besides, this is a free country, any man can come into this room any time. But I'm here to tell you men are chicken.
CAROL:	Shut up and play poker. Ante up!
NANCY:	Let me see those cards.

BETTY:	(*Enters, heads straight for the couch and lights a cigarette.*) I wish in the world you could just walk around without shoes. When I was a kid I went barefoot all summer.
CAROL:	Pull up a beer.
RICKY:	Imagine if you started teaching class barefooted.
NANCY:	You can't be yourself anymore, let's face it. You see that Gauguin, Betty?
BETTY:	Hey, you couldn't have waited for me two minutes before starting to play? What kind of pizza did you order?
NANCY:	Isn't that a beautiful painting?
BETTY:	Yeah, sure. Say have you read that memo proposal or whatever the hell it is?
CAROL:	Sure we read it. They want to control you. They don't want you to think for yourself. They want you to yes them to death.
NANCY:	Do you see anything wrong with that Gauguin?
RICKY:	We definitely need men at these parties, but I'm locking the door.
NANCY:	What are you doing?
RICKY:	Jane and Donna are going to walk in that door.
NANCY:	So what?
RICKY:	We're drinking and gambling and smoking.
CAROL:	Big deal. Sit down and ante up.
BETTY:	I think she better lock the door.
NANCY:	Look at it, would you, and answer me. (*Staring at the Gauguin.*)

CAROL: They wouldn't step into this room in a million years. Besides, this is a public faculty smoking lounge.

RICKY: I don't feel like playing.

CAROL: Are you kidding? You have to play.

BETTY: Jane and Donna are going to walk in that door any minute and we are all going to get fired.

NANCY: Good. Let them fire us. We're only the best goddamn teachers in the place. They just can't stand the fact that we know what we're doing.

CAROL: Am I playing alone here?

RICKY: Quiet! Someone's coming.

NANCY: I don't hear anything. Carol's right. Quit worrying. Besides, I'm the guy in the goddamn dog house this week.

BETTY: Shut up. I hear footsteps.

RICKY: I'm locking the door.

BETTY: Lock the door. Those are footsteps!

NANCY: You can't lock the door.

RICKY: Yes, I can.

NANCY: No, you're not.

RICKY: Get away from that door.

NANCY: Don't tell me what to do.

RICKY: Then I'll get rid of this stuff. I'm not losing my job because you're an idiot!

CAROL:	Don't touch those chips! Pick up your cards and play.
BETTY:	Get away from that door, Nancy!
NANCY:	This is a public room. Anybody can walk in here, sit on that couch, have a cigarette, or join this friendly game of penny-poker.
CAROL:	Penny-poker! Are you kidding? I'm hungry. Give me the phone, Betty.
BETTY:	Get it yourself.
RICKY:	I'm going home.
NANCY:	Wait a minute, Ricky, you can't leave now.
RICKY:	Try and stop me.
BETTY:	Let her go, Nancy.
NANCY:	Paul Gauguin, Ricky, Paul Gauguin.
RICKY:	What the hell are you talking about?
BETTY:	I was talking to them. They told me, Nancy. You are in trouble.
NANCY:	I know I'm in trouble. I know they're coming here. I invited them. That memo is about me.
CAROL:	Who else?
RICKY:	These friendly Friday night sessions do not include meetings with the dean and the vice president of whatever. So, good night, ladies.
CAROL:	What the hell are you afraid of?
RICKY:	I'm not afraid of anything.
BETTY:	She doesn't have to explain to you.

NANCY: Say, what's going on here, there's something you're not . . .

                  (NICK *nonchalantly strolls into the room, sits on the couch, lights a cigarette, pulls a book from his briefcase and starts to read.*)

CAROL: Would you like to play a friendly game of poker?

NICK: Are you talking to me?

BETTY: I'm Betty Jones. Business.

NANCY: Nancy Johnson. Drama. You ever act?

NICK: Act?

NANCY: How do you like that Gauguin over there?

BETTY: Who are you?

NICK: Oh, I teach history. Nick Davis.

CAROL: Beer?

NICK: Beer?

NANCY: Scotch?

NICK: Scotch? Are we allowed to drink on campus?

CAROL: We're over twenty-one.

BETTY: Yeah, what's the big deal?

CAROL: Can we trust you?

NICK: Is this the faculty smoking lounge?

NANCY: It ain't the nursery school.

NICK:	Am I interrupting something? I can go outside. I was going home anyway. I.
BETTY:	Sit down. Relax. Are you married?
NICK:	Married?
CAROL:	Have you got a girlfriend? Come on, pal, talk to us.
NICK:	I just came in for a cigarette.
NANCY:	Nobody comes in here just for a cigarette, buddy.
NICK:	Buddy? What is this?
RICKY:	Never mind them, Nick. I'm Erica Leland. My friends call me Ricky. You can call me Ricky. I teach poetry. And I'm not talking about crap poetry either.
NANCY:	Because of that Gauguin and due to the fact of the way I teach, two things will result. One. I will get fired; and B. some new cheap little fascist policy will be instituted. They're going to tell us what good teaching is, and whether or not our students learn anything. Exhibit three, said memo proposal amendment type thing. You've read it I presume.
NICK:	There is a third possibility.
NANCY:	Is that so?
NICK:	Yes, but you and I are going to have to discuss the details of this academic crisis, say, over dinner. I know a swell little bistro right on Gloucester Harbor.
NANCY:	Who said anything about a crisis?
BETTY:	Slow down there big fella.
NANCY:	Yeah, I don't have to have dinner with you. I can spill it in about two seconds.
RICKY:	That's right. Besides, you can cut the dinner euphemisms with us. Everybody knows what a guy means when he asks a woman to dinner. But why'd you ask her instead of me?

Danny Sklar

423

NICK:	I didn't mean anything by it.
CAROL:	Too late to apologize. Have a drink. I'll deal you in.
BETTY:	Tell us exactly what's on your mind, Nick—besides dinner.
NICK:	Nothing's on my mind.
RICKY:	Well, dinner is on my mind.
NICK:	Are you talking about the euphemism of dinner?
RICKY:	I think I could get to like you.
NICK:	You do?
RICKY:	I just said so, didn't I?
NICK:	What could you tell me if I asked you to dinner?
RICKY:	Plenty.
NANCY:	Wait a minute! What's the third thing you were talking about? Not that I really care—just curious, that's all.
RICKY:	Quit crowding me, Nanc'. I'm working here.
BETTY:	Footsteps!
CAROL:	Ditch the cards.
NICK:	Why?
BETTY:	Two sets of 'em, The pace is quick. It's them!
RICKY:	Put out that cigarette!
NICK:	This is the smoking lounge!

RICKY:	Doesn't matter, Don't let them know you smoke.

(JANE *and* DONNA *enter and stand together just inside the door. They are both in suit-type dresses and their hair is pulled tightly back or cut short.*)

JANE:	Well?
DONNA:	I see.
JANE:	Have you anything to say?
DONNA:	Yes. Do you mind if I smoke?
JANE:	I wasn't talking to you.
DONNA:	Oh. Sorry.
JANE:	You wanted to see me, Nancy?
NANCY:	Not really.
DONNA:	Well, we wanted to talk to you about your methods. You know, we have meetings every Tuesday on the latest teaching techniques and theories and methods and instructional technology management systems. Several of the faculty attend and find it most—
NANCY:	Stupid.
DONNA:	Enlightening. I was going to say that or informative.
JANE:	You asked me to meet you here, Nancy.
NANCY:	Right, but I don't want to see you, I have to.
JANE:	Why won't you speak to that student?
NANCY:	I'll speak to her.

JANE: I don't want to take disciplinary action against you.

NANCY: Don't.

DONNA: Perhaps it would be wise to talk somewhere else? If not, I hope you don't mind, Jane, if I have a cigarette?

CAROL: Would you like a drink.

DONNA: A drink?

JANE: I will be frank with you.

NANCY: Be anybody you like.

JANE: I understand you did speak to the student in question.

NANCY: Sure, if you mean the student who ratted on me. Wait a minute! Hey pal, did you say bistro before?

NICK: What? I did. I think? Did I say bistro?

NANCY: You did say bistro. Couldn't you have said small bar or tavern or nightclub or informal restaurant? I hate that bistro crap! Who are you trying to impress?

RICKY: I like that kind of talk.

BETTY: I like it too. We have to demand romance in men, even if it's just in the things they say.

RICKY: Yes, and words are the best place to start. I love romance. Give me a candlelight dinner in a quiet out of the way restaurant, the two of us looking into each other's eyes. Saying everything with our eyes. It's dangerous I suppose, but bistro is fine with me.

CAROL: Yes, but how can you keep it from being corny?

RICKY: That's a good question. Maybe it has to be a little corny. And how can you believe them when they are romantic? It's easy to be romantic when you don't mean it.

And if you're married they say you should be suspicious of them when they get romantic. But how can you know the truth?

DONNA: You have to get them good and drunk, you see. That's how you can find out the truth. You're Nick Davis, right, History? I'm Donna Mirabella, vice president of academic learning, whatever that is, here at Cape Ann College. Why did I just say Cape Ann College? Just saying here was enough. You're pretty cute. Give me a cigarette, would you?

JANE: Donna, what the hell are you doing? We are not here to pick up men.

DONNA: Oh, sorry. Never mind the cigarette, Nick. (*Whispers.*) Later, Nick, we'll do it later.

CAROL: Here's a cigarette, Donna. Give her a light, Betty.

BETTY: Okay.

JANE: Don't take that cigarette, Donna! What is the matter with you, anyway? Look, Nancy, let's not drag this thing out. The student is not satisfied. What did you say to her?

NANCY: I think you should let Donna have a cigarette.

DONNA: Is that the Gauguin? Is that what this is all about?

JANE: Yes and the fact that Nancy said the word that starts with *F* in class. And furthermore she told the said student in question that the paper said student was writing was written like someone in middle school.

DONNA: What is it about this Gauguin? What's the student complaining about?

NANCY: You tell me.

JANE: The point is you did not apologize to the student, Nancy.

DONNA: I understand the student was offended. Our job is not to offend students, Nancy. Teaching and learning is not about offending students. Why don't we have a drink, Jane?

JANE:	Donna!
DONNA:	Sorry, sorry.
JANE:	Have you anything to say?
CAROL:	What do you mean it's not about offending students? Why not? There aren't enough students being offended around here. Why don't you relax, Jane, and have a drink with us?
BETTY:	You're forgetting what this is really about, Carol. It's about money. They haven't the guts to tell this kid to grow up because they're afraid she'll transfer out. When I taught at Northeastern and a kid complained about me, my dean told the kid he had some nerve talking behind my back and that he should go and see me if he had a problem and furthermore he was being a big baby about it all.
CAROL:	Did you get some sort of thrill listening to the girl's story about how Nancy said fuck in class? Is that why you . . .
JANE:	That is not all she said. Besides, students need to have someone to whom they can address complaints.
DONNA:	I agree with Jane.
BETTY:	But before anything is said, don't you think the student should be sent to the professor?
RICKY:	What if the student is intimidated by the professor? I mean, let's face it, Nancy, you come on strong.
CAROL:	Are you taking Jane's side on this thing?
RICKY:	I'm not taking any sides. It's not a question of sides.
NANCY:	Oh, yes it is. It's them against us. Get that straight and you won't be confused about the world.
RICKY:	I'm not confused about the world. You think things are black and white like that?

NANCY: You bet I do!

RICKY: Where did you go to college, anyway?

NANCY: Hard knocks!

RICKY: Funny. Maybe Jane and Donna and the rest of them are right about this
              probation thing. I mean, what if a professor loses sight of her purpose here?

BETTY: What the hell are you talking about?

CAROL: She's saying, basically, that if a professor suddenly goes batty, the way Nancy
              always appears to be heading, then the college should have the right to terminate
              her teaching tenure. In plain English, fire her.

RICKY: No, that's not what I'm saying.

NICK: I beg your pardon, Nancy, but didn't you say you teach acting, that theater is your
              field?

NANCY: Did you have to say "I beg your pardon"? Couldn't you have asked me plain and
              straight out?

RICKY: What's wrong with saying "I beg your pardon"? I don't see anything wrong with
              that. But what I'm saying is this: there are two sides or even more than two sides
              to everything.

DONNA: Ricky is making sense. Isn't that the kind of thing we are trying to do with critical
              thinking and problem solving and group work and case studies here at Cape Ann
              College? Cape Ann College is on the cutting edge of education, state of the art
              methods and techniques as well as computers. Cape Ann College has become a
              committed and dedicated center for—for—

NANCY: Bullshit.

CAROL: Give a kid a book, a pencil, a piece of paper—that's all you need, and someone
              to talk about it with.

JANE: Are you anti-technology?

CAROL: No, but someone has to be.

NANCY: I am. I'm anti-everything. You name it, I'm anti-it.

DONNA: What kind of influence can that be on the young developing minds of our students here at Cape Ann College? Why do I keep saying Cape Ann College? I could just say here. Oh my god, I've been brainwashed!

CAROL: Have a swig of this. It'll wash your brain.

DONNA: (*Takes a drink of scotch.*) Thank you, Carol.

JANE: Donna!

BETTY: Be yourself for five minutes, would you, Jane, instead of a robot programmed on the company line.

NANCY: Brainwashed is right. Brainwashed because of fear. That's how they do it. They make you afraid of something. What? Losing your job? Not working hard enough? Not getting some sort of approval? What are you afraid of?

JANE: I have a tough call to make here. But I am up to the challenge.

NICK: Look, I just started working here and it seems to me that, you know, being an objective observer as I am . . .

NANCY: Get to the point.

NICK: My point is because you are a drama teacher you act the way you act. Drama is a heightened kind of reality; I mean loaded with extremes, so therefore you act extremely. You are intense, just as drama has to be intense and somewhat radical.

RICKY: "Be radical, be radical, but not too damn radical!" Walt Whitman!

JANE: Nevertheless that does not change the fact that Nancy has not apologized to said girl, and continues to use said Gauguin as some sort of writing exercise in said playwriting class when she was asked not to use it anymore.

RICKY: I don't like Gauguin. I prefer Vincent van Gogh.

CAROL: Who asked you?

RICKY: Don't you believe in teamwork and that people should cooperate? I mean if someone asks me to do something, and it is a reasonable thing, I do it.

BETTY: Nazis cooperated. That was a real team effort.

RICKY: Shut up.

BETTY: Tell us all of the things Nancy has done. Let us judge her. We're her peers. We'll be fair.

NANCY: Don't call me radical, buddy! And don't give me that *furthermore, moreover, thus, therefore,* and *on the other hand* language garbage. You don't know what you're talking about. A girl walks into a Chinese restaurant, it's raining, late Sunday night. She's got on a green dress, short, sleeveless. She orders fried rice to go. She stands there and waits for maybe fifteen or twenty minutes. She says nothing else. Maybe she crosses her arms or taps her foot. She looks around—up, down, straight ahead. There's a man at a booth. He's smoking a Lucky Strike cigarette and eating chop suey at the same time. Maybe he looks at the girl. She does not look at him. She pays for her fried rice, takes it and exits. She does nothing for fifteen minutes and you forget your life. I mean you have just seen the greatest actress of the twenty-first century. That's acting pal. The life is inside of her. So don't tell me about drama.

RICKY: What is that supposed to mean?

NANCY: Nothing, just a speech from a third-rate play by my old professor, Professor Myles D. Cooper.

JANE: This is all just ducky! You want to hear every rule Nancy has broken? You want a list?

DONNA: Yes, give us a list.

NANCY: I'll give you the list.

JANE:	No, I want to give the list.
CAROL:	Why don't you give us a song instead?
BETTY:	Yes, sing it, Jane, Better yet—let's have a toast and the we'll sing a song and dance too. What should we sing?
JANE:	You think I don't know what you're doing? I am not going to stand here and be humiliated.
CAROL:	Why not? There's not enough humiliating going on around here. "I think, therefore I am humiliated!"
BETTY:	Sure, you know our motto: "To live is to be humiliated."
NANCY:	Yes, and "Humiliate me today!" That's my motto.
DONNA:	You realize that Jane is your superior, don't you?
NANCY:	What did you say?
DONNA:	Jane is your superior.
JANE:	And insubordination is "just cause" for release from any contract. I think I know where you stand on this matter.
NANCY:	Jane is my superior? What is this, the goddamn army?
JANE:	Come, Donna, we shall draft a letter together.
DONNA:	Draft a letter? For what?
JANE:	What do you think?
DONNA:	Oh, yes, I forgot. Mind if I finish this cigarette first?
JANE:	Yes, I do mind!

DONNA: Okay, okay. See you, Nick. (*Whispering to* NICK.) Say, listen, I know a neat little place on Route One Twenty-Seven. I'll be there nine tonight. It's—

JANE: Coming, Donna? (*To the others*.) The president of the college shall hear of this. You can rest assured I will relate to her the details of the events of this evening.

(JANE *and* DONNA *exit*.)

NANCY: (*Hollers down the hall after them*.) Don't give us that *rest assured* crap!

CAROL: All right, all right, everyone concentrate on the game. You playing, Nick?

RICKY: You had to antagonize her, didn't you?

NANCY: I had to.

BETTY: That's her nature.

RICKY: She's going to fire you. And us too maybe.

CAROL: Yeah, yeah, quit brooding.

BETTY: Hell, I guess you can't have a job for life.

NICK: Why not? Why not have a job for life? Why not expect loyalty from an employer? We expect it when we get married. Why shouldn't a job be as sacred as a marriage?

BETTY: What world do you come from?

RICKY: I don't want to lose my job. I am a good teacher and I like it. I mean, friendship is one thing, but—

NANCY: But what? Right is right.

RICKY: Sure, but you could have been more diplomatic. You could have taken the high road. It wouldn't have killed you to apologize to that student. I mean what exactly is the cause?

NANCY: You want to know what the cause is?

RICKY: Yes. I want to know what the cause is.

NANCY: I'll tell you what the cause is.

RICKY: Go ahead, tell me.

NANCY: I'll tell you.

RICKY: Tell me.

NANCY: I'm going to tell you.

RICKY: When?

NANCY: When?

RICKY: When?

NANCY: I'll tell you when.

RICKY: Tell me.

CAROL: Tell her the cause so we can play poker!

NANCY: You want me to tell her the cause?

BETTY: Tell her the damn cause. I'm ordering the pizza. Hello, Joe's Pizza? Yes. I'd like to place an order.

NICK: The cause is Paul Gauguin. That's the cause.

NANCY: Yeah. Paul Gauguin! Hey, who asked you? Keep out of this, pal.

NICK: The cause is freedom.

NANCY: Yeah, freedom.

NICK:	The cause is liberty.
NANCY:	Right. Liberty. I don't believe in nothing but liberty!
CAROL:	Yeah, yeah, and the American way. Make sure you get pepperoni on that pizza, Betty. Someone put the radio on. How about a dance, Nick, you wanna dance?
BETTY:	What are you driving at, Nick?
RICKY:	Wait a minute. You've got something to say. You've had something to say the whole time, haven't you?
BETTY:	Yeah. You come in here all innocent and all the time there's been something on your mind.
NICK:	You're right, Betty. There is something on my mind.
RICKY:	What is it Nicky?
NICK:	There are several possible scenarios here. A. You could all get fired. B. Only Nancy could get fired. And last but not least, the most horrible possibility of all: C. They could take the smoking lounge away and make it into a game room.
NANCY:	What? Lose the smoking lounge!
BETTY:	They would never do a thing like that!
CAROL:	That would be cruel and unusual punishment.
RICKY:	Just the thought of it is frightening.
NICK:	That's right. Even worse than losing your jobs, you could lose the faculty smoking room.
NANCY:	You better not say that again, bub!
RICKY:	No, no. It's too fantastic to think about.

Danny Sklar

435

NICK: Nevertheless.

BETTY: He's right, you know. The truth hurts.

NICK: And it is the truth. But it doesn't have to be that way. Things don't have to be the way they are. You may never beat the Janes of this world, but there is a way to deal with them. Moreover, small-minded institutions get what they deserve.

NANCY: Don't give us that *nevertheless* and *moreover* garbage. You must have your doctorate. I bet you used the word *moreover* fifty times in your dopey little two-bit dissertation.

CAROL: What do these institutions deserve, Nick?

NICK: I was hoping you figured it out yourselves. You seem to me to be a pretty unified group. Oh, you have your minor quarrels, but basically you agree on things.

BETTY: Yeah, so?

NICK: Look, do I have to spell it out for you?

NANCY: I don't dig guessing games, mister.

NICK: Builds the drama though, doesn't it?

NANCY: No. It makes me hate your red, communist, union-organizing guts!

CAROL: Bingo!

RICKY: Union?

NICK: Union.

BETTY: Union?

NANCY: Union, eh? Do we look like dirty little joiners to you? My father used to pay off union officials. He had a painting contracting company and to keep the union out he'd meet them at Belmont Race track. Five hundred bucks a year. It was a business expense. The painter's union officials used the horse track as their office. My old man was fair and decent. You could trust him.

NICK: Can you trust your bosses? Are your bosses fair and decent?

CAROL: You can't trust anyone.

NICK: You can trust your union brothers and sisters.

BETTY: Is this what it takes to keep the smoking lounge?

NICK: Wages, hours, and working conditions. And to keep your jobs.

NANCY: Saving the smoking lounge makes me think! And if it will keep Mary Poppins off my back.

CAROL: I wouldn't mind being in a union with you, Nick. So what do we have to do?

NICK: First, Nancy has to square things with the student. Let Jane write that letter about the Gauguin. It'll prove she's interfering with academic freedom. Then we smack them with unfair labor practices. But we have to talk somewhere else.

RICKY: I'll be the president, which means you and I will have to discuss the intimate details of these arrangement, say, over that dinner we were talking about.

BETTY: Let's drink to our right to be bad and to teach with bare feet!

CAROL: Here's to our right to make stupid mistakes.

NANCY: To our right to use Paul Gauguin or any damn artist we please.

RICKY: And to the first amendment to the Constitution of the United States of America which says: "Congress shall make no law respecting an establishment of religion, or prohibiting the free exercise thereof; of abridging freedom of speech, or of the press; or the right of the people peaceably to assemble, and to petition the government for a redress of grievances."

CAROL: And that goes for third-rate little colleges too! All right, this game is five card draw. You in, Nick?

NICK: Deal me in sister! We'll talk of union later.

DONNA: (*Enters.*) Union? Yes, Nick, union. I didn't know you were so romantic. Deal me in too, Carol, and I think I'll have that drink as well, please.

NANCY: I hate that "as well" crap. Gimme those cards. Someone give me a cigarette.

BETTY: Where the hell is the pizza? Gimme another beer, Carol.

CAROL: What am I, the damn bartender? Get it yourself.

RICKY: We really, really, really have to get more men to these parties.

(*The lights fade to black.*)

END

Danny Sklar teaches writing at Endicott College
where he tries to get his students to write
in a natural and spontaneous way. Recent
publications include *Poetry East, Square Lake,
The Village Rambler, bowwow, Paper Street,* and
the *Mid-America Poetry Review.*

Danny Sklar

Devoted

Claudia Barnett writes clear, simple dialogue, and in three short scenes turns a seemingly simple play about relationships into an investigation of the sinister subversion of truth. Simple dialogue about looking tired, having trouble sleeping, or not being hungry is repeated so that distinctions blur between friend or enemy, and lover or dangerous acquaintance. Reversals of simple statements and gossip lead the characters to question the truth about their relationships with each other.

As Aristotle has amply demonstrated, discovery or revelation leading to reversal is a strong dramatic device essential to successful plays. In *Devoted* Keith tells Julia an unpleasant story; later, her friend Melissa tells the same story with a different spin. When Julia challenges the truth of his tale, Keith first denies that he has lied, then strangely gives in to Julia, creating a sinister ending to what might have been an innocuous sequence of events. Who is telling the truth? Who is lying? Who is vulnerable? Who is in danger? Barnett uses the simplest of means—talk of donuts, who hit whom, ordinary details about daily routines—to create this dark and troubling play about the tenuousness of human relationships.

Claudia Barnett

Devoted

CHARACTERS	KEITH: early to mid-twenties.
	JULIA: early to mid-twenties.
	MELISSA: early to mid-twenties.
SETTING	The living room. Furnishings are slightly upscale.

(*Darkness.* JULIA *is asleep on the couch. The sound of a door slamming as* KEITH *enters. The lights come up.* JULIA *buries her head beneath her pillow.*)

KEITH: What are you doing here? (JULIA *makes indiscernible noises from under the pillow.* KEITH *grabs the pillow from her.*) What?

JULIA: I'm sleeping.

KEITH: Why here? Why aren't you in bed?

JULIA: I want to sleep here.

KEITH: Go to bed.

JULIA: I'm asleep.

KEITH: No you're not.

JULIA: I want my pillow

KEITH: Why do I live with you if you're going to sleep on the couch?

JULIA: Please. Let me sleep.

KEITH: What's the point?

JULIA: Please.

KEITH: I'll move out. I can move out any time. It's your name on the lease.

JULIA: I'm sorry.

KEITH: Just remember. Any time.

JULIA: I was depressed. Please. I'm sorry.

KEITH: What were you doing there?

JULIA:	On the couch?
KEITH:	At Ray's.
JULIA:	He invited me.
KEITH:	He invited you.
JULIA:	He called. He said I should come.
KEITH:	What about me?
JULIA:	He said you'd be there. I thought you'd drive me home. I had to walk.
KEITH:	Those are my friends.
JULIA:	They're my friends too.
KEITH:	No. Those are my friends.
JULIA:	They like me. They invited me.
KEITH:	I go there to get away.
JULIA:	(*A pause.*) From me?
KEITH:	And then there you are.
JULIA:	You go there to get away from me. (*A pause.*) I thought you loved me.
KEITH:	I need my space.
JULIA:	I'll make us some coffee.
KEITH:	No.
JULIA:	There's ice cream. Chocolate. I bought it for you.

KEITH: No.

JULIA: Are you hungry? There's fried chicken.

KEITH: I don't want you waiting on me.

JULIA: Can I have my pillow?

KEITH: (*He throws the pillow at her.*) Here.

JULIA: (*She clutches the pillow.*) Are you going to leave? (*A pause.*) When are you going to leave? I know you're going to leave. Where have you been? (*A pause.*) Are you going to leave?

KEITH: Leave?

JULIA: Are you moving out?

KEITH: Let's go to bed.

JULIA: Are you moving out?

KEITH: No.

JULIA: What about your . . . space?

KEITH: You have your friends. I have my friends.

JULIA: You want me to stay away from your friends.

KEITH: You have your own friends.

JULIA: But they like me. Ray invited me.

KEITH: You think they like you?

JULIA: They invited me. They laughed at my jokes.

Devoted

KEITH: They laughed at you.

JULIA: What?

KEITH: They always laugh at you. As soon as you're out the door.

JULIA: (*A pause.*) They do? Why? (*A pause.*) What are they laughing at?

KEITH: You, baby.

JULIA: No they don't.

KEITH: Just look at yourself. Your fancy clothes, your fancy car, your fancy ideas.

JULIA: They don't. (*A pause.*) Why don't you stick up for me?

KEITH: I do.

JULIA: You do?

KEITH: How do you think I got that black eye?

JULIA: You said it was an accident.

KEITH: Ray insulted you. I defended you.

JULIA: You defended me?

KEITH: Sure I did, baby.

JULIA: From Ray?

KEITH: From Ray.

JULIA: Then why did he invite me?

KEITH: That's Ray.

JULIA: Why are you friends with him?

KEITH: We've been friends all our lives.

JULIA: And he punched you?

KEITH: Yeah. He punched me.

JULIA: You did that for me? Does it hurt?

KEITH: Shhhhhhhh. It'll be fine. Come to bed.

JULIA: Okay. You love me. Don't you?

                        (*The lights fade to black.*)

Devoted

Scene 2

(*Lights rise on the next morning. JULIA is straightening the apartment, folding blankets. There's a knock at the door. JULIA opens it and finds MELISSA standing there with a box of donuts.*)

MELISSA: You look like shit.

JULIA: Good morning.

MELISSA: No, really. You do.

JULIA: So do you.

MELISSA: Are you kidding? I look fantastic. This is the best I've looked in years. But you look like shit. Aren't you getting any sleep?

JULIA: Not lately.

MELISSA:	Oh, honey, you've got to take care of yourself. Are you eating? Look, I brought breakfast.
JULIA:	Thanks. I'm not hungry.
MELISSA:	But you've got to eat. You're just wasting away. Look at you.
JULIA:	I've never weighed more. This is the most I've weighed in my entire life. So no thank you. I don't want any donuts.
MELISSA:	They're your favorite kinds. French crullers. Chocolate and vanilla. Two of each. One for each of us. Like when we were kids.
JULIA:	I never liked donuts.
MELISSA:	I know a guy ate donuts for breakfast every day of his life. Lived to be a hundred. I saw him on the news. I don't really know him. I saw him interviewed. He said donuts are the health food of the future. (*A pause.*) So, tell me about it.
JULIA:	About what?
MELISSA:	What's going on with you. Why you look like crap. Is that why you're home today? I didn't think you'd be home.
JULIA:	Then why'd you come?
MELISSA:	You never know. Aren't you sleeping?
JULIA:	I guess not.
MELISSA:	Fighting with——? (*She motions towards the offstage bedroom.*)
JULIA:	What? Oh. He's not here.
MELISSA:	He's not? Out all night?
JULIA:	He's working breakfast this week. We had to get up at four-thirty.

MELISSA: We?

JULIA: I can't let him tiptoe around in the dark.

MELISSA: No. Of course not. You look like this because Keith is working breakfast? You think his dinky little minimum-wage job is worth your health? Why don't you at least go to bed earlier?

JULIA: I—

MELISSA: You've been fighting. I know you have.

JULIA: Of course we haven't.

MELISSA: (*She mimics* JULIA.) Of course we haven't.

JULIA: We hardly ever fight.

MELISSA: Right. That's why you look like this.

JULIA: We hardly ever fight.

MELISSA: Last time I was here you argued about the piano.

JULIA: That was just a disagreement.

MELISSA: What kind of man doesn't like the piano?

JULIA: Well, Keith, I guess.

MELISSA: So where is it? You got rid of it.

JULIA: I couldn't play it if he didn't like it.

MELISSA: See. That's what's the matter with you right there. You shouldn't have gotten rid of the piano. You should have gotten rid of Keith.

JULIA: I don't care that much about the piano. Besides, we got a good price for it.

MELISSA:	You shouldn't care so much about Keith. (*A pause.*) *We* got a good price for it? It was *your* piano! You think this is none of my business, don't you? Well, it's not. You're my best friend. I have to look out for you. Just look at yourself! Someone has to look out for you.
JULIA:	I can take care of myself.
MELISSA:	I'm sorry. Of course you can. You're a grown woman, aren't you?
JULIA:	Same as you.
MELISSA:	I wouldn't mind so much if someone wanted to look after me.
JULIA:	You wouldn't . . . ? You mean, you want someone to?
MELISSA:	Sure. Why not? Makes life easier.
JULIA:	Do you need help? Are you okay?
MELISSA:	I'm fine. This isn't about me. This is about you.
JULIA:	I'm fine.
MELISSA:	It's time you found someone who was good for you. Keith is not good for you. He's not a bad person. That's not what I'm saying. It's just that you and he together are not a good combination. You both look like shit.
JULIA:	Keith looks like shit? When did you see him?
MELISSA:	Oh. I don't know. Around. He had a black eye.
JULIA:	I know. (*A pause.*) Ray punched him.
MELISSA:	Ray? His best friend? Why?
JULIA:	He was defending me.
MELISSA:	Ray was defending you.

JULIA:	No. Keith was defending me. Against Ray.
MELISSA:	Really?
JULIA:	Yes. Really. Keith told me.
MELISSA:	Well. If Keith told you.
JULIA:	I believe him.
MELISSA:	Why would Keith have to defend you against Ray? Ray adores you.
JULIA:	I always thought he liked me. But he makes fun of me.
MELISSA:	When?
JULIA:	When I leave. When I'm not there.
MELISSA:	Oh really.
JULIA:	He laughs at me.
MELISSA:	I've never heard him laugh at you. I've heard him talk behind your back and he never laughs. You want to know what he says?
JULIA:	No.
MELISSA:	He says he wishes you'd dump Keith and go out with him instead.
JULIA:	He's Keith's best friend.
MELISSA:	So what?
JULIA:	He would never say that.
MELISSA:	Well he has. And you know what else? He punched Keith in the eye for making fun of you. I was there.

JULIA: You were there?

MELISSA: Yes.

              (*The lights fade to black.*)

                          Scene 3

              (*Lights rise on that evening.* JULIA *is setting the table for dinner.* KEITH
              walks in from the bedroom dressed to go out.)

JULIA: Dinner's almost ready.

KEITH: Dinner?

JULIA: I cooked.

KEITH: What?

JULIA: Steaks—Porterhouses. Potatoes. Brussels sprouts. Your favorites.

KEITH: I'm not hungry.

JULIA: It'll be ready soon.

KEITH: I'm going out.

JULIA: First there's soup. Cream of mushroom. Not from a can.

KEITH: I said I was going out.

JULIA: Can't you go out after? I cooked. You won't have to buy dinner.

KEITH: I'm going out now.

JULIA:	Please. It won't be good as leftovers.
KEITH:	You should have thought of that before. I told you I was busy.
JULIA:	You didn't.
KEITH:	Yes. I told you yesterday.
JULIA:	You didn't. I told you I'd make Porterhouse steaks. You said good. You said they were your favorite cut. You talked about the shape of the bone. Meat on both sides of the T.
KEITH:	I told you I had to go out.
JULIA:	Maybe you were drunk. Maybe you forgot.
KEITH:	Maybe you're just wrong.
JULIA:	Okay. Maybe I'm wrong. Can't we have dinner? Then you can go out. Where are you going?
KEITH:	Out.
JULIA:	Who are you going with?
KEITH:	What are you, my mother?
JULIA:	Fine. Go out. (*A pause.*) Melissa was here today. She said I should break up with you. (KEITH *laughs*.) What's so funny?
KEITH:	That bitch. She's always had it in for me. What'd I ever do to her?
JULIA:	She says I look like shit.
KEITH:	Well you do, baby.
JULIA:	I do?
KEITH:	Your face is puffy. You need a haircut.

JULIA: I had a haircut last week.

KEITH: Yeah? You should go get a refund. Who cut it?

JULIA: I don't know.

KEITH: Tell me and I'll deck him.

JULIA: You'll deck him?

KEITH: Yeah.

JULIA: Like you decked Ray?

KEITH: Yeah. See, baby, I defend you.

JULIA: How come Ray didn't get a black eye? How come only you got a black eye?

KEITH: (A pause.) Because I hit him in the stomach.

JULIA: You didn't hit him, did you?

KEITH: Sure I hit him.

JULIA: Why?

KEITH: I told you. He made fun of you. So I decked him.

JULIA: So why did he punch you?

KEITH: He hit me when I hit him. What do you think, he'd just stand there?

JULIA: What did he say, exactly, that made you hit him?

KEITH: I don't like to repeat it. I don't want you to feel bad.

JULIA: Just tell me. (A pause.) He didn't say anything about me, did he? Melissa told me what happened.

KEITH: Oh, she did?

JULIA: She told me everything.

KEITH: What did she tell you?

JULIA: She told me. The whole thing.

KEITH: She's a liar.

JULIA: You don't even know what she said.

KEITH: It wasn't about her.

JULIA: What wasn't?

KEITH: It was never about her. It was about you. I defended you.

JULIA: The black eye?

KEITH: It had nothing to do with Melissa. She was just there.

JULIA: Why was she there?

KEITH: She's always there. She's like a parasite.

JULIA: She's always where?

KEITH: Around. She brings me donuts.

JULIA: Donuts?

KEITH: Those twisty ones. With the frosting. My favorites.

JULIA: The black eye was about Melissa?

KEITH: Melissa. She's your friend.

JULIA: Is she?

KEITH: Ray said she's a whore.

JULIA: He did? (*A pause.*) Is she?

KEITH: Look. You want to have dinner? Let's have dinner.

JULIA: You're not going to go out?

KEITH: First let's have dinner.

JULIA: Then you'll go out?

KEITH: Let's have those steaks. Cooked rare.

JULIA: They're already cooked. They're getting cold.

KEITH: Then let's eat.

JULIA: And then you'll go out.

KEITH: It's Saturday night.

JULIA: But then you'll come home?

KEITH: Sure. Then I'll come home.

JULIA: And tomorrow we can see a movie.

KEITH: Maybe. Sure. Tomorrow.

(*The lights fade to black.*)

END

Claudia Barnett

Claudia Barnett teaches playwriting at Middle Tennessee State University, where students performed *Devoted* at the Women and Power Conference luncheon in 1997. Her first full-length play *Feather* won the 2004 Brick Playhouse Award. She is currently writing *Another Manhattan,* a historical drama set in 1642-43.

The Artist

Michael Hohnstein's chillingly comic satire turns on the theatrical truism that if a gun appears onstage it must be used before the final curtain. Many playwrights have planted objects (gun, knife, diary, whatever) early in a play's action to prepare for their use after the initial appearance is all but forgotten. In *The Artist*, however, the rifle on its tripod is a literal pointer aimed at the heart of the title character, and remains the focus of the audience's attention from start to finish. The play's ending is implicit in the piece of performance art at center stage, as well as in the dramatic convention it embodies.

As the play begins, the artist, Ted, and his performance piece catch the attention of George, an unwilling gallery patron engaged in domestic bickering with his wife Helen. Lingering as Helen moves on with the tour group, George conducts a one-sided conversation with the silent Ted and reveals himself as something more formidable than the "okay Joe" he claims to be. Upon the entrance of Gus, a naïve young would-be artist, George sets into motion a catastrophic sequence of events worthy of a Mephistopheles. Hohnstein's dialogue, characterization, and complications are witty and diverting, but underlying the laughter they earn is a feeling of dread much like that evoked by the inexorable progress of a classic tragedy toward its inevitable ending.

Michael Hohnstein

The Artist

(Lights on to reveal TED seated on the floor, left, slightly up from center, facing right. He is dressed only in a white loincloth. His legs are crossed and his arms rest on his knees. Unless indicated otherwise, he is oblivious to everything around him. Directly at his back, against which he can lean, is a partition. It is important only that the partition be sturdy and its surface white. At right, aimed at TED, is a rifle mounted on a tripod. The areas immediately around TED and the rifle are well-lit. The MUSEUM GUIDE is heard speaking a moment before entering, right. He moves toward center speaking to persons apparently filing in behind him.)

GUIDE: . . . which is essentially what this gallery is all about. When we select pieces to exhibit, we look for those artists who define the obscure and make it relevant. We look for the artist whose work dramatically redefines art simply by revealing, then defining the artist himself. (*Pause. He waits at center a moment for everyone to enter. As he resumes speaking, GEORGE and HELEN enter right and stop. They are both carrying pamphlets. HELEN intently studies hers and tries hard to listen. GEORGE has his pamphlet rolled up and absently plays with it, bored and disinterested. As he speaks, the GUIDE will alternately address the audience, persons to his right and left, and turn to TED when appropriate.*) The piece before us is an excellent example of what I've been talking about. But what makes this an extraordinary piece? Art is the artist painting the painting. He has stripped art to the act, to himself. He is the sculpture. (*Short pause.*) Incidentally, copies of his new catalog in both the hardcover, limited edition and soft cover edition are available downstairs in our gift shop. They contain prints and photographs—

GEORGE: (*To* TED) Autographed as well?

(HELEN *elbows him in the side*)

GUIDE: —of many of his previous works. He has secured his reputation primarily on the West Coast. He has had numerous showings in the Bay area and in Los Angeles. We are proud to be the first to give him exposure here in the Midwest. (*Pause*) As we leave for the next exhibit, remember that sculpture is a response to space. As you pass, focus on the way this piece utilizes space. (GEORGE *and* HELEN *begin to move left,* GEORGE *trailing.* GEORGE *has his rolled-up pamphlet to his eye and is looking up, presumably at space. Until* HELEN *grabs it, he keeps the pamphlet to his eye.* HELEN *looks alternately at the different elements pointed out by the* GUIDE *and the* GUIDE *himself, who is oblivious to both.*) Look not only at the space the piece occupies in the room, (GEORGE *looks quickly around the room.*) but at the spaces within the piece itself. (GEORGE *looks back to the piece*.) Notice the space between objects in the piece. The artist and his texture as one object, (GEORGE *looks at* TED.) the gun and its texture as another, (GEORGE *looks at the rifle*.) and how the space between them and the movement that space suggests, (GEORGE *looks rapidly back and forth between the rifle and* TED.) creates metaphor and meaning.

GEORGE: Ahh. Yep.

GUIDE: (*As he exits left*.) Which is what art and this gallery is all about.

              (HELEN *stops to consult her pamphlet*.)

HELEN: This next one sounds pretty interesting.

              (GEORGE *bumps into her back*.)

GEORGE: Whoops, sorry. What is it? What's the next one about?

HELEN: Well, it says here (GEORGE *leans over her shoulder and looks at her pamphlet through his*.) that it's a reconstruction—(*She grabs his pamphlet away. Then angrily*.) What are you trying to do?

GEORGE: I was trying to focus.

HELEN: What you were trying to do, and doing very well, is embarrass me.

GEORGE: I wasn't trying to embarrass you, Helen.

HELEN: No, of course not. Like you've never done it before. You're always trying to embarrass me.

GEORGE: I am not. That's ridiculous.

HELEN: You're ridiculous.

GEORGE: Oh. We're having that type of discussion. (HELEN *turns away*. GEORGE *follows*.) Listen, hon, I wasn't trying to embarrass you. If I did, I'm sorry. Really. I admit I was indulging in a little creative play, but—

HELEN:	(*Turning on* GEORGE.) Just like a goddam kid, George. (*She looks at* TED, *smiles, then back to* GEORGE.) Worse, in fact. Our kids behave better than you do.
GEORGE:	That's ridiculous. No, wait. I'm ridiculous. The kids, for your information, don't happen to think I'm ridiculous. They happen to think I'm an okay Joe. I wonder why? It causes no end of confusion.
HELEN:	This is all just a big joke to you, isn't it? Everything.
GEORGE:	No. No, it isn't. It's just hard for me to take something seriously when I'm among a horde of people. It's very distracting. You can't see or hear anything. Everybody stands around and nods their head when somebody else nods theirs. Very seriously, too. Like they're at an autopsy or something.
HELEN:	I know you're not crazy about art, George, or taking me to see it, but it's important to me. So you can at least act like an adult, can't you?
GEORGE:	Yes. Yes, I'll behave. I promise. (*He pats her on her shoulder.*)
HELEN:	Let's go, then. I think they've already started.
GEORGE:	Would you mind if I stayed here? I'll catch up to you in a minute. This thing actually kind of intrigues me.
HELEN:	You're not going to try to talk to him, are you? Grill him on his childhood? Ask him what his parents do?
GEORGE:	Of course not. Why? Is it against the rules?
HELEN:	You're just not supposed to, infant. So, don't.
GEORGE:	I won't. I'll just look. Take it in. Immerse myself. (*He turns to* TED, *thoughtful, and slowly nods*).
HELEN:	Spare me, please. (*Short pause.*) Not too long, all right? They'll be closing soon.
GEORGE:	Right. (*She turns to leave.*) Helen?

HELEN: (*Turning back.*) What?

GEORGE: Can I have my pamphlet back? (*She hands it to him.*) Thank you. (*He unrolls it, studies it. She watches a moment, turns and exits left. He studies the pamphlet a moment longer, then rolls it up, puts it to his eye, looks left, then looks at* TED. *He walks right, toward the rifle, tapping the pamphlet in his open hand. He stops behind the rifle, sights, raises his head, then sights again. He steps back and regards* TED.) Yep. It's pointed at your heart, all right. (*He moves up, a few steps closer to* TED.) So tell me, Ted—can I call you Ted?—how does it feel to be exposed in the Midwest? (*Pause.*) Is it like being exposed on the Coast? In the Bay? (*Pause.*) We here in the Midwest are tickled to have you, I can tell you that. I think I can speak for the Midwest. I have the accent. (*Pause.*) Have you exposed yourself in the East? I know they'd be delighted to have you. And then there're other places. You know, in the South and in the North. (*Pause.*) Well, Ted—are you sure Ted's all right?—I've got to admit that you've gotten me a little curious. Not you exactly. You seem a little dull to me. I don't really care about what kind of friends you have, you childhood, nor do I care about what it is your parents do. No, I don't care for you much, but—(*He moves alongside the rifle, regards it briefly, then turns to* TED.) let's assume for the moment this gun is loaded. Now, what does that suggest? (*Pause. He jumps up and down hard a couple of times.*) Okay. We know it doesn't have a hair trigger. (*He turns and walks behind the rifle, slightly upstage.*) Notice where I am, Theodore, or would you prefer Ted? I'm behind the gun. When I'm assuming it's not loaded, I'll feel free to walk in front of it. Clues, Ted. (*Pause.*) You know what, Simpkins? I'm having a lot of trouble with the idea that this thing is loaded. It would show a somewhat unjustified optimism on your part in human nature. We read in the paper, every other day it seems, stories about someone getting plugged by a gun found lying around the house. As I understand it, it doesn't make any difference whether the gun is loaded, or not. It fires anyway. But that's beside the point. What about the stories of intentional mayhem we read about on almost every page? The point is that people can't wait to do themselves or others in when there's a gun lying around. Or mounted on a stand. But then those people probably don't appreciate art like you and me. (*Pause. He turns and moves slowly upstage.*) Us serious gallery-goers wouldn't dream of pulling the trigger, of course. But I don't think it very likely you could absolutely count on that. Say for instance, some guy walks in here off the street. Maybe he's looking for a cup of coffee or a bathroom, or maybe he's just never been in an art gallery before. Anyway, he comes in here, sees the gun, walks up to it, and pulls the trigger. Pow! Now, that poor bastard doesn't have murder in his heart. Maybe he just has a heightened sense of play. Or maybe he thinks he's supposed to. There aren't any signs telling him not to, for Pete's sake. He just has the wrong attitude. He's not a serious gallery-goer. (*Pause. He moves downstage.*) See what I mean, Teddy? But the real clincher here is that the museum wouldn't allow it. They couldn't take the chance. The publicity, the lawsuits. Ergo—that's nice, isn't it? Ergo? Yes. Well, ergo, Ted, the gun isn't loaded. The evidence is overwhelming. (*He moves up in front of the gun.*)

But if we're supposed to wonder if the gun is loaded, then whoa!—(*He hops back.*)—and we've just determined it's not, (*He hops forward back in front of the rifle.*) then what's the point? (*Pause. He reflects.*) Wait. I'm supposed to pretend, in my mind, I think, that this thing is loaded and then become overwhelmed by the possibilities. Right. But I just can't get excited when I know the gun's not loaded. You with me, Ted? (*He walks upstage.*) And how does this thing end? Ted, are you listening to me? I mean, are you hired by the gallery for an ex number of days? Do you punch out every night and go home with your empty lunch box? Or does it end when somebody pulls the trigger? Does it go click? Or is there a blank? Or does a flag come out? A blank and a flag? Do you just get up, grab the gun, go home and cash the check? Or are you paid in cash? Are you paid a set fee? Or by how long the piece lasts? Piece-work, Ted. (*He begins to walk downstage, stopping farther down and left than before.*) You see? I have a lot of questions about art. There are a lot of things about art I don't understand. (*Pause.*) You know, Ted—please, I'm George—I dabble a little in art myself. I may just look like a guy who owns an appliance store, but I dabble. I appreciate art. Oh sure, there's a lot I don't understand, but I have a capacity for it. (*Pointing to his heart.*) Mostly, art gets me right here. It's like a yearning. So I dabble. I help Karen, she's our youngest one, with her art. She tells me which colors to use and I help her fill in the spaces. I can stay in the lines pretty well. (*Motioning for silence.*) Now, I know you and others of you ilk—that's nice, isn't it? Ilk?—you and others of your ilk may say that what we do is just so much garbage, but we are damn proud of it, mister. We've got our stuff hanging all over. In the hallway, on the refrigerator, and the walls of her room are just covered with it. (*Pause.*) You'd like our family. Why don't you come over for dinner? Would you like that? I could invite the Jensens, they're friends of ours. Neighbors. I could borrow a gun, clamp it to the dining room table, and prop you up against the far wall. We could get a separate table for the kids, they like that anyway, and maybe get them a BB gun. Tommy, he's our oldest, has been badgering me for one and I think he's old enough. We'd be tickled to have you.

(*Pause.* HELEN *enters, left.*)

HELEN:	You're still here.
GEORGE:	(*Turning to her.*) Hi, Helen. Yep, still here. This guy is really fascinating. I've invited him for dinner.
HELEN:	You what? (*She turns to* TED *and smiles.*) I mean, of course we'd be delighted to have, uh, Mr.—
GEORGE:	Ted. Mr. Ted. He prefers that to anything else. So do I.
HELEN:	I'd be tickled to have Mr. Ted over for dinner—
GEORGE:	(*To* TED.) See?
HELEN:	—but I wish you would have checked with me first.
GEORGE:	Don't worry, honey, he won't be able to make it. Otherwise engaged and all that.
HELEN:	Oh. So you have talked to him.
GEORGE:	Just briefly. He asked me about the show, whether I liked it or not. I assured him I've been simply fascinated. And then I asked him to dinner and that's about it. He's pretty reticent. Almost taciturn.
HELEN:	Yes. Well, I stopped by to tell you that we're on our way to the last exhibit. It's upstairs. Are you coming? They're closing soon.
GEORGE:	Why don't you go ahead? Do you mind? I want to stay a little longer.
HELEN:	No, I don't mind. I just wanted you to know where I'd be.
GEORGE:	I appreciate that. I'll catch up in a bit.
HELEN:	Fine. Don't pester Mr. Ted.
GEORGE:	I won't. (*She turns and exits left.* GEORGE *watches her leave through his pamphlet. The turning back to* TED.) Lovely woman, isn't she? Have I told you how we met?

It was at a party. She was standing by herself. Great legs. So I walked over and asked her if she was a Gemini. She had to mull this one over because she didn't know what to say. Finally she said she was. Then I said, "Isn't that remarkable? My horoscope told me today I should hitch my wagon to a Gemini, even though yesterday it told me to kiss and make up. I don't have a wagon, but it's plain we're meant for each other." And Helen said, "I happen to be a Pisces." And do you know what I told her? I told her, "It doesn't matter. You've got great instincts." And that's what she's got. Great instincts. Great legs. (*Pause.*) She's a frustrated artist, you know. That's her one great desire. Her consuming vision. To be an artist. I try in my own way to encourage her, but still she despairs. Her skill cannot match her yearning. (*Pause. He walks upstage right, apparently deep in thought. He walks in front of the rifle and stops, then turns to* TED. *Pause.* GUS *enters, right. He walks to center and stops. He looks at* TED, *steps back, looks at the rifle, looks back at* TED *and otherwise contemplates the scene. He notices that* GEORGE *is staring at him.* GEORGE *smiles and they both regard* TED. GUS *pulls a pamphlet from his pocket and studies it.*) Well?

GUS: What?

GEORGE: Well? What do you think?

GUS: About what?

GEORGE: The piece. What do you think about the piece?

GUS: Oh. (*Pause.*) It's obviously a statement.

GEORGE: Really?

GUS: Yes.

GEORGE: About what?

GUS: Well, the contrasting elements are quite vivid. Very powerful.

GEORGE: Yes. I can see that. Now that you mention it. (GUS *looks at the rifle, then at* TED, *then down to his pamphlet, then at* GEORGE.)

GUS: I think it's a plea for gun control. (GEORGE *pulls his head back, then leans forward and squints.*)

GEORGE: (*Straightening.*) That is powerful. And vivid. You know what? I've been standing here at least three minutes and I never thought of that. Amazing. (*Pause. They both reflect.*)

GUS: What do you think?

GEORGE: About what?

GUS : The piece.

GEORGE: Shit, I'm no artist. No way.

GUS: You don't have to be an artist to appreciate art.

GEORGE: That's easy for you to say. You're an artist.

GUS: How do you know that?

GEORGE: I'm just guessing by the way you approached the piece. Carefully. And by the way you stopped and immersed yourself in it and saw everything at a glance. You are, aren't you?

GUS: Well, yes.

GEORGE: You see? What kind of work do you do?

GUS: I'm a sculptor.

GEORGE: Really? Isn't that fascinating. What's your medium? Is that the term?

GUS: Ceramics. You know, clay. That's the term.

GEORGE: You mean like urns and bowls.

GUS: No, not exactly. I do busts.

GEORGE: That doesn't sound too hard. A scoop of ice cream and a cherry. Or do you mean heads?

GUS: Busts in sculpture are heads.

GEORGE: Oh. (*Pause*.) What did you say your name was?

GUS: I didn't. It's Gus.

GEORGE: Gus?

GUS: Gus. What's yours?

GEORGE: Gus.

GUS: That's pretty funny.

GEORGE: Yeah. And I thought I was the only one. (*Pause*.)

GUS: You must have some response to the piece, Gus.

GEORGE: Well, I guess I do. (*Pause*.) You won't laugh?

GUS: Of course not.

GEORGE: I'm a little dense about these things, but the only way I can respond to sculpture is to think of it—aw, hell, you're the sculptor . . .

GUS: Go ahead.

GEORGE: Well, Gus, I look at sculpture as a response to space. And not just the space the piece occupies in the room, though that is important. I try to focus on the spaces within the piece itself. In this case, the space between objects. As one object we have the artist dressed only in swaddling clothes. To me, that suggests the Christ child. And the backdrop, smooth and white. Virginal. Virtuous. Together, I see an image of purity. Of innocence. Now, I see the rifle as the other object. And I see the space between. I see the movement that space suggests. The two objects are at opposite ends of the same line. Ergo—sorry, I hate that word—anyway, that suggests to me that the rifle is a pure and innocent object. It is we that render the rifle murderous. I see the piece as a metaphor for the human condition. It appeals to the murderous instinct that is a part of every man. At least, we're supposed to pretend that it does. (*Long Pause*.)

GUS:	Well, that was pretty good. Quite remarkable, in fact. Is that what you do for fun? Wait around so you can make fun of people? Is that what you do?
GEORGE:	What are you talking about?
GUS:	Is that how you get off? Trying to embarrass people?
GEORGE:	I was just talking garbage. Residue.
GUS:	Because I don't think it's too funny myself. (*He turns left to leave.*)
GEORGE:	(*Crossing over in front of the rifle to* GUS.) Wait a second. Hold on. I've got to let you in on a little secret. (*He stands in front of* GUS.) Please? I'm sorry. I was saying all that stuff for Ted here. I wasn't trying to make fun of you. There's something you should know. You being an artist and all. (GUS *stops. Pause.*) Well, my wife is quite an artist. My daughter, too. She's done some really fine work.
GUS:	Really? I wouldn't have thought you were that old. Is that the secret?
GEORGE:	From another marriage. It's not really a secret, but you see my wife went to school on the West Coast and she was quite active in the art community around the Bay area, which is where this guy comes from. She knows all about him. She filled me in on this bird. Well, have you thought at all about how this piece ends?
GUS:	No. What do you mean?
GEORGE:	It's gotta end. And I know, for a fact, that this piece ends when somebody walks up and pulls the trigger.
GUS:	You're crazy.
GEORGE:	No. Really. I know. Nothing happens, of course. It just goes click and the guy gets up, grabs his gun and his check and goes home. Or maybe it's cash, I don't know. He did the same thing in L.A. My wife saw it.
GUS:	Really.
GEORGE:	Don't you see? The piece is incomplete. The fact that the gun is so accessible is supposed to make us acutely aware of our potential involvement, like we're supposed to fall over at the mere thought of it. But the whole thing is a sham.

The gun just goes click. It remains, however, that the piece isn't complete until somebody pulls the trigger. Now, if I was the artist, I'd have a friend if mine come up about five minutes after I sat down and shoot. Then I'd get up, pocket the money, and take a powder. But I'm no artist. Artists have scruples.

GUS: I'll be damned. (*Pause. They reflect.*)

GEORGE: Come over here a minute. (GEORGE *indicates the rifle and moves toward it.* GUS *hesitates.*) Come on. I want you to look at something. (GUS *follows. They stop behind the rifle.*) Now. Sight down the barrel.

GUS: (*Looking nervously around.*) What?

GEORGE: Go ahead. Everybody that walks by does it. Gives them a real feel for their potentiality. (GUS *timidly sights down the barrel.*) What does that remind you of?

GUS: Well?

GEORGE: Go ahead. Take another look. (GUS *does so.*) Well?

GUS: I don't know. Target practice?

GEORGE: In a way. But I'll bet you've never sighted down a real gun at a person before.

GUS: No. No, I haven't. (*He sights again.*)

GEORGE: The penny arcade.

GUS: What?

GEORGE: The arcade. The shooting gallery. Sometimes the guns are mounted like this to the counter. So you can't steal them. You shoot at ducks.

GUS: I see what you mean. (*He straightens and turns to* GEORGE.) I lived by a penny arcade when I was a kid. It was on a boardwalk that was built out into the ocean. It was best at night. The lights on the water and the girls. I haven't been back in years. It's still there. They even had clowns.

GEORGE: Exactly. (*He walks left, stops and turns.*) I thought also of a carnival, a fair. Where they have the cage with a guy inside on a plank over some water. If you hit the target, the plank collapses and the guy falls in. I was a deadeye. (*Pause. GUS sights down the rifle.*) Art is all around us. That's why I admire artists. They see things. Ordinary things most of us don't notice. But an artist, he'll notice something and boom! (TED *raises an arm, his palm to the gun.*) it triggers something in his mind—

> (*The rifle fires. It should be done as realistically as possible: the shot is loud, the rifle recoils, etc. TED is slammed back against the partition, then falls away to his right. GUS stands stunned for a moment, then takes a few cautious steps toward TED.*)

GUS: Oh, my God. (*Pause.*) You said it wasn't loaded.

GEORGE: I'm shocked.

GUS: (*Louder.*) You said it wasn't loaded!

GEORGE: I'm very shocked. I was expecting a flag.

GUS: You said!

GEORGE: And my wife has a lot to answer for, I can tell you. Meanwhile, we don't need to hang around here.

GUS: Don't you see what's happened?

GEORGE: Yes, I do. And I think you've done enough.

GUS: What? (*He looks at* TED, *then begins to back away.*) My God. I'm going to be sick.

GEORGE: Buck up, Gus. The gallery wouldn't stand for it. Here, I'll give you a hand.

> (*He advances.* GUS *keeps backing right.*)

GUS: Stay away from me. (*Pause.*) Who are you?

GEORGE:	(*Still advancing.*) "Your name is my name, too. And when we all go out you can hear the people shout—"
GUS:	Stay away from me.
	(*He turns and exits right. GEORGE stops. Pause. He turns and walks toward TED. He stays upstage from the rifle and stops near center. He consults his pamphlet, then rolls it up and walks nearer TED. Pause.*)
GEORGE:	I must say that was a pretty good joke we played on each other. We're two of a kind, you and me. (*Pause.*) But the best joke was the one we played on that poor bastard. He's had enough art for one day.
	(*Pause. He steps away from TED and moves downstage. He glances right, then left. Seeing HELEN approaching, he moves to her and stops her as she enters far left.*)
GEORGE:	Hello, dear. I was just coming to find you.
HELEN:	They're getting ready to close.
GEORGE:	How were the other exhibits? What were they like?
HELEN:	Well, in the next room they have a collection of ceramics. Frankly, it looked like stuff Karen could do. Upstairs they had a neo-Dada exhibit. Very strange.
GEORGE:	Neo-what?
HELEN:	Dada.
GEORGE:	Dada. Well, we'll just have to give them some time. Look, we've got a few minutes left. Why don't you take through the rest on the way out? Show me the highlights. I'd really like to see them.
HELEN:	I guess we could.
GEORGE:	Good. You know what? I learned a lot about art today. I really did. I like art. I understand art.

HELEN: That's great, George. (*Consulting her pamphlet.*) Let's go upstairs first. Then we can see the ceramics on our way out.

GEORGE: Fine. You know, we'll have to come again soon. We don't do this nearly as often as we should.

HELEN: (*Doubtful, looking at him.*) Well. I'm surprised to hear you say something like that.

GEORGE: I can see now that I've been approaching art with the wrong attitude. Shall we? (HELEN *moves left, consulting her pamphlet.* GEORGE *follows with his rolled-up pamphlet to his eye.*) Helen. You know what I like about art?

HELEN: What's that, George?

GEORGE: (*Regarding space through his pamphlet.*) Art is all around us. Wherever you look.

HELEN: We're in an art gallery.

GEORGE: Yes. Yes we are.

(*They exit. Pause. The lights fade to black.*)

END

Michael Hohnstein wrote *The Artist* in 1983,
and it was first produced at the York Arena
Theatre, Western Michigan University, in
1984. Another of his plays, *The Contract*,
has also been published and produced,
and he is a published short-story writer as
well. He is married and lives in Stevensville,
Michigan, where he works as a construction
superintendent.

Heart of Hearts

Jim Daniels brings his working-class characters together in the waiting room of an abortion clinic. The opening tableau seems self-explanatory: a middle-aged couple and a teenaged girl. What we're actually seeing, however, is the unlikely setting for a pregnant woman's reluctant introduction of her unborn child's father to her judgmental daughter. The mother, Betty, is about to have an abortion, with Carl and Ann as doubtful sources of moral support.

Daniels depicts each character thoroughly, giving attention to their endearing qualities as well as their shortcomings, but he refuses to force the play to a facile optimistic ending. The likeable but emotionally clumsy and heavy-drinking Carl is clearly not the answer to Betty's prayers, if indeed she still believes in prayers or answers. Ann's moral stance is undermined by the revelation that she, too, has ended a pregnancy. And Betty in turn makes no last-minute decision against abortion.

As the play ends, mother and daughter find their way to a tentative reconciliation that allows them to face together an uncertain future. Daniels's clear-eyed vision allows him to give the ordinary its due, in a complex and moving drama that neither condescends to nor romanticizes its characters' working-class status.

Jim Daniels

Heart of Hearts

CHARACTERS   BETTY: an attractive woman in her mid-thirties, prematurely hardened and aged.

CARL: a large, heavy-set man around forty, with the look of an athlete gone to seed.

ANN: a thin, mousy woman in her late teens.

SETTING   The waiting room of an abortion clinic, the present.

(BETTY *sits alone on a couch, facing the audience, head down, hands clasped between her legs. She wears a flashy, low-cut blouse. On one side of her,* CARL. *He is wearing a T-shirt and jeans. On the other side of* BETTY, *in a chair facing* CARL, *sits* ANN, BETTY's *daughter from her first marriage.* ANN *is dressed conservatively in plain skirt and blouse.* ANN's *arms are folded across her chest. In front of the couch sits a low table covered with magazines. A long silence.* CARL *squirms uncomfortably in his chair. He holds a set of keys in his hands and jingles them nervously.*)

ANN: How did you two meet, anyway?

(CARL *and* BETTY *speak simultaneously.*)

CARL: In a bar.

BETTY: In the supermarket.

CARL: Well, both. First in a bar, then in the supermarket.

ANN: How come I never met him before? Were you ashamed to bring your "boyfriend" home?

BETTY: After the way you treated the last man in my life . . .

ANN: (*Interrupting.*) Lucky Larry?

(*She shakes her head, laughs derisively.*)

BETTY: (*Louder.*) After the way you treated the last man in my life, you think I'm going to bring anybody home to meet you . . . ? I was waiting till it seemed right . . . (*Quietly.*) Lucky Larry, by the way, wasn't so bad. I wouldn't go so far as to call him lucky, but he was decent enough for a Larry.

(*She chuckles softly to herself.* ANN *rolls her eyes.* CARL *loudly jingles his keys again.*)

Yeah, Lucky Larry, if only . . .

CARL:	(*Interrupting. Facing* ANN.) I told your mom I wanted to meet you. We haven't known each other that long. A few months is all.
ANN:	Long enough, it seems . . . Lucky Larry, now Lucky Carl. Mom, I wish you'd quit getting so lucky . . . It seems like it takes an abortion to get your attention these days.
BETTY:	Oh, shut up. Why did you want to come here? I really don't get it. I mean, I didn't even have to tell you. I'm trying to treat you like a goddamn adult, and here you are treating me like . . . Just don't judge me like this. It's not fair. I can't take it.
ANN:	(*Gets closer to* BETTY, *lowers voice.*) Mom, I just want to help turn things around a little bit—for you, for us. (*Louder.*) Besides, it's not like you haven't been judging everything I've done for the last eighteen years.
BETTY:	(*Pausing, speaking slowly.*) Not everything. Sometimes it's better to leave things alone. Sometimes it's better not to know.
ANN:	What are you talking about?
CARL:	I always wanted to have kids. My first wife, we couldn't get pregnant. That was part of the problem, why we split up. Hell, I half-thought I couldn't make anybody pregnant.
BETTY:	It's those half-thoughts of yours that get you into trouble, Carl. We already talked about all this. You think I'd make a good mother at this point in my life? Ask Ann. Annie, haven't I been a total fuck-up as your mother?
ANN:	Mom, you amaze me. (*She straightens the magazines into neat piles.*)
CARL:	(*Standing up, walking around.*) Betty, you sure they know you're still here?
BETTY:	Christ, Carl, we're the only ones in the room.
ANN:	(*To* CARL.) You're kind of an asshole, aren't you?
BETTY:	Ann, you're supposed to be offering moral support here.

ANN:	For you, not for him.
CARL:	(*Sighing*.) Maybe, maybe I am. Everybody is sometimes. Is an asshole.
ANN:	You didn't pick Carl for his brains, I take it.
CARL:	Hey, I'm a good fireman. You can ask anybody . . . So, how 'bout those Buccos?

(ANN *and* BETTY *both turn and stare at him.* CARL *continues nervously.*)

	They took three from the Braves . . . Braves are a damn good team . . . Good pitching . . .
BETTY:	Carl . . .
ANN:	(*Sarcastically*.) Yeah, how about those Buccos?
CARL:	Well, what the hell are we supposed to be talking about? We all know why we're here.
ANN:	Why are you here, Carl?
BETTY:	He said he wanted to be here.
ANN:	He can speak for himself. Why are you here, Carl? Why?
CARL:	I don't know what it's like, having something alive inside of you, but getting rid of it, that can't be no easy thing.
BETTY:	. . . So, how about those Buccos?
ANN:	What I want to talk about is, how exactly did this happen? I don't get it. Mom, you've been preaching protection since I was thirteen. How many times have I heard, "You don't want to end up a mother at eighteen like I did." I bet you were both drunk.
BETTY:	Look, I just went through all that with the counselor back there. The "how" doesn't really matter. It was an accident. I know better. I mean, I made a mistake eighteen years ago, and I did pretty good since then. Till now.

(A beat.)

ANN: . . . Mom, did you and Dad think about having an abortion when—when you got pregnant with me?

BETTY: I think your dad thought it made him a stud or something, getting me knocked up. He's a strange man. He wouldn't hear of it. Said we had to get married right away. So, we did. It was what everybody wanted, both our families.

ANN: Was it what you wanted? You said "mistake" a minute ago. You think it was a mistake to have me?

BETTY: Now, don't get me wrong. I . . . I never . . . I was your age. Are you ready to be a mother?

ANN: When is somebody ready?

BETTY: It looks like I'm never gonna know. Listen, Annie, one thing I can say for sure, it was a mistake marrying your father. Oh, I loved him alright, but we were just kids.

ANN: At least he got wise and got fixed. Not like the big stud Carl here.

CARL: Now wait a minute . . . I never . . .

BETTY: (Interrupting CARL.) What?

ANN: Dad had a vasectomy.

BETTY: You're kidding? When?

CARL: (Putting his hands between his legs.) This is getting a little too weird for me.

ANN: A vasectomy, Carl. They don't cut your dick off. They just fix it so you can't get anyone pregnant. Didn't they used to sterilize idiots? You might look into it.

CARL: Hey, I know what a vaselectomy is. Doesn't mean it don't hurt.

BETTY: Ann, I won't have you talking to Carl like that. And Carl—you think a vasectomy's tough? In a few minutes I've got to go through that door and get a kid sucked out of me. Goddamn it, I should have just come here by myself. (*She buries her face in her hands.*)

CARL: Aw Betty, I'm sorry.

ANN: Me too, Mom. I just wanted to be alone with you today. Of all days.

> (CARL *and* ANN *both sit on the couch with* BETTY *and put their arms around her. Their hands touch behind* BETTY, *and they each pull back.*)

BETTY: I need a drink.

> (BETTY *rifles through the magazines, messing up* ANN's *piles.*)

ANN: Mom. That's how you got into this mess in the first place.

CARL: Your mom can hold her liquor.

ANN: Forget it, Mom. I'm sorry. Can I get you a pop or something?

BETTY: If you don't mind running the gauntlet again, I could use a pack of cigarettes.

CARL: I got smokes.

BETTY: No thanks, Carl. You know I'm not a Marlboro man like you.

ANN: (*Sarcastically.*) Yeah, she's a Kool customer—everybody knows that . . . I'll go see what I can find.

> (ANN *gets up and walks offstage left.*)

BETTY: Carl, listen, you don't have to stick around.

CARL: I just feel so lousy. It's my duty.

BETTY: Your duty to be hanging around with that sad-dog face making me feel worse?

CARL: (*Putting his keys in his pocket.*) Okay, I'll try and cheer up.

              (CARL *tries to smile, fails.* BETTY *bursts out laughing.*)

BETTY: That's better, Carl. You're always good for a laugh.

CARL: (*Quietly, perplexed.*) Yeah, I suppose . . . (*A beat. Louder.*) So. What should we do?

BETTY: I don't know, Carl. We haven't known each other that long. Can we talk after this is over?

CARL: I meant right now. What do you want to do right now?

              (BETTY *sighs but does not answer.* CARL *gets off the couch and moves back to his seat.*)

              Maybe we could think of some of the fun times we've had, take our mind off this.

BETTY: I don't think that's gonna work . . . What fun times?

CARL: C'mon, we've had some fun times hanging out together down at the Redwood.

BETTY: Yeah, well, I don't always remember them. Or else, when I do, they don't seem as much fun as when they were happening. Sometimes I lay there in bed the next day wondering, "What was it that was so funny I was laughing about last night?"

CARL: (*Shrugs.*) I don't know, I always remember pretty good. I don't spend time thinking, "Well, I was laughing a lot last night, was it really funny enough, maybe I shouldn't of been laughing so hard." Hey, laughs, take 'em where you can get 'em. What else have you got? Some measly bank account, a tough job . . .

BETTY: A poor fucking baby you don't want.

CARL: (*Glares at her.*) Speak for yourself.

BETTY: I am. I am speaking for myself.

              (CARL *takes his keys out and starts jingling them again.*)

	I'm sorry. You're right, I guess. We've had some fun together, eh Carl?
CARL:	You know my favorite thing? My favorite thing to do with you?
BETTY:	Well, it might of been screwing before all this . . . I think it'd be hard to do it now, without thinking. The first time, with Ann's daddy, we made our mistake, then got married. I had Ann, got on the pill and off we went. If that man would've got paid for screwing, he might have been able to get somewhere in life . . . He went to the trouble to get himself fixed—he still must be making the rounds . . . I used to tell him, the problem is you got a dick for a brain . . . Sorry, Carl. You were saying?
CARL:	It wasn't sex. My favorite thing with you.
BETTY:	(*Sighing.*) Listen, I'm sorry. I don't know where I'm at today. I know where I'm at, but I'm trying to be anywhere but here.

(*She stands up and sits on the arm of* CARL's *chair.*)

Tell me what your favorite thing is. It must be listening to me sing.

(BETTY *starts to sing, but her voice cracks, and she starts to laugh and cough.* CARL *laughs.*)

CARL:	No, that ain't it. My favorite thing is . . . is dancing with you. Late at night, after we've had a few. When there's hardly anybody in the place.
BETTY:	And we got the jukebox to ourselves.
CARL:	Yeah.
BETTY:	You ain't a bad dancer—for a fireman.
CARL:	How many firemen you danced with?
BETTY:	Firemen? Quite a few. Doctors? Never. Lawyers? Never. Firemen, janitors, candy salesmen, mechanics . . .

CARL: Hey, don't be lumping firemen in with candy salesmen.

BETTY: Okay, low blow. What I'm saying is, for a big guy, you're pretty graceful.

CARL: (*Blushing.*) No one ever called me graceful before.

           (CARL *takes* BETTY's *hand.*)

BETTY: You're such a ham . . . And I'm a sentimental drunk.

CARL: Maybe we should keep trying after this.

BETTY: I don't know . . . This isn't the time to talk about it.

           (CARL *stands up, begins to pace, looks at his watch.*)

CARL: What's the hold up here?

           (BETTY *stands up and bumps into* CARL. *They stop and hang on to each other to keep from falling.*)

BETTY: Maybe you're not as graceful as I remember.

CARL: Don't take that back—it's the only nice thing you've said to me today.

BETTY: I'm just joking. C'mon, let's dance right here. It'll keep us from pissing each other off.

CARL: You . . . you . . . okay.

           (CARL *and* BETTY *lean into each other and shuffle their feet like dancers in a bar at closing time.* BETTY *hums softly.* ANN *reenters room with a pack of cigarettes.* BETTY *and* CARL *quickly separate.*)

ANN: (*Softly.*) Here's your cigarettes, Mom.

BETTY: (*Backing slowly away from both of them.*) Save it for me. I'm starting to lose my nerve—it's time—they better be ready for me, because I'm going back there.

ANN: Oh, Mom.

(*She starts to choke up.*)

BETTY: Don't say another word.

CARL: But . . .

BETTY: (*Raising her voice.*) Either of you!

(*She gets up and quickly walks offstage right. ANN holds her head in her hands. CARL gets up off the couch and starts to move toward her, but then stops, goes back to his own seat. Silence as CARL and ANN look everywhere but at each other. Then they both start to talk at the same time.*)

ANN: Well . . .

CARL: So . . .

Go ahead.

ANN: (*Composing herself.*) I . . . I was just going to say there's this crazy part of me that wants a brother or sister. It's stupid. I mean, I know in my heart of hearts that my mom can't afford to . . . that she doesn't have her shit together enough to . . . I should know . . .

CARL: I wanted to pay. She won't even let me pay for this. Only half, she said, when it's probably my fault.

ANN: (*Glaring.*) I suspected as much . . . I've learned one thing about men—when they say "probably my fault" it's damn sure their fault. What the hell happened?

CARL: Well, see . . . This is embarrassing. You don't need to know.

ANN: C'mon, Carl—it's too late to get embarrassed.

CARL: (*Slowly.*) We were both a little drunk. I can't exactly remember it all. We weren't very careful.

ANN: That's a teenager's excuse.

CARL: It's the best I can do. What's done is done.

ANN: And getting done. Right now.

CARL: Oh, man. Let's talk about something else.

ANN: My Mom, a little drunk. That's like saying she's just a little pregnant. She should start getting her mail at that damn bar.

CARL: The Redwood?

ANN: Where else? Christ, you should know, Carl. Sounds like you have some knowledge of the place. I call it the Deadwood.

CARL: (*Laughing*.) So do I. You know, a fireman's hours are kinda strange. We get a lot of time off. I used to have a side job to keep me busy. Then one day the side job lets out early, I go home and get the big surprise. Got divorced, and started hanging out down there.

ANN: Sounds like you and my mom have a lot in common.

CARL: (*Brightening*.) Yeah, see, that's what I always tell her.

ANN: And now this. Maybe it'll sober her up some. My dad even had a talk with her about it. I mean, he's turned his life around, why can't she?

CARL: Turning things around, it's not so easy. The older you get, the wider the turn you have to make . . .

(*He rubs his beer gut*.)

Gee, I wonder how long this is going to take.

ANN: It depends—I don't know. Ask the receptionist.

CARL: (*Looks OS R, but stays seated*.) Ann, your mom tells me you got a boyfriend.

ANN: Oh—what'd she'd tell you?

CARL: Not much, just that you've been seeing some guy.

ANN: That's all she said about you. "I'm seeing this guy—a fireman."

CARL: Yeah, but she told you about this.

ANN: So?

CARL: (*Slightly angry.*) I thought it was just gonna be me and her. She didn't say nothing
                about you coming.

                (*He stacks the magazines into one tall pile.*)

ANN: Yeah, how romantic . . .

CARL: Ann, you've got a mouth on you. No wonder Betty didn't want me meeting you.

ANN: Maybe she just didn't want to bother me with someone she's not serious about.

CARL: There's different kinds of serious. You'll find that out when you get older.

ANN: I think I know all about that, now. Thanks to my "boyfriend" . . . Are you going to
                stop seeing my mother after this?

CARL: (*Caught off-guard, responds slowly.*) It ain't just my call, you know. Look, I'm here,
                ain't I? A lot of guys, they wouldn't . . .

ANN: That's because all men are shits. You think you deserve a medal for coming
                down here? She doesn't need you, Carl. We could have handled this ourselves.
                You going to dump her now?

CARL: We walk out that door, who knows which way we're gonna be turning? This
                makes things tough. We only been seeing each other a few months. This place
                gives me the creeps. How long we have to wait?

                (CARL *searches his pockets for his keys, but cannot find them. He becomes
                a bit frantic.*)

Hey, you seen my keys?

ANN: Leaving already? We came in separate cars. Doesn't that tell you which way we're turning? If you're going to run out on her, you might as well do it now.

CARL: (*Continuing his search, looking under his chair.*) I can't figure you out. Do you want me to keep seeing your mom?

(CARL *finds the keys, holds them between his hands.*)

ANN: Relax, read a magazine. They have some nice pamphlets here on birth control . . . Maybe you'll learn something.

CARL: (*Losing his composure.*) Fuck this. I'm outta . . . I gotta get some fresh air. Going out for a smoke.

ANN: That's what I want to see, the real Carl . . . Asshole.

(CARL *gets up and stomps toward the door. He starts to slam the door, but stops, grabs it, gently pulls it closed.*)

(*Softly.*) See ya.

(ANN *leans her head back and stares at the ceiling. She lets out a deep sigh, then stands up, begins pacing.* CARL *re-enters the room.*)

CARL: Hey, I'm sorry.

ANN: Me too. What are you sorry for?

CARL: Everything. Everything. I fucked up, what can I say . . . What are you sorry for?

ANN: (*Sitting down.*) For being born . . . I feel like a ball that can't stop bouncing. I'm mad. I'm sad. I'm jealous. I'm disappointed. I want to help my mom. Being nice doesn't seem to help . . . She keeps missing the hints, but when I get pushy, she gets mad . . . (*Looks at* CARL.) Sit down, Carl. It'll be over soon.

CARL: I can't. This is too much for me. I don't believe in this. In my heart of hearts,

I know it's killing going on in there. I tried to talk to her. Even adoption for chrissakes, give the kid a chance. Those protesters, they've got pictures and stuff. It's a real baby in there.

ANN: Carl, those people out there are nuts. Do we really need to talk about this? What's done is done. Or will be soon . . .

(*Uncomfortable silence.* CARL *and* ANN *both look away from each other.*)

Why don't you tell me about being a fireman?

CARL: I just can't stop thinking . . . Betty's a stubborn woman.

ANN: She's a strong woman. When she really needs to be. She's been on her own a long time now. We have—together.

CARL: The last thing that baby's going to remember is swaying in her momma's belly, my beer gut pushing into her . . .

ANN: Carl! Quit it! Did they brainwash you out there? What the hell are you talking about?

CARL: (*Pausing.*) Okay. Okay . . . A fireman. Well, yeah, okay . . . I'm gonna tell you a story. You let me finish, okay? No smartass comments, okay?

ANN: (*Looking at her watch.*) Okay, Carl.

CARL: One time we got called to this fire in a rundown building over on the North Side—a goddamn fire trap. It was really cooking when we got there. This was about ten years ago—right after my marriage broke up. The people outside in their underwear and robes start yelling, "Third floor, third floor, a family up there." So me and Tony put on our tanks and go running up the stairs. The stairwell's still pretty clear—a little smoky. We get up there and start shouting to see if anybody answers.

ANN: This isn't going to be one of those hokey stories about a fireman rescuing a baby, is it?

CARL: (*Dead serious.*) Yes, yes it is. It's the best story I've got, and I'm going to finish it . . . So. We hear noises on both sides of the hall. Tony turns right and I turn left and we're pounding on doors and whacking with our axes as fast as we can. I hear a whining behind the last door and it turns out to be a cat. I'm no cat-lover, but I grab it and run back down the hall. It's hard to see 'cause of the smoke—Tony's in another apartment calling to me. I run in and find him cradling a baby. He tells me to search the rest of the place and takes off with the baby, an infant—no bigger than a football. Nobody else in the apartment—no sign of the parents. By this time, a big crowd's outside and lots more fire trucks. Ladders and hoses everywhere. I grab the cat, find a ladder, and climb down. I hit the ground, the cat jumps out of my arms and takes off. Tony's standing on the grass across the street holding the baby. Fire's under control, so I go over to him. I've never held a baby before in my life. Never, if you can believe that. Not an infant. I don't know why, I just never had my chances. So I ask him, "Tony, can I hold the baby just for a minute?" He says "Sure, EMS needs to check her out, but she seems just fine."

So I take off some of my gear and cradle that baby to my chest. You ever hold a baby, Ann?

ANN: (*Quietly.*) Sure. Sure I have.

CARL: So the newspaper guy finds me holding her and snaps this picture and it gets blasted all over the papers the next day and it wasn't even me who saved her. In the station, Tony taped a picture of a cat over the baby on the bulletin board. Everybody got a good laugh out of it. Tony wasn't too sore about me getting the glory.

ANN: What happened to the baby?

CARL: I held her there. Trying not to get her dirty, so I didn't touch her skin. I could feel her warm through the blanket. Her eyes wide open, staring at me. She wasn't making a sound. Around us, all this commotion, and she was just staring at me. It was a moment. I said to her, "I wished I woulda saved you and not the stupid cat . . ." I didn't want to give that baby up. I got other pictures in my head, you know. The ones we didn't save . . .

ANN: (*Her voice cracking.*) Carl, that's enough . . . Hey, what happened to the cat?

CARL: I don't know. It took off . . . Took them two weeks to find the baby's mother. She was hiding 'cause of not wanting people to know she left the baby alone. And the people who owned the cat, they filed a fucking complaint that I let it get away. See, 'cause they never found it . . . Interesting, huh? I sent it in to *Reader's Digest* for that "Personal Glimpses" section, but they never printed it. Can you believe it? My best story too.

ANN: Carl, look, I do appreciate you coming, for my mom. You have to understand—I just want her back. It isn't you that's taken her away. She'd be out there with somebody. Or not with somebody. Sitting there laughing too loud at her own jokes.

CARL: You mean the Deadwood?

ANN: The Deadwood. The Grand Duchess. The Tel-Star. Wherever.

CARL: The Tel-Star? Shit, I don't even go in there. Rough joint.

ANN: Yeah, she found that out.

(CARL *winces.*)

CARL: Damn, I wish she'd let me pay.

(CARL *pulls a wad of bills from his wallet.*)

ANN: It's not so important who pays.

CARL: What do you know about it?

ANN: What do you know about it?

CARL: Shit, Ann. Not much. I feel like I'm at a fire, but nobody will let me do anything . . . Why don't you tell me a story?

(CARL *puts his wallet in his back pocket.*)

ANN: (*Pausing, sighing. She looks at her watch again.*) Okay, my story is . . . my story is I lost a friend in a fire. Artie Marks.

(ANN *closes her eyes and leans back.*)

First boy I ever kissed. Lived down the street. Hanging out with his friends in the basement one of those hot summer days where everybody's just looking for a hole to crawl into. Somebody knocked over a gas can and it caught on the drier pilot light. Everybody else got out. He slipped and fell.

CARL: Never store gasoline in the house.

ANN: He was twelve. We gave each other hickeys and my mom slapped me when she saw . . . He had this crooked smile . . . My first funeral. Poor, sweet Artie, comb sticking out of his back pocket, bouncing in his sneakers like the world couldn't hold him down . . . (*A beat.*) I ran down the street when the fire engines passed. This fireman brought him out wrapped up in a blanket. I stood in the street crying. Some kids were cracking jokes . . . Aw, he probably would've grown up to be a shit like all his friends.

CARL: What've you got against guys? What happened with that boyfriend?

ANN: I don't see that asshole anymore. I keep telling my mom we're going out, then I just go walking around. Hell, I even hang out at the library some nights. (ANN *laughs.*) Next thing you know, I'll be hanging out in church like my dad. Not that my mom cares where I am. She cares, but . . . it's like drinking's her other kid or something.

CARL: Like a part-time job. That's what my friend Ted called it when he quit. He said drinking was like a part-time job.

ANN: Whatever you call it, I hope this sobers her up some. She always talks about how she can handle it, that it doesn't affect her work. I tell her, "But it's affecting me, Mom. It's affecting me."

CARL: Betty can hold her liquor, that's the truth. I've never seen a woman drink like that. But she gets a little nasty sometimes.

ANN: That's when you can tell she's really drunk.

CARL: I haven't been much help to her. I can see that now. Buying her drinks and all. When we're sober, though, we don't have much to say to each other.

ANN: That's funny—when she's drunk, we don't have much to say to each other.

CARL: You two need to do some talking, then. I'm not going to be of much use. You're not gonna see me quit drinking any time soon.

ANN: She won't listen to my dad, and she won't listen to me. They should've never gotten divorced. They got married too young is all. On account of me. This "sowing your wild oats thing" is definitely overrated. Now, my dad spends all his time trying to look younger, and my mom spends all her time in bars.

CARL: My ex-wife, she was a handful too. And now she's living with some guy I work with.

ANN: Oh.

CARL: (*He pushes over his tower of magazines.*) "Oh" is right. I've sure screwed up a few things in this life.

ANN: Hey, nobody's perfect . . . Geez, Carl, now you've got me talking in clichés.

CARL: Better watch it—maybe it's contagious.

>   (CARL *and* ANN *share a small smile. A beat.* ANN *looks at her watch.*)

ANN: Let's go check and see if we can go back and see her.

CARL: You go, Ann. I'll wait out here.

>   (ANN *stands, hesitates, looks at* CARL, *then walks OS R.* CARL *gets up slowly. He realizes he's still holding the cash and stuffs it in his pocket. He takes his keys out, looks at them. He tosses them high in the air, catches them, then walks OS L.*)
>
>   (ANN *sits in a chair next to* BETTY, *who is sitting up on a small bed drinking a glass of juice.* BETTY *appears tired, subdued.*)

BETTY: Carl's right, Annie. Everybody is an asshole sometimes.

ANN: That Carl, he sure is profound.

BETTY: Is he still out there?

ANN: Yeah. He said I should come in and he'd wait.

BETTY: That was nice of him. I look at him, and it's like "mistake" is tattooed on his forehead . . . I'm never going through this again, let me tell you.

ANN: Yeah, I know what you mean.

BETTY: I know, Ann.

ANN: (*Nervously*.) How do you feel, Mom?

BETTY: I don't know. Empty. Sad. Relieved . . . Sober. How did you feel?

ANN: What do you mean?

BETTY: I know, Ann. I know what you been through.

ANN: What?

BETTY: I'm telling you, I know. Maybe I should have tried to help. They called home, the clinic did, on a follow-up. And here you are with me when I wasn't there for you. You being here now, it makes a difference. My child, the one I kept.

ANN: You know. Jesus Christ, Mom. You know . . . But I didn't tell you before—I didn't want you to know. I wanted to do it alone.

BETTY: But after—after, I could've helped . . . When I got pregnant with you, all these people were telling me what to do. It was out of my hands. You took control. You chose not to tell me. I wanted to respect that.

ANN: Mom, it wasn't so bad. Isn't so bad . . . You did the right thing. I know you would've been there—if I asked. You've got enough problems . . .

BETTY: You don't think I can handle anything. I've been around. I know a few things. I know about men . . . Did Al come with you?

ANN: No, he had basketball practice.

BETTY: Uh-huh . . . You're still seeing him?

ANN: No. I just pretend. Well, once or twice. I kept giving him chances.

BETTY: You got any more of those chances left for me?

                        (ANN *puts her head in her hands. Runs her fingers through her hair.*)

ANN: Mom, you just have to . . . I miss having you home with me, talking—hell, even watching bad TV together—anything. I get up and find you asleep on the couch in your clothes, stinking like the bar. You used to tell me stories, gossip from work . . .

BETTY: Ann, I'm forty years old. I'm tired of waiting tables. Sucking up for tips—you know that ain't me. After work, I got all that cash, only thing open's the bar . . . You're gonna be leaving me soon anyway.

ANN: For school, Mom, for school. What you always told me to do. What you could have done if . . . You're no dummy, Mom.

BETTY: Well, I ain't getting any smarter, that's for sure . . . Your father doesn't know, does he? You didn't have to go to him for money, did you?

ANN: (*Sighing.*) No, no. Al's father paid.

BETTY: Shit . . . The men, they always want to pay to clean up their messes. Think throwing a few bucks at it will solve everything.

ANN: Carl and I had a pretty good talk.

BETTY: I bet . . . He's a real talker, that Carl. He asked me to marry him one night.

ANN: (*Irritated.*) What?

BETTY: (*Laughing slightly.*) I said "yes" too. The whole bar was buying us drinks. We had such a good party that night . . . Woke up the next day—you were up at your father's—and we felt like shit. Thank God Vegas is so far away or we might've done it, the whole bar as witnesses.

ANN: Thank God.

BETTY: Carl's a nice guy, I guess. I sure as hell don't love him though.

ANN: I don't think you're going to find anyone to love down at the Deadwood. Mom, you're gonna end up killing yourself. What are we going to do?

BETTY: Ever since your dad and I split, I haven't quite got my balance.

ANN: But it's been six years. You should see Dad, he's lifting weights. Going to church.

BETTY: (*Sarcastically*.) Yeah, I bet he thinks he's going to live forever. Going to church?

ANN: He says it gives him peace.

BETTY: (*Softly*.) Peace, huh? I wish I could find some of that . . . In my heart of hearts, I still love your father. Geez, that little punk lifting weights. I can just see him strutting his stuff. And puffing himself up with prayers like money in the bank.

            (*A beat.*)

ANN: You know, these last few months it's been like I have this little ghost. Just a little wisp of life floating around me, a little shadow.

BETTY: Annie, did you think at all of keeping it—the baby?

ANN: No . . . No way. I'm going into debt up to my neck, but I'm getting out. I am not going to end up—forgive me—like you.

BETTY: (*After a long pause*.) I wouldn't want you to end up like me either. You made the right choice . . . We made the right choice . . . Shit, I hope I don't get your ghost—I've already got enough of them floating around.

ANN: Ghosts don't drown, Mom.

BETTY: Sometimes I get home late from the bar, I just want to call your father up and cry.

ANN: You have, Mom.

BETTY: Have I? Maybe I have. Not as often as I've thought about it. I usually hang up. I guess he knows it's me, huh?

                (ANN *nods.*)

                Well, where do we go from here, little girl? My little girl.

ANN: Home to rest.

BETTY: And then?

ANN: It's up to you.

BETTY: I guess we got a few months left. Before you leave.

ANN: Home. Rest.

BETTY: I've stopped expecting miracles. Don't believe in them.

ANN: No. I'd like to though. I think you can nudge things a little bit. Give them these little pushes. Before you know it, it's a whole new place.

BETTY: (*Laughing, shaking her head.*) What? Sometimes I don't understand you . . . I know you're in here though. (BETTY *touches her heart.*) Come give your stupid old mom a hug.

ANN: (*Hugging* BETTY.) You're not old. (*They both laugh softly.*) You don't have to love Carl, but you have to love me.

BETTY: I didn't have it in me to love another. I know that's cruel to say, but it's just not in me . . . It's hard enough sometimes . . .

ANN: I know, Mom. But I need to hear you say it.

                (ANN *starts to cry.* BETTY *rocks her in her arms.*)

BETTY: I'd be dead without you, that's the truth.

ANN: There's no looking back. It's not allowed . . . Ha.

BETTY: Ha yourself.

              (*Getting slowly to her feet.*)

              C'mon Annie, let's go say good-bye to a nice man.

              (*The lights fade to black.*)

                            END

Jim Daniels

Jim Daniels's most recent books include *Show and Tell: New and Selected Poems*, University of Wisconsin Press (2003) and *Detroit Tales*, fiction, Michigan State University Press (2003). He also wrote the screenplay for *No Pets*, an independent feature film. *Heart of Hearts* was produced at the 13th Street Repertory Theater in New York.

APPENDICES

POINTS TO CONSIDER IN ANALYZING A PLAY

1. How do the specifics of setting generate action and reveal or affect character? Consider that places where we *must* be create obvious pressures, while those where we *choose* to be act on us more subtly. What physical *stuff* (including props, set pieces, clothing, and the like) can you recall as affecting action because of the playwright's choice of setting? What stuff affects the action for reasons other than setting (such as character or some external factor)?

2. What—and how—do we learn about the nature, the backgrounds, and the relationships of the characters in the play's opening scene or sequence (the first ten to twenty percent of its running time)? How does each character's nature (strengths, weaknesses, personality, disposition—the way he or she habitually confronts the world) cause him or her to respond to—or create—complication and conflict? Distinguish the wants and needs that drive the characters and create conflict. What are their short-term goals (within individual scenes, larger segments)? What are their long-term goals (for the end of the play, perhaps even beyond the play's end)?

3. What disturbs the play's balance (the situation and relationships of the characters) near the beginning, triggering action and making the audience aware that a process of change has begun? For each play, we should be able to ask—and answer—the question, "Why today?" What makes this day different from all others in these characters' lives? The answer reveals why the playwright has chosen to begin the play at this point.

4. What discoveries does each character make as a result of complication(s) and conflict(s)? And what changes (or "reversals," to use Aristotle's term) arise from how each character acts—or refuses or fails to act—on those discoveries or realizations? Are the changes internal or external? Which characters drive the action, which are driven? Who attacks, who defends?

6. How does the playwright use beats (sequences of dialogue analogous to paragraphs) to provide exposition or preparation, reveal and contrast character, introduce complication or discovery, create conflict, advance the action, create tension, humor, mood, echoes, or connections? Note that good writers don't just introduce a subject, then drop it after one exchange. They use the subject and develop it, making it work for the play as a whole by making sure that the dialogue accomplishes several tasks at once.

7. How does the playwright use techniques of preparation to prepare the audience for later developments, to create tension, suspense, or surprise? Distinguish between *pointers* (which let the audience know something or someone is coming) and *plants* (which unobtrusively prepare for some later development). Trace the ways in which the playwright uses these devices to give

the audience a *hint* of something to come, then makes them *wait* until they've almost forgotten the hint, then gives them a *surprise* by delivering on the hint in an unexpected way.

8. Trace the number of echoes or connections in the play and consider how they may affect the audience's responses, as well as the play's unity and coherence. These echoes or connections may appear in character, action, setting, dialogue, or production elements (like costuming, setting, lighting, sound, and the like).

9. Note how strong plays heighten tension and story movement by keeping the complications and discoveries coming, rather than making you wait through endless minutes of dialogue that seem designed to postpone some surefire dramatic moment. Trace the pattern of complications and discoveries, noting how they affect situation, character, and action.

10. Note the ways in which the playwright provides opportunities for laughter, even in a serious play. Find the places where the playwright relieves tension with a lighter moment, or creates a highly dramatic effect by following a lighter moment with something serious.

11. And, again, note the playwright's use of *stuff*, what he or she knows from experience or research—about people, places, things, memories, dreams—and how he or she uses it to give substance and credibility to the play.

PLOT STRUCTURE

Commentators frequently represent the essential dynamic of dramatic action by means of Freytag's Pyramid or later modifications thereof, all of which cite the pattern of complication leading through rising action to crisis (or climax), followed by falling action leading to resolution (see diagram A).

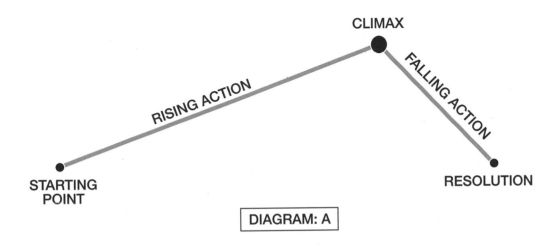

DIAGRAM: A

This language of rise and fall suggests the forceful launch of a missile and its subsequent gravity-bound descent toward its target. The ballistic precision of these models is attractive, and certainly captures a good play's movement toward a seemingly inevitable conclusion. But the models also convey the dramatically unfortunate implication that after the play reaches its high point (its apogee or climax), its force is spent and all that's left is the fall to earth. However useful this dynamic may be for audiences (including critics), we would propose our own diagram for the dramatic process from the playwright's viewpoint.

Wherever and however a play may begin, and however much its forward momentum toward change may concern the writer, that dynamic is only part of what fills the play's world. The pattern also comprises setting, character, language, movement, spectacle—the myriad details that bring life to the stage. For the playwright, a more useful visualization of the process may be seen from diagram B: here the play grows from its starting point in what we've represented as an expanding cone of detail, language, and structural connection driven by, but not exclusively focused, on action.

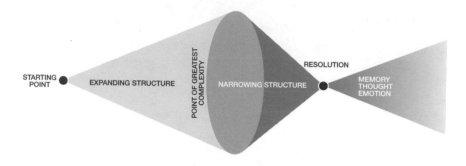

STARTING POINT

EXPANDING STRUCTURE

POINT OF GREATEST COMPLEXITY

NARROWING STRUCTURE

RESOLUTION

MEMORY THOUGHT EMOTION

DIAGRAM: B

The playwright's feel for the play's development, then, depends not merely on its reaching a "high point" or climax, but on its having attained a level of complexity that virtually demands the relatively swift narrowing of its structure to an ending point or resolution. That narrowing invariably calls for attention to connections that will enable the audience to feel, if not immediately comprehend, the aptness of the movement toward the play's inevitable final moments. And, at best, those final moments are not simply the last things the audience sees and hears before the lights fade to black. If the playwright creates those final moments with full attention to all that precedes them, the audience will recall the ways in which the resolution resonates with the complete experience of the play. We have represented this resonance in diagram B by a "phantom" cone of memory, thought, and emotion that leaves the theatre in the minds of the audience.

Though diagrams tend to be reductive, we believe this one gives a fuller sense of the demands of the playwright's craft, of how much depends on a "feel" for one's material, and of why the perfect ending is so difficult to write.

SOME NOTES ON COMEDY

Writing good comedy is not easy. Here are a few thoughts on the subject culled from numerous sources.

What makes people laugh? Consider the following suggestions, and look for them the next time you watch a comedy on stage, on film, or on television—or when you read or reread the comedies in this collection.

1. Derision. Ridiculing or making fun of something or someone. The most frequent targets are stupidity, hypocrisy, pomposity, and sanctimoniousness.

2. Incongruity. Any laughable contrast involving situation, character, or language between the expected and unexpected, intention and realization, normal and abnormal.

3. Automatism. Henri Bergson's term, exemplified when a character becomes rigid and machinelike through an obsession or preoccupation that controls his or her actions and reactions, causing loss of self-control or humanity. This loss of control often emerges in repetitive dialogue or behavior.

What techniques do writers employ to make people laugh? Again, here's a list of things to watch (and listen) for. Knowing about and recognizing such techniques will help you to appreciate them and, if you're a writer, to use them. Again, you'll be able to see these techniques on stage and screen; you'll notice, too, how often they are causally interrelated.

1. Teasing. This one needs no real explanation. We do it openly with our friends and more covertly with people we dislike.

2. Reversal or inversion. This is a frequent technique in situation comedy, as when a timid character is called upon to behave heroically, the servant becomes the master, and so forth.

3. The unfamiliar. Place a character in a new and demanding job, or among other characters speaking a foreign language. Consider the possibilities.

4. Mistaken identity. In Gogol's play *The Inspector General,* a bumbling peasant is mistaken for a visiting dignitary with unlimited powers (see also reversal or inversion above.) In Shakespeare's *The Comedy of Errors,* almost everyone is mistaken for someone else.

5. Violence. Just think about The Three Stooges, Laurel and Hardy, Wile E. Coyote and the Roadrunner, even *Pulp Fiction*.

6. Deception, pretending. This often follows the occurrence of mistaken identity, when the person mistaken—as in *The Inspector General*—realizes the mistake, but can't afford to admit it.

7. Fancy footwork, skillful recovery. Again, we enjoy seeing authority being expertly deceived and admire someone who can convert disaster into triumph (however temporary).

8. Jeopardy. Strangely, life-threatening situations that we fear in real life can be hilarious in a comedy when we know everything will end well.

9. Exaggeration. Extravagant language and behavior often provoke laughter, as in tall tales, lies or excuses that go too far, and so forth.

10. Grilling. Think of Laurel and Hardy or Abbott and Costello being questioned by cops or gangsters; in fact, think of Abbott and Costello's "Who's On First" routine, which is based on question-and-answer.

11. Exposure or discovery. What happens when true identity is revealed or deception and fancy footwork prove unsuccessful. In the case of Laurel and Hardy, this often involved buckshot applied to Ollie's rear end (see also jeopardy and violence).

For examples of these techniques, check out videotapes of John Cleese's hilarious *Fawlty Towers* series or episodes of *Seinfeld*, which provide a virtual clinic in writing comedy.

PLAYWRITING—SOME RECOMMENDATIONS

The following list covers some of the same ground as "Some Points to Consider in Analyzing Plays," but does so from a playwright's—rather than a reader's or audience's—viewpoint. These recommendations may seem to oversimplify to some extent the way plays work, but they're intended as a way of helping a playwright to get started, or to help pinpoint where and why a particular draft does or doesn't succeed.

1. Put your characters in a specific setting, not only physically, but geographically and chronologically. Place can generate action. The places where we *must be* create obvious pressures, those where we *choose* to be act on us more subtly. *Our* places are often an outgrowth of ourselves, or at least reflect ourselves. In any case, when you've chosen a setting, don't forget to take inventory of the *stuff* that would, should, or could be there. And make sure you get the details right.

2. By and large, keep your characters' focus *physical*—on setting, objects, clothing and the like—or at least *external*. By doing so, you'll find many opportunities to get what's inside your characters to emerge in dialogue and/or action. Objects can trigger memories, emotions, conflicts, can reveal wants and needs. Again, to help external focus, give each character an occupation and make him or her care about someone or something. The more stuff in your play, the less pure talk.

3. Make sure your characters *want* or *need* something in each scene (or short play). Each character should have both a *short-term goal* (or goals) within the scene and a *longer-term goal* (or goals) beyond the scene. As writer, you too will have goals for the scene and larger play; think about the point of action toward which you want to move the scene. As David Mamet says, "If your characters don't want something, why write the play?" Though what we want can often bring us into open conflict with others, consider how many times people try to get what they want by negotiating or by creating conditions favorable to themselves while concealing their goals.

4. Disturb the play's balance (the situation and relationships of the characters) near the beginning, so that the audience has a sense that some sort of process has begun. Remember that the best sort of balance for a play is *uneasy*, containing the seeds of the play's ending by suggesting the potential for imminent change. In considering when to open a play and how to disturb the balance, ask yourself, "Why today? What will make this day different from all others for these characters?"

5. You'll usually find the play's central *complication*—the force that makes it move—by looking at your characters, not only at what they want or need, but at their natures: their strengths and weaknesses, their personalities and dispositions, the ways in which they habitually confront the world.

6. Complication growing out of character will lead naturally to *conflict,* with characters confronting each other as their natures dictate.

7. Conflict will lead to *change*—in situation, character, or both—by causing characters to make *discoveries,* to learn, and to act—or refuse to act—on that information or realization. Try to make sure that each scene involves at least one discovery for one or more characters. As Aristotle said, discovery usually brings about change or reversal. Life is full of surprises; good plays usually are, too.

8. In creating strong scenes, remember the value of *beats.* Not "beat" as in "pause," but "beat" as in paragraph of dialogue. Like good paragraphs, good scenes, and good plays, good beats have a beginning, a middle and an end (or a point of transition) to which they build. If a subject comes up between your characters, don't just drop it after one exchange: use it and develop it; the process will force you to make it work for the scene or play as a whole.

9. Remember the value of *echoes* and *connections*—of all sorts (character, action, setting, dialogue and so forth). As with beats, if something is important enough to get into your play, it's probably important enough to use again.

10. *Preparation* is a particularly important aspect of connection, accomplished largely through *pointers* (which let the audience know something or someone is coming) and *plants* (with which you unobtrusively prepare for some later development). Typically, a good playwright will give the audience a *hint* of something to come, make them *wait* until they've almost forgotten the hint, then *surprise* them by delivering on the hint in an unexpected way.

11. Don't hoard invention. In early drafts, a playwright often has one surefire dramatic moment in mind, and because he/she doesn't want to waste it too soon, keeps postponing it. Resist this temptation. It will lead you to dead stage time. If you have something good, get it out there. Doing so will force you to come up with something else. And you will.

12. Provide opportunities for laughter. Even in a serious play (maybe *particularly* in a serious play) the audience needs lighter moments to relieve the tension and to make the serious moments more effective. Moreover, if you *don't* provide the opportunities for laughter, the audience will find their own, and you won't be pleased about it.

13. Remember your resources: your daily experience of people, places, things; your memories; your dreams; research. Pay attention to what's around you. And don't be afraid to go looking for what you need.

14. Don't be afraid to trust your instincts, to let the process of writing the play, and the techniques of playwriting, help you to discover what the play wants to be about. With a first draft finished, and some discoveries made, you can then revise to make sure the play *is* about what you've discovered.

NOTES ON SCRIPT FORMAT AND RELATED MATTERS

The plays in this collection appear in print format, which is designed mainly to save space and allow for the inclusion of as many plays as possible. The format playwrights use when submitting plays to theatres for production, an example of which appears after these notes, has two main aims: separating dialogue clearly from stage directions and emotional cues; and providing directors and producers with a dependable way of gauging how much time the play will take to perform. The format shown in our example—an excerpt from *Hands for Toast*—calls for only one tab setting and averages one minute of stage time per page. The following observations merely clarify, reinforce or anticipate questions about the format shown in the excerpt. When in doubt, cross-check with that example.

1. *Stage directions.* Use "up" for what moves away from the audience, "down" for what moves toward them, "off" for what they can't see. Use L (no period) for left, R for right, and C for center. No need, in general, to use "stage" with any of these, since that's understood. Example: "We see a table and four chairs up L and a sofa down RC."

2. Use all caps for character names when they appear in dialogue tags (speaker identifications) and stage directions, but not when a name occurs as part of dialogue. And—to avoid confusion—underline dialogue you want emphasized, rather than using all caps.

3. Use *one tab setting* for dialogue tags, stage directions and emotional cues. Even if your direction or cue is just one word—like (Pause.)—set it off on a separate line and tab it. You don't need to italicize or underline directions or emotional cues. Only dialogue runs from margin to margin, except for the description of SETTING and TIME at the beginning of each scene. *Double space* between the end of a speech by one character and the next speaker's dialogue tag.

4. Place all directions and emotional cues within parentheses. No matter how long or short a direction may be, *one set of parentheses will suffice;* and for consistency's sake, *use a cap and period,* even for one word—(Beat.)—or a fragment—(Crossing to the table.). And try not to mix fragmentary directions with complete sentences. You're writing directions to be read; be concise, yes, but make them clear, thorough, and correct.

5. If a direction occurs *within a speech by one character,* you don't need to double-space between dialogue and direction. If a direction occurs *between dialogue by two different characters,* double space after the end of the first speech and before the next speaker's dialogue tag.

6. *Don't* use a dialogue tag unless the character actually speaks; if the character merely *does something,* that's a direction, and the character's name should appear with the action, within parentheses. *Don't* immediately follow a dialogue tag with a long direction before the character speaks; keep such directions to one line where possible. If you need a long direction, set it off before or after the tag and dialogue. *Don't* strand a dialogue tag at the bottom of one page and begin the dialogue on the next. And you needn't repeat a dialogue tag if a speech spills over onto a new page, but make sure you can get at least one line of dialogue on the new page for the continuing speech; i.e., *don't* strand a word or two of dialogue as the first thing on a new page (this is known in the printing trade as a "widow").

7. Use a 1.25" margin on the left of the page (to allow for binding) and 1" margins on the right, top, and bottom. And use ragged (unjustified) right margins to avoid eccentric spacing.

8. Page numbers should appear in the upper right corner of all pages except the first; numbering should begin with a 2 on the second page. Number consecutively throughout (no need to give each scene or act its own pagination). Scene designations (e.g., Scene One, Scene Two, etc.) should be centered above a scene's first direction (which, as we've noted earlier, usually identifies SETTING and TIME). If you have room on a page at the end of one scene, drop three spaces, tab, and begin the next. NOTE: if your play runs fewer than sixty pages, it's generally a one-act, in which case you won't need an act number; if the play has two or more acts, ACT ONE (or TWO) should appear only once, above the act's first scene.

9. Signal the end of a scene (or a play) with a direction (e.g., He sits in the armchair as the lights fade slowly to black.), rather than just stopping. "Curtain" is pretty outmoded; lots of theatres don't use them even if they have them. Use END for the finish of a play, centered three spaces down from your final direction.

10. For readability, use *two spaces* between all sentences (or fragments used as sentences). In general, avoid using colons or semi-colons to punctuate dialogue: they're too "literary."

11. Use a dash—two hyphens, no spaces—for interjections or interruptions; most word processors will convert the hyphens to a dash. Save ellipses . . . three spaced periods . . . for dialogue that trails off or proceeds by fits and starts. In general, though, go easy on ellipses; you'll find that (Pause.), (Beat.), or a simple period will often. Do more. To establish. Rhythm.

12. Listen to your own dialogue; read it aloud if need be. If your characters are speaking colloquially, use contractions where appropriate. Write out numbers within the dialogue so that you'll be in

control: "666" could be read "six-sixty-six," "six-six-six" or "six hundred and sixty-six"; you want it read your way. Don't get hung up on phonetic renderings of speech. Use accepted forms for colloquialisms (e.g., yeah, rather than ya, yah, yea, or other fanciful variations). Keep it readable. Keep it sayable. Don't confuse the actor. If you want an accent, you can handle most of it with a stage direction (e.g., "She speaks with a slight Spanish accent."), sentence rhythms and phrasing, and perhaps an occasional unusual word or pronunciation by way of suggestion.

HANDS FOR TOAST
A Ten Minute Play
By
Carey Daniels

CHARACTERS

CHESTER: a man in his mid-fifties, a corrections
officer, built and fit like a man twenty years
younger, wears glasses and a moustache, perpetually
angry and dissatisfied but able to maintain a sense
of civility on occasion.

DARLENE: Chester's wife, 40, with the demeanor
and maturity of a seventeen-year-old, alternating
between self-righteousness and petulance.

BABY BABY: Chester and Darlene's nine-year-old
daughter, as yet unnamed.

SETTING

Chester and Darlene's modest two-bedroom one-story
house. It looks like something out of Levittown,
slightly homey and with the exception of an
expensive entertainment center, it hasn't quite
moved out of the 1960s in terms of décor. A beige
afghan rests on the back of a beat up old armchair
that obviously belongs to Chester. A decorative
table sits next to the armchair, adorned with a
white doily and overgrown spider plant. Antique
lamps with dusty lampshades rest on both end
tables flanking a brown plaid upholstered sofa.
Mainly we see the living room. Passageways in
the back on either side of the stage lead to the
kitchen R and bedroom/bathroom area L. Alongside
the house L a dark blue '88 Cadillac rusts away
through the seasons, sadly missing one of its back

tires. An eight-foot-tall fence, fashioned from old lumber and obviously constructed by hand by Chester separates the Caddy and rest of the house from whatever lies on the other side. Chester and Darlene would be able to look out the window facing the car and fence if the blinds were not always drawn.

TIME

A fine spring day. The present.

                              (The bang of a screen door
                              slamming shut is heard.
                              CHESTER enters from the
                              kitchen, in uniform, his
                              jacket slung over one
                              arm, sorting through a
                              small stack of mail. He
                              stops in the center of the
                              living room, sorting the
                              envelopes and frowning.
                              He pauses to loosen his
                              tie and toss his jacket
                              onto his armchair.)

                         CHESTER
It's hot in here.
                              (Pauses, looking around.)
Darlene! It's hot in here!

                         DARLENE
                         (Off.)
What?

                         CHESTER
It's hot in here! Are you deaf?

                              (DARLENE enters. She's
                              wearing a pair of cut off
                              shorts and a tube top.
                              Her skin is overly tan
                              almost to the point of
                              crispiness and her hair,
                              naturally a medium brown,
                              has been streaked blonde.
                              She is barefoot, but gaudy
                              gold chains adorn her
                              neck and wrists, her long
                              nailed fingers glittering

with gold and jewels.)

                    CHESTER
Damn woman, how hard is it to open a few windows in
here? This place is like an oven.

                              (DARLENE reaches under the
                              blinds to open the window,
                              then leaves through the
                              kitchen to open more in
                              there.)

                    DARLENE
                    (Off.)
Don't start with me first thing, Chester! You just
got home from work and haven't even been fuckin'
drinkin' yet! I swear to Christ if you drink
tonight I'm leaving you!
                              (CHESTER ignores this and
                              looking through his mail,
                              he pulls out an envelope
                              and tears it open,
                              thoughtlessly handing the
                              envelope to DARLENE as she
                              re-enters.)
And your mother called today.
                              (DARLENE takes a cigarette
                              out of the pack she got
                              from the kitchen and
                              lights up. She inhales as
                              CHESTER reads his letter,
                              blowing smoke out of the
                              side of her mouth and
                              picking up where she left
                              off.)
Your mother is a real piece of work, Chester. She
was on about the kids again, bitching that you
forgot Jason's birthday and didn't even call him-

                    CHESTER
                    (Reading his letter,
                    mumbling.)
If he wanted me to talk to him on his birthday he
would've called me. Him and his sister know how to
pick up the damn phone and use it. If they want me
to talk to them, they'll call.

                    DARLENE
                    (Taking another drag off
                    her cigarette.)
Ungrateful brats. After all you did for them.
Heather's been getting' a lot of use outta that
lawn chair you bought her for Christmas three years
ago and not a word of thanks since. What kind of
father buys something as useful as a lawn chair
for his kids? One with a cup holder even? A damn
thoughtful one, I tell you. No fucking respect.
                    (Pausing to smoke as
                    CHESTER ignores her,
                    reading his letter.)
What's in the mail?

                    CHESTER
                    (Throws the letter to the
                    floor in a rage.)
Fucking bitch!

                    (DARLENE moves to pick
                    up the letter as CHESTER
                    stomps into the kitchen
                    with the rest of the
                    mail. He returns quickly,
                    opening a can of beer and
                    taking a long drink.)
That bitch wants me to help pay for Jason's college
tuition.

                              (CHESTER drinks his beer,
                              fuming, as DARLENE reads
                              the letter.)

                         DARLENE
She says she'll take you to court to fight for it.
Fucking bitch.

                              (Beat. Then, confused.)

Which wife is this?

...

Arnold Johnston's plays, and others written in collaboration with his wife, Deborah Ann Percy, have won awards, production, and publication across the country. His poetry, fiction, non-fiction, and translations have appeared widely in literary journals. His books include *What the Earth Taught Us*, *The Witching Voice: A Play About Robert Burns*, and *Of Earth and Darkness: The Novels of William Golding*. Johnston is also a member of the Dramatists Guild and a resident playwright with the Off-Off Broadway theatre company AAI Productions. Arnold Johnston lives in Kalamazoo, Michigan, where he is chairman of the English Department and teaches in the creative writing program at Western Michigan University.

Deborah Ann Percy earned the MFA in Creative Writing at Western Michigan University. Her plays, and those written in collaboration with her husband, Arnold Johnston, have won awards, publication, and production nationwide. Their books include a play, *Rasputin in New York*, and (with Dona Rosu) translations of Romanian playwright Hristache Popescu's *Night of the Passions* and *Sons of Cain*. Winner of major playwriting grants from the Michigan Council for Arts & Cultural Affairs and the Gilmore Foundation, Ms. Percy was named as a 1999 recipient of Kalamazoo's Community Medal of the Arts. She is also a member of the Dramatists Guild and a resident playwright with AAI Productions.